HENRY PAOLUCCI

SELECTED WRITINGS ON LITERATURE AND THE ARTS; SCIENCE AND ASTRONOMY; LAW, GOVERNMENT, AND POLITICAL PHILOSOPHY

EDITED WITH A PREFACE BY ANNE PAOLUCCI

Published by *Griffon House Publications for*
THE BAGEHOT COUNCIL

Distributed by GRIFFON HOUSE PRESS
1401 Pennsylvania Avenue, Wilmington DE 19806

Library of Congress Cataloging–in–Publication Data

Paolucci, Henry.
    [Essays.   Selections]
    Henry Paolucci : selected writings on literature and the arts,
  science, astronomy, law, government, political philosophy /
  edited with a preface by Anne Paolucci
        p.   cm.
    Includes bibliographical references.
    ISBN 0-918680-79-4 (cloth). — ISBN 0-918680-81-6 (pbk.)
    I. Paolucci, Anne.   II. Title.
  AC8.P262   1999
  081—dc21
                                                        99-38479
                                                           CIP

Published for
The Bagehot Council
by Griffon House Publications

Distributed by
GRIFFON HOUSE PRESS, INC.
1401 Pennsylvania Ave., Suite 105, Wilmington, DE 19806

CONTENTS

HENRY PAOLUCCI

RESPICE, ADSPICE, PROSPICE

(A Song for the Last Days)

YES, I came to City College
To acquire heaps of knowledge
And to spare myself the coarser kinds of labor;
For the many lores of learning
I had in me quite a yearning
And an idle life at college met my favor.

But I found on my arrival
That the struggle for survival
Was much keener there than I'd anticipated;
So instead of all the pleasures
That a college student treasures
I had to go on grinding unabated.

On the day of registration
I was filled with jubilation
Til I learned about the closing of the classes;
Every time I made selections
They would quickly close the sections
Til my hours were like those of toiling masses.

My indomitable spirit
Was still able then to bear it
So courageously I undertook my studies;
While the sun on high was riding
Til the moment of its hiding
I was busy grinding with my college buddies.

Oh I learned much self reliance
Taking first a course in science
Then across the hall to study mathematics;
From a class in foreign language
I'd go down to buy a "sanguage"
Then directly to the gym for acrobatics.

After sweating there an hour
I was pushed into a shower
Then descended to the subway feeling dizzy;
When a worker homeward hurries
He can leave behind his worries
But at home a City student must keep busy.

Still I'm really not complaining;
With few college days remaining
I look back upon those days that used to be;
With a kind of pleasant sadness
With some tears and yet with gladness
For with age, tis now a mellow memory!

[Written in 1941. From *City at the Center. A Collection of Writings by CCNY Alumni and Faculty.* Ed. by Betty Rizzo and Barry Wallenstein, CCNY, New York, 1983.]

PREFACE

During his lifetime, Henry Paolucci taught and wrote in several academic disciplines. He was a rare teacher in that he was able to present any subject as part of a total picture, enabling students and readers to adjust their sights as they moved with him into often unfamiliar intellectual territory. He was always ready to help colleagues and students, never trimming his time with them but giving as much as they could take. He often said that he learned a great deal by helping others. Perhaps he did, for he could take in the most disparate subjects and find a place for them in the wide expanse of his learning.

As a lecturer or in debates he was mesmerizing. In 1964, when he ran for the United States Senate on the New York State Conservative Party line, the *New York Times* quickly recognized him as a "Scholarly Candidate" worth following. They assigned a special writer to cover his campaign, almost to the end. In his public speaking and in the classroom, he used whatever he could muster to gain and retain the attention of his audience: humor, irony, mime, parody, the rough language of the streets, acting out parts as he spoke. He drew audiences and students with his histrionics but never at the expense of serious argument. In this context, his students remember him as a brilliant scholar but, also, affectionately, as an "entertainer."

Students remember him also as talking "in the third person" when referring to arguments not his own. He had a profound respect for sources, for writers before him, and presented in the best possible light even those with whom he did not agree. He was meticulous about giving credit where it was called for, a habit he communicated to his students as a discipline to be honored and followed.

He trained his students well. Many who were present at the Henry Paolucci Memorial Celebration held May 7, 1999, in New York, recalled instances of his flair, his humor in the classroom, his brilliant lectures. Equally moving were letters from students who wanted to share — in some cases, at a distance of thirty and forty years — anecdotes about his compelling manner and intellectual fervor.

This first volume is a representative one in that it sweeps through a number of disciplines, providing an impressive record of Henry Paolucci's comprehensive approach to knowledge. Much else could have been included in each section, but what is presented here is quite enough as an introduction to an unusual scholar and teacher, a keen statesman, a political realist who was also, always, at ease as a philosopher.

> What a remarkable life he led! What contributions he made: As a patriot who flew combat missions for his country, as a scholar whose written works ranged over the spectrum of ancient and modern history and philosophy, as a political leader and as a public man who stepped into the political arena and engaged in thoughtful and rewarding debate.[1]

His former colleagues, students, and friends remember his multi-faceted talent for different reasons, in different ways, a true Renaissance man.

> While it's hard to believe that I last sat in his class approximately 36 years ago, I can recall as if it happened yesterday: Dr. Paolucci, parodying some rich industrialist ... with feet up on the desk and cigar in his mouth, voicing contempt for the underprivileged. Long before Stephen E. Ambrose won fame for his book *Citizen Soldiers* in 1997, Dr. Paolucci conveyed to us in his class the responsibilities incumbent upon members of the "polis" and shared with us the thoughts and feelings of a young man as he peered through his Norden bombsight and observed the lights of the city below appear as the plane made its bomb run. I particularly recall his love of St. Augustine and how, in a flash, he could intertwine the experience of Augustine and Thomas Merton and his own experience to produce a memorable lecture which had the added advantage of strengthening us in our faith. He was an Orator who could hold a class enthralled .... He also had a sense of humor, which made him all the more believable.[2]

Those who knew him as a writer and teacher were invariably struck by his "unpretentious scholarship," his natural talent for communicating not just ideas but his own passionate convictions.

> My favorite memory of Old New York was, during my first summer nights at Columbia, encountering Henry at 111th and Broadway discoursing on Dante, Augustine, St. Thomas, et al. I thought I was in Athens — or at least Hyde Park. The street life of upper Broadway has not been so elevated since — a little touch of Henry in the night.[3]

> He galvanized the intellectual life at Iona during my years there. The rides home from New Rochelle that I shared with Henry and Willard Maas were like Platonic dialogues (Henry as Socrates, of course). His irony, depth. and humor made the 17-mile trip an educational treat. I witnessed his strength on many other occasions, including his Senatorial candidacy, but for me the years at Iona with Henry were seminal.[4]

> Because at my seldom best, I remain, as he called me a "jewel in the rough," I will put it succinctly and unadorned. I first met him in Roman History class as a freshman at Iona. I was spellbound. His words, gestures, and beliefs had a cathartic effect on me. In a moment, I realized that it was OK to feel the way I did. He gave an intellectual fig-eaf to my passions. He gave me the self-confidence, critical to every man to successfully complete the journey from adolescence into manhood . . . . Every year on 15 July, St. Henry's day, I have thought of him . . . . I have taught all of our sons the "Band of Brothers" speech as I remember, like yesterday, the very first time I heard it.[5]

My own debt to him is personal and professional. A born teacher, he was generous in sharing with me the subjects and authors he loved — Hegel, Greek and Roman history, aesthetics, theater, political theory, Goethe, music, especially the German songs of Schubert and Brahms, the political realism of Machiavelli — and, for a period of two or three years, spent many hours every week helping me to master English. He taught me also to appreciate Christian doctrine and, by his own example, the power of prayer. But his greatest lesson, for all who knew him, was his humanity, his deep sense of compassion, his quiet dignity. He was "a kind and gentle man," a friend recalled. "I never heard him utter a hostile word or make an unpleasant observation about anyone. "6

The variety of subjects represented in this volume is but a small measure of the man-scholar, who humanized learning and raised personal emotions to the level of poetic sensibility. Henry Paolucci was impeccable as a researcher; as a writer, he was precise and thorough. The most difficult subjects were rendered with a clarity that insures easy reading. All these things are evident in the selections included in this volume. But his true worth must be sought, finally, not simply in his excellence as a teacher, a scholar, a writer, but in the life of thought which he embodied. His example encouraged others to aim higher to hit that mark.

To his credit, all of us tried.

ANNE PAOLUCCI

1. Letter by New York State Senator John Marchi, January 6, 1999.

2. Letter by Dr. Frederic Eder, January 4, 1999.

3. Letter from Robert Rosenbaum, January 6, 1999.

4. Letter from Professor Vincent Quinn, January 10, 1999.

5. Letter from Dr. Larry Franklin, January 12, 1999.

6. Letter from Nicholas John Stathis, Esq., January 13, 1999.

PART ONE

◇◀◀◀◀◆▶▶▶◇

LITERATURE AND THE ARTS

ITALIAN AND ENGLISH "MODELS" FOR THE MODERN VERNACULAR LITERATURES OF INDIA

As a point of departure, linking my subject with more familiar materials, I draw, for a sort of text, upon a commencement address of 1953, delivered at Washington University in his native St. Louis, by T. S. Eliot. The address is titled "American Literature and the American Language."[1] In its early paragraphs, the leading Anglo-American poet-critic of his day raised the question whether "speech in England and speech in America" might actually develop in time into distinct languages. "Perhaps," he added, "we can draw some conclusions from the transformations of languages in the past." And he cited as obviously suggestive examples how the "decline of Latin" had brought about its "transmutation into the several Romance languages," and how the "development of Sanskrit, through Pali," had apparently brought into being the modern Aryan vernaculars of India. "I make no pretense of being a philologist," he next protested; "but even to a person untrained in that science there is a striking parallel between the relation of Italian to Latin, and the relation of Pali to Sanskrit. It would at first sight seem within the bounds of possibility, that in the course of time American speech and writing might come to differ as much from present-day English, as Italian and Bengali differ from Latin and Sanskrit." ([1] 48)

The address from which those words are drawn can be said to be Eliot's small-scale equivalent of Dante's *De Vulgari Eloquentia,* and it ought, I think, to be prized as such. By 1953, Eliot had already completed his notorious *altro viaggio* – his

[From *The Emergence of National Literatures,* ed. Aldo Scaglione, A. Longo, Editore, Ravenna, Italy, 1983]

"other" journey — which had taken him "eastward," physicallyand spiritually, to "recover his past" as poet, citizen, and Christian. His return to St. Louis in 1953, to address a graduating class on the hundredth anniversary of a university his grandfather had helped to found, and which his father, uncles, brother, and several cousins had attended, must have been something like Dante's longed-for but never realized return from exile to his *bel San Giovanni,* to be crowned finally with the poet's laurel by his fellow Florentines.

The author of *The Waste Land* had been the first of the St. Louis Eliots to leave the banks of that most American of rivers, the Mississippi, to retrace his grandfather's steps back to Boston and Harvard. From Harvard, he had gone farther East, to London, and even to the little town from which his ancestors, for religious reasons, had set out for their westward journey across the Atlantic in the seventeenth century. Young Eliot had been the most promising American modernist poet. Yet he had chosen, at a certain point, to give up his American birthright, to become a British subject, and to gain acceptance as a classicizing British poet-critic and High Churchman. Then, after decades of world-wide fame as chief arbiter of literary taste for the entire English-speaking world, Eliot had come back to his native St. Louis to talk to the "folks back home" about his native American speech and the prospects that it and the speech in England might separate into mutually unintelligible languages.

But Eliot doubts that the Latin and Sanskrit parallels are valid. Before Bengali and Italian emerged as viable vernaculars, the Sanskritic and Latin civilizations had collapsed. Is there any likelihood, he asks, that the civilization of the English-speaking peoples of the world today can suffer a comparable collapse? Even if England were somehow to fail, America would still be there to fill the vacuum. And waiting to take their turns would be the English-speakers of Australia, Canada, etc. Indeed, says Eliot, echoing the phrase Winston Churchill had used in that same St. Louis only a few years before, "unless you yourselves draw a linguistic iron curtain, you cannot keep the American language out of England. At present the current of language flows from west to east . . . but, whatever happens, I believe that there will always be movement in one direction or the other. So that, against the influences toward the development of separate languages, there will always be other influences tending towards fusion." ([1] 51)

With the question of a distinctively American language out of the way, Eliot turns to explain what he means by American literature: "as I believe," he says, "that we are now justified in speaking of what has never, I think, been found before, two literatures in the same language." That was said in 1953. Since then claims of the same sort have been made for other emergent literatures in English, as well as in Spanish and Portuguese and several other "imperial" languages, Western, Eastern, and Middle-Eastern. But independent national literary maturity isn't easily attained. As Eliot illustrates in the rest of his address, it came for American writing, not with James Fenimore Cooper or Washington Irving, nor with the "flowering of New England," which remained regional, but, tentatively, only with Poe, Whitman, and Mark Twain, as major facets of an emergent truly American national identity, and, definitively, only with the many first and second rate modernist American poets (including Pound, Williams, Stevens, Marianna Moore, and, of course, Eliot himself) who came out of the Anglo-American Imagist movement, vied with their British counterparts for leadership, and won!

Still, the question is: How does it actually happen? How does a provincial branch of a parent literature extending itself over a distant land put down a trunk of its own, rooted in the soil below it, to become an independent tree? Doesn't that do violence to the very idea of organic growth? A highly suggestive answer has recently come to us from distant Australia, which is now experiencing the phenomenon for itself. Back in 1930, that former penal colony's greatest literary historian, H. M. Green, had insisted in a widely read book on local writing, that "Australian literature is a branch of English literature, and however great it may become and whatever characteristics it may develop, it will remain a branch." But, almost a generation later, when he got around to completing his monumental *History of Australian Literature* in two volumes (Sidney, 1961), literary-historian Green had changed his mind. The Australian branch, he said, had ceased, in the course of that generation, to be a mere branch. And with that he supplied an image that helps greatly to make sense out of Australia's experience, and America's, and, I dare say, that of all other peoples who developed national literatures of their own in whatever speech they may have learned from their mothers' lips or been otherwise taught. "It is scarcely necessary to argue nowadays," Green wrote, "that the literature of Australia is worth discussing on its own account, and not merely as a part of the great literature in English of which it is an outgrowth." The great literature in our shared language, he went on,

> is like a banyan-tree, whose branches bend down, and, striking the ground, take root and grow up as independent individuals. The largest of these is of course the literature of the United States, though there has been some cross-fertilization here; but apart from this and the rapidly developing literatures of English-speaking Canada and South Africa, and also of New Zealand, we hear of those of New England and of the deep South, and of Scottish plays and Welsh short stories; and there has even appeared in this country a book on the poets of Queensland. Few traces still survive of the tradition that Britain, like ancient Rome, must remain the social, political and literary center of her world; and though writers from Australia and the other dominions do still migrate to London and settle there, there have been some signs lately of a reversal of the process. (xi-xii)

In a supporting footnote, Green added that of course the parallel with the growth process of the banyan "extends much further than literature."

The banyan, as we know, is the great "down-growing" fig tree of India: the *ficus indica* or *bengalensis,* called in Sanskrit the *nyagrodha,* which means literally "the down-grower." Foreigners came to call it the banyan tree because the Hindu merchant-caste of that name, the *bania,* often set up their colorfully-festive bazaars, or flea-markets, as we now call our own equivalents, under its grand crown, and around its many trunks, for shelter against the heat and rain. How suggestive a cultural symbol the tree has been for India from the remotest times down to the present reveals itself in the fact that, when the Royal Asiatic Society of Great Britain and Ireland was founded in 1823, as the London branch of the original Asiatic Society founded by Sir William Jones in Calcutta in 1784, its heads adopted for it the motto *quot rami tot arbores:* "as many trees as branches." With the four Latin words, they meant to indicate that the London branch, which had been preceded by branches in Bombay and Madras, was destined to become a bigger tree than its prototype in Bengal, and that, perhaps with new branches of its own striking roots in Europe and America, it might soon take on the appearance of having been from the beginning the massive central trunk of a forest of trees which is yet a single tree.

In its natural state, not as cultivated, the banyan is an epiphyte. Its seed is usually deposited, by birds, squirrels, or monkeys, on the top-most branches of another tree. There, it first forms a sort of basket of branch-roots — like the ornate capital of a Corinthian column — to secure itself. Then it sends thinner aerial roots down to the ground all around the supporting trunk. Ideally, the relationship is supposed to be symbiotic, because the banyan is not a parasite. But in fact the down-growing aerial-roots usually end up squeezing or strangling the supportive trunk and eventually replacing it. Meanwhile, other branches have been arching themselves outward and putting down root-branches of their own, which will become supportive trunks.

The cultural-linguistic suggestiveness of the image is obvious. In the *India* issue of *Review of National Literatures* (Volume 10, New York, 1980), the introductory essay titled "India's Banyan: 'As Many Trees as Branches' " (pp. 10-17), traces the modern use of the image as an organizing principle for India studies. Cited there is the striking instance of its use by the eminent Oxford Sanskritist F. W. Thomas to suggest that Sanskrit, too, may originally have been a down-growing branch, like the living vernaculars. "In a measure," he writes,[2] "the formal literature of India may be viewed as having roots in the common life. Though the principle of its growth is mainly innate, it has from time to time incorporated independent products from the same soil; and, like the banyan, it has sent down branches which have themselves taken root." ([2] 50-51)

The banyan-image should therefore be kept in mind as we proceed to consider the process of emergence of three Indo-Aryan vernaculars as modern literary languages. It suggests, as Thomas says, the organic, innate principle of their organic growth. But, at least initially, our focus must be rather on the *external* principles of their cultivation as distinct literary languages. Historically, those principles were represented by the two great foreign conquests of India which have had abiding consequences. There was, first, the Muslim-Arab-Turkish conquest, from the eighth to the twelfth centuries, which produced a vernacular flowering in the fourteenth, fifteenth, and sixteenth centuries of our era; and then the English conquest of the eighteenth and nineteenth centuries, which had the effect of turning vast India into the world's largest laboratory of linguistic-literary experimentation — with Italian and English very consciously introduced to serve as "models" in guiding the experimentation.

What linked the Italian and English models together was the fact that they had, of course, both been, in large measure, direct consequences of the two great Norman conquests of the eleventh century; "conquests wrought," as a modern historian of the Normans has put it, "in the great island of the ocean, and the great island of the Mediterranean." They had been very different kinds of conquests. William the Bastard of Normandy had crossed the channel into England to impose his rule on the Anglo-Saxons there. The sons of Tancred of Hauteville and their successors (including the great Rogers) went to Southern Italy and Sicily to defeat the reigning Saracens and Byzantine Greeks. The natives saw them as emancipators. In fact, from an Italian standpoint, the Norman Mediterranean conquest brought on — again in the words of a modern historian of the Normans — the "most brilliant time for Sicily as a power in the world," conferring upon it a prominence the likes of which it had never known, even in ancient Greek times.

It needs to be borne in mind that the Norse raiders who descended upon Northern France at the close of the glorious age of the Vikings (after some of their peers had ventured eastward to the Volga, to give that vast expanse of Euro-Asian land a name and a political order) were not overly attached to their native tongue. In France, they had soon given up their old Norse to speak a variety of French instead. When they went to Southern Italy, they quickly took up the local varieties of Italian. And while they held on to their adoptive French in England for several centuries, they eventually gave it up to speak the language of their Anglo-Saxon subjects — heavily Normanized, to be sure — even as, with a kind of *noblesse,* they began to call themselves Englishmen, and their land England. Since then, they have held on more tightly, as Anglicized Normans, to what became theirs in those days. Thus, when they conquered French Canada, for instance, they pretended that they had somehow never been French-speaking Norman conquerors of England. And when they conquered India, at about the same time, they did not in the least think of themselves as French.

The point to be stressed here is that, for the Hindus of India, especially in the province of Bengal, the English conquest of the eighteenth and nineteenth centuries was like the Norman Mediterranean conquest, not like the Norman English conquest. The Indian equivalent of the Norman-English conquest was, in fact, the Muslim conquest that started a thousand years earlier, in the first century after the death of Mohammed. When the Muslims first entered India, Sanskrit was still what it had been for centuries before: the perfect, cherished, sacred language of ancient Brahman-Hinduism. Actually, in its cherished perfection, Sanskrit had in fact ceased to be a *living* language, in the strict sense, perhaps as far back as 400 BC, when, largely as a consequence of the great labors of the grammarian Panini, it was apparently frozen "for all time," as Hinduism's "ritually perfected and intellectually cultivated language" par excellence. As independent India's first Prime Minister, Jawaharlal Nehru, put it in his widely-read *Discovery of India* (New York, 1946), certainly when the great playwright Kalidasa wrote his celebrated *Shakuntala* in it (fourth-fifth century BC), Sanskrit was "not the people's language," as it perhaps had never been, though it was still then "the language of educated people throughout India" (158-159). For brevity's sake we can refer here to the concise characterization of the

entire history of Sanskrit that Sir Percival Spear gives us in his
India, Pakistan, and the West (Oxford, 1967). At one time, he
there reminds us, Sanskrit

> was thought to be the parent of all the Aryan languages,
> but it is now accepted as the sister of Greek and Latin, of
> Ancient Persian and Avestic. As the (Aryan) invaders
> spread over Northern India the tribal dialects tended to
> develop into local languages; one of them thus became the
> Sanskrit language, which, standardized in the early Hindu
> scriptures, became first the speech of the polite, and then
> a dead language for priests and scholars. Learned men
> can still converse in Sanskrit as Renaissance scholars
> talked in Latin. (24-25)

The parallel at the close, we see, is with Renaissance Latin,
not with classical or medieval Latin. The point is that what
happened in the West to the Latin of Cicero and Virgil when
the German tribes invaded the Christianized empire in the
fourth and fifth centuries AD is the opposite of what happened
to the language of the Vedas, the *Mahabharata,* the *Ramayana,*
and *Shakuntala* when it found itself confronted by invading
Muslims in the seventh and eighth centuries of our era.

The ancient Church in the West flirted briefly with the idea
of shutting itself in protectively in the face of the so-called
northern barbarians. The disdain of St. Ambrose in this regard
is a matter of record. But that soon passed. Once the decision
was taken to extend the "pastoral care" of the Church to the
new peoples, its inherited Latin, so masterfully adapted to the
needs of Christianity by St. Jerome, St. Ambrose, and St.
Augustine, was immediately transformed into a "mission"
language. Soon the Church was recruiting even its Latin-
educated clergy — which is not hereditary, like the Brahman-
Hindu priesthood — from the ranks of the Germanic converts.
Efforts were made from time to time to hold to the standard of
some early treasured Christian texts, like the Vulgate Bible of
St. Jerome. But before long, scholar, priest, and layman alike
came to understand that "biblical Latin is one thing and the
Latin he believed he was speaking quite another." The latter, as
Giacomo Devoto aptly observes in his *Languages of Italy* (Chi-
cago, 1978), "was no longer Latin, though he still called it

Latin." (146)

The response of the Sanskrit-Hindu priesthood to the invading Muslims took an exactly opposite course. It is true that the Turkish Muslims who completed the conquest of India had a native speech so crude in their own view that they early adopted, for official use, a language as foreign to them, namely classical Persian, as it was to their Hindu subjects. Like the reigning Sanskrit, that Persian, too, was a "dead" language. The learned Brahman-Hindus soon learned to live with it in their dealings with the Muslims, while they retreated, with their own ritually perfected language, into sanctuaries of silent safety from which the sacred classical texts did not re-emerge until the English began to pry things loose a thousand years later, in the late eighteenth century. When Sir William Jones and Charles Wilkins and their peers finally battered their way into the Sanskrit sanctuaries, and began to praise its sophisticated forms and literary qualities to the heavens, its traditional custodians eagerly impressed upon the English scholars the fact that Sanskrit hadn't changed at all since the days of Kalidasa, that it certainly had never been reduced to anything like Latin's task of trying to convert barbaric invaders to the faith of the conquered.

How then did Hindu India defend its Hindu identity and heritage from the conquering Turkish Muslims and their Muslimized classical Persian? The answer is: by means of their humblest popular speeches, which were very numerous indeed. Something similar had happened in the Dravidian lands of South India when Aryan tribes of the North first overwhelmed them. The Dravidian speakers accepted Sanskrit as their sacred language when they became Hindus; but they also, in cultural self-defense, produced a vernacular expression of the same to give it a popular and essentially devotional local coloring. That accounts for the pre-Muslim flowering of the Dravidian literatures in Kanarese, Telugu, and Tamil, "all of which," as Professor Thomas could still say half a century ago, "are older and more important than the Indo-Aryan vernaculars." And of Tamil in particular, Thomas added, it can be said that it "is undoubtedly, next to Sanskrit, the greatest Indian literature." ([2] 214)

Centuries after that early flowering of Dravidian vernaculars, it is in response to the Muslim "intrusion" that the Northern Aryan vernaculars made their first literary bow. From the eighth to the twelfth centuries, we get a body of heroic songs celebrating the struggles of the *Rajput* (prince-led) tribes against the invaders. But by the end of the twelfth century the Rajputs are all subdued, and the heroic songs cease. The vernaculars are silent for a time. When they reappear, it is to do the work of defending the Hindu identity that sacred Sanskrit had refused to attempt. What provoked the vernaculars was Muslim proselytizing, which came relatively late. Islam in not a caste-religion like Hinduism, but a democratic or egalitarian faith. Initially it offers the faithless the choice of Islam or the sword, submission or death. But in India, the Hindus were far too many, and the foreign Muslims never amounted to more than a light sprinkling of salt, as it was said, on a vast native dish. Islamic rulers couldn't possibly expect seriously to "cut" their way through to a majority position, since their faithless subjects could reproduce themselves faster than they could be killed. It seemed more prudent in time simply to tax the natives rather than kill them, and to leave the mission of converting them to the more persuasive arts of the traditional mystic reformers. The greatest of the mystic-reformer sects of Islam in those days was that of the Sufis, who at one time numbered in their ranks the great Perso-Arabic poets Sadi, Jalal-ud-din Rumi, and Hafiz.

Sufism in India directed its mission particularly to the conversion of lower-caste Hindus, including the untouchables, for whom the appeal of Islamic brotherhood was very strong. Most of the natives around the major centers of Muslim power spoke varieties of the Hindi vernacular, and so the Sufis learned to preach primarily in that, transforming it into a hybrid by introducing the essential terms of Islam, in Arabic and Persian. There was much pairing of Perso-Arabic and roughly equivalent Hindi vernacular terms. Islam was stripped to its essentials and assimilated as far as possible to the fundamental beliefs of popular Hinduism. The Hindu response was to preach the same simple doctrine with the claim that it was indeed native to Hinduism, once the ritualistic accretions of Brahman Hinduism were stripped away. Thus there was no need to convert to get what one already had. South Indian devotionalism or *Bhakti* was of great help here. What the Sufi-Bhakti encounter was like, making use of the same sort of hybrid local vernacular, is admirably summed up by the Muslim-Indian scholar Aziz Ahmad in his authoritative *Studies of Islamic Culture in the Indian Environment* (Oxford, 1964). "In the fourteenth and fifteenth centuries," he writes,

> as Sufism penetrated into the masses of converts and semi-converts from Hinduism, the Bhakti movement rose as a popular Hindu counter-challenge to the proselytizing pull of Sufi humanism . . . . Historically the growth of the Bhakti movement can be divided into two phases: the first, from its development in South India to the thirteenth century; the second, from the thirteenth to the seventeenth, when in North India it came in contact with Islam, was inspired by its monotheism and stimulated by its challenge, and developed against it a system of self-defense and self-preservation for Hindu spirituality by borrowing Islam's monotheistic egalitarianism. (136, 140)

The great poet-saints of Bhakti are Ramananda, who came up to Benares from the South, Kabir, who was among his first twelve disciples, and then Kabir's disciple Nanak, who went on to found the sectarian religion of the fierce Sikhs. Of the three, from a linguistic literary perspective, Kabir is undoubtedly the greatest. There can be no doubt that with his preaching and poetry in a hybrid form of Hindi and Persian, his purpose was to "save Hinduism" among the lower castes, where millions of converts were being made. But his verses have indeed enjoyed a wide popularity among Muslims and Hindus alike, among the educated as well as the uneducated. Some of his best-known verses stress the underlying identity of the two faiths. Of his linguistically important verses, one notes especially this: "Sanskrit is like the water of a deep well, but the vernacular is like a running brook."[3]

Legend has it that when Kabir died, in c. 1518 AD, Hindu and Muslim disciples disputed with one another over the disposal of the body. Then the "spirit of the Master appeared and told them to lift up the shroud. They did so, and lo! there was no corpse, but only a heap of rose petals. Half of these were buried in Muslim fashion at Maghar, the remainder were taken to Benares and burnt, and the ashes scattered upon the broad bosom of Mother Ganges." This perfectly symbolizes what became of that first attempted fusion of Muslim and Hindu faiths and languages in India. Many Hindus were converted to Islam, and many more were kept from converting. But through it all, and since, the Muslim and Hindu communities managed to maintain their distinctiveness. The pull of a universal faith, of a global Islam, was strong among the Muslims of India; while the Hindus, for their part, simply absorbed as much of the foreign faith as was compatible with their traditional Hindu eclecticism. Kabir's high literary-linguistic fusion of Hindi and Persian bore little fruit in subsequent times. During the next century, a more political kind of eclecticism was encouraged under the rule of the great Akbar, a contemporary of Elizabeth of England, the first of the Muslim rulers who tried to gain the allegiance of all his subjects. He came to profess a faith that fused Islam and Hinduism, Jainism and Buddhism, and even Roman Catholicism. He patronized Sanskrit learning, and drew its Brahman elitist priesthood for the first time into the highest levels of Turko-Muslim public administration.

An immediate consequence was that popular-reformist Bhakti Hinduism lost much of its appeal before the force of Brahman orthodoxy which encouraged the expression of or-thodoxy in several of the vernaculars. The "Hindi version of the *Ramayana* by Tulasi Das" was an orthodox work of that time. Its continued popularity among the Hindi-speaking faithful ever since, it has been said, has amply earned for it "the title of the Bible of the Hindi-speaking people of India." Linguistic fusion thereafter ceased to be cultivated for literary expression, limiting itself almost exclusively to lower, purely utilitarian uses. It needs to be noted that, from beginning to end, Muslim rule in India remained essentially military in general character, and especially in administrative structure. Its centers of power everywhere could be called, in fact, military encampments. Thus, the people who came to linger around such centers, seeking jobs, or pressing petitions, were soon enough called "camp-followers," and the hybrid speech they used to make themselves understood by the administrators came to be called the "language of the camp-followers," or *Urdu,* the accepted Turkish term for army or army camp, deriving from the same root as the English term *horde.*

The development of the camp-followers' variety of Hindi under the Muslims was certainly a language transformation on the Norman-English model. We recall the opening pages of Sir Walter Scott's *Ivanhoe,* where social relations in the times of Richard Coeur de Lion are pictured for us: "Four generations had not sufficed to blend the hostile bloods of the Normans and the Anglo-Saxons, or to unite by common language and mutual interests, two hostile races, one of which felt the elation of triumph, while the other groaned under all the consequences of defeat." Conquerors and conquered at first had their separate languages. "French," writes Scott, "was the language of honor, of chivalry, and even of justice, while . . . Anglo-Saxon was abandoned to the use of rustics and hinds." And what little fusion there was proved initially to be even more humiliating than the original stratified isolation of the two languages.

A few paragraphs later comes the once notorious exchange between Wamba the fool and Girth the swineherd on the humiliations of linguistic fusion for the lowly. Wamba explains how *swine, ox,* and *calf* are "good Saxon" when running on all fours, "in the charge of a Saxon slave," but become Norman *pork, beef,* and *veal* once they have been "flayed and drawn and quartered and hung up by the heels," later to be cooked and carved and served up for some Norman noble's feast in the castle hall.[4] Similar humiliations were at the base of the early Persian-Hindi fusions in India. At first it is all confined to speech; but soon enough the need arises for the lowly to address pleas and petitions to their masters in writing. That is when professional scribes and advocates appear, usually Brahman-Hindus already employed in the lower echelons of the Muslim public-administration bureaucracy. It is they who first write the hybrid Hindustani in the Perso-Arabic script of their masters, and who "enrich" it with a heavily-Persianized vocabulary to facilitate its comprehension by the foreign officials. Thus a gulf begins to yawn between the spoken hybrid, which is the same for low-caste Hindus and Hindu-converts to Islam, and the same hybrid as written in the script of the Muslims.

But, to be sure, what later happened to England's hybrid *lingua franca* did not happen to India's. Once they gave up their old ambition to conquer France, England's Norman rulers adopted the language of their subjects, and, in the process, took to calling themselves Englishmen and their land England. But hybrid English had by then been so thoroughly suffused with Norman-French terms that, with regard to public law and government, at any rate, as much as 90% of the entire vocabulary was French. The Mughal-Muslim rulers of India were tempted to do the same in the late seventeenth and early eighteenth centuries. But the religious obstacles and, even more, the barriers of the Brahman-Hindu caste system were too great. The Mughals in fact made Hindustani the official language in many parts of northern India; but by the time they did, it was too late. The major European powers were already on the scene, struggling to determine the succession.

The English, who triumphed in that struggle for succession, at first re-installed Persian as the administrative language for the natives, even as they sought, successfully, to maintain the forms of administration that Akbar had so ably structured several centuries before. Had old Delhi, the traditional Moghul capital in the heart of Hindi-speaking Hindustan, been made the British power-center, instead of Calcutta in Bengal, India's subsequent linguistic-literary fate might have been different. In Hindustan, the British would probably have felt more like conquerors than they did in Bengal, where they had previously quite amiably carried on their commerce. At any rate, when the Moghul rule fell, the Bengal Hindus of the classes with which they had previously dealt received them as emancipators. Their rule was, of course, foreign to Bengal Hindus and Muslims alike. But as the poet critic and one-time Indian Minister for Culture, Humayun Kabir, has observed: "There were however circumstances which led a large section of the people to accept the position without protest. The possibility that Bengal might, for the first time in history, win national leadership helped to reconcile the people to British hegemony." It was upperclass Muslims who felt the British presence as a demoralizing defeat. Cooperating middle-class Hindus, on the contrary, were soon enjoying what has deservedly been called India's "Bengal Renaissance" — a time when Bengal's Calcutta became for India what ancient Athens had been for Greece. But a better parallel, as we have been suggesting, is obviously what Sicily's Palermo became for all of Italy in the century before Dante.

The British in India immediately set about mastering the languages of their subjects. Sir William Jones's Royal Asiatic Society was founded in 1784, the famous College of Fort William followed in 1800. That college was intended to be, and for a time actually was, India's "Oxford of the East." One of its chief assignments was to make possible translations of the major documents and traditional sources of Hindu and Muslim custom and law, first of all into English, but also into the living vernaculars. In the very first Fort William College bulletin it was stressed that "all the Eastern languages were to be taught," including not only *learned* Arabic, *classic* Persian, and *primaeval* Sanskrit — the qualifying adjectives are those of William Carey, Christian missionary at Serampore and first professor of Sanskrit and Bengali at Fort William — but also the chief vernaculars of the people. At this point in the bulletin, "the five great vernaculars of India" at that time —Bengali, Marathi, Telugu, Tamil, and Kannada — "were accordingly named, and the greatest of all, Hindi" (I am still quoting) "was provided for under the mixed dialect or *lingua franca* known as Hindustani." William Carey's adjective for Bengali, interestingly enough, was *commercial,* while he aptly characterized the *lingua franca* as colloquial Hindustani.[5]

The ultimate purpose of setting up language studies at the college was, however, to "promote the rise of printing and publishing" in the oriental languages. And so their teaching was from the beginning departmentalized not according to the essential characteristics of the languages as spoken but according to their scripts. Hindustani as spoken, for instance, is as much an Aryan vernacular as Bengali. But because it was then written mostly in Arabic script, it was assigned not to William Carey's Sanskrit-Bengali department but to the Perso-Arabic department headed by the talented but enigmatic Dr. John Gilchrist. Yet hybrid Hindustani was briefly well-served by Gilchrist. He saw at once the potential parallel between

Hindustani under the Muslims and English under the Normans; and he boldly tried to do for it at the dawn of the nineteenth century what the Mughals had only half-heartedly tried and therefore failed to do in previous centuries.

To get past the obstacle of Hindu prejudice against Arabic script and Muslim prejudice against Hindi's traditional Nagari — the script now used for sacred Sanskrit — Gilchrist proposed the obvious solution long-since adopted in many Muslim lands of mixed populations: transliteration into Roman characters, especially for printing and publishing, and for early schooling of illiterates. He also favored immediate substitution of Hindustani for Persian as the official language. The British then had the power to do such a thing; but, in Bengal, they hadn't the will. The moment passed. Gilchrist had to content himself with simply developing the language as spoken by both communities into a superior but still popular educational-literary instrument. He brought together at Fort William expert native speakers of all significant Hindustani dialects, and, with their help, prepared grammars, dictionaries, and graded readers printed in fonts of native scripts of his own simplified design. In a late plea for funds, he thus defined his aims and expectations:

> I shall engage to form such a body of useful and entertaining literature in that language as will ultimately raise it to that estimate among the natives which it would many years ago have attained among a more enlightened and energetic people . . . . May we not reason thus from analogy, that the Hindustani will ascend as high on the Indian scale . . . as the English has done in a similar predicament in our own country? ([5] 95)

Unfortunately, Gilchrist's tenure at the college didn't last long. By 1804, four years after its founding, he was gone, and with him went the hope of establishing Hindustani on the English model as the national vernacular. In a score of years after his departure, Gilchrist's Perso-Arabic department had five successive heads, none of whom was ever a match for William Carey, head of the rival Sanskrit-Bengali department, who remained at his post for over thirty years. As a Christian missionary, Carey's chief concern was the conversion of Hindus to Christianity. He seems to have followed St. Francis's example in walking away from the Muslims and dusting his sandals, at least for the present. Hindus were to be converted by preaching in their language and by offering them the Christian Holy Scriptures in attractive translations. Bengal, however, was his immediate mission land. So his first translation of the Bible was into Bengali, and his overriding concern from the beginning was to make Bengali an adequate instrument for Christian instruction.

Carey devoted himself so completely to his aim of refining the local vernacular that, before long, it was to be said of him that at his touch Bengali "arose from the tomb of Sanskrit as Italian did from Latin under Dante's inspiration." Certainly his approach to the refinement of Bengali resembles Dante's approach to a similar task in the *De Vulgari Eloquentia*. He first of all recommended taking the language in its purest spoken forms, as children learn it from their mothers' lips. But beyond that, he urged enrichment by extensive lateral borrowing, drawing on the actual usage of the various native classes and crafts, sampled over as wide an area as possible. And that in turn was to be supplemented, he insisted, by steep vertical borrowing which meant drawing on classical Sanskrit to raise the horizontally-broadened basic speech to heights worthy of the sublime message of the Christian Gospels.

Dante, too, as we know, had urged vertical and horizontal borrowings to enrich the purity of vernaculars learned from the lips of mothers. But he also warned against what he accused the Sardinians of having done. They had gone too far, Dante said, in *aping* Latin. The same could be said about Carey's enrichment of Bengali by reaching up into Sanskrit. Before he was done, Bengali's Sanskrit borrowings amounted to over 88%. Chiding the Sardinians for surrendering their linguistic birthright by taking up too much Latin, Dante had said: "Incapable of creating a dialect of their own, they imitate Latin as if they were not men but monkeys." Similarly, when it was perceived that Carey's approach, in which he was encouraged by his Brahman pandits, had resulted in a split between the popular version of the language and a literary dialect "known only through the press and not intelligible to those who do not know Sanskrit," the great linguist Sir George A. Grierson wrote in his monumental, many-volumed *Linguistic Survey of India* (Calcutta, 1903-1928): "Bengali, as a vernacular, has been stunted in its growth by this process of cramming it with a class of food it is unable to assimilate" when native Bengali terms of beauty and simplicity were always ready at hand. ([5] 98)

It may be said that the history of Bengali writing after Carey's time is the history of efforts to arrive at a proper fusion or balance of the two extremes. The landmark figures in that history are first of all Rammohun Roy (1772-1833), Bengal's great modernist pioneer, then Iswar Chandra Sarma (1820-1891), later honored under the title Vidyasagar, followed by that 'marvelous-boy' poet in both Bengali and English, Michael Madhusudan Datta (1824-1873), then Bankim Chandra Chatterji (1838-1894), founder of the modern school of Indian fiction, and finally Rabindranath Tagore (1861-1941) who, with his Bengali poetry and English translations, earned for Asia, in 1913, its first Nobel Prize for literature. Tagore, many have said, brought to completion the Dante-Bengali parallel. With a Dantesque touch, Carey had brought the language into existence; Tagore, it is claimed, with a similar touch, brought it to a full literary flowering. Humayun Kabir, whom we cited earlier on Bengal's sense of emancipation under the British, has put it this way:

> Dante in Europe offers an example where the work of a single poet lifted the dialect of a province to the status of a world language. The achievement of Tagore is in some ways even more striking. Dante was born in the expansive days of the Italian Renaissance. Italy was divided into a hundred principalities but stirred with a new consciousness of freedom. . . . Dante's genius shone the more brightly in the context of his surroundings. In the case of Tagore, the contribution of the environment was at times negative. His influence on the environment was in fact greater than that of the environment on him. Renascent Bengal found in Tagore's work a message of liberation. He brought the message of a new awakening to India just as Dante had done to a resurgent Italy. ([5] 90-91)

But, of course, by the time Tagore died in 1941, India was

just five and a half years short of gaining independence from its foreign British rulers. After Dante's death in 1321, his Italy was to enjoy two centuries more of its "divided freedom" only to experience an added three and a half centuries of "divided subjugation" under foreigners as contemptuous of the Italian political character as the British may ever have been of the Hindu political character. A truer parallel for what happened to the Bengali vernacular from the time of Carey to that of Tagore is to be sought, rather, in what happened to "emergent" Italian at the "court of emperors" in Palermo. We call the literary Italian that developed at that court Sicilian, Dante says, even though the court under the Hohenstaufens attracted poets from all over Italy, as well as French, German, and even Arab, Persian, and Greek-speaking poets, to say nothing of would-be Latin classicists. That Palermo court was truly a prototype for the literary flowering that Bengal's Calcutta enjoyed under the British in the nineteenth century.

It is conceivable that, had Palermo become the capital of a reconstituted Holy Roman Empire, Sicilian Italian might have been elevated to the status of court vernacular, and thus the national vernacular, for all of Italy as the traditional national "garden of the empire." Or the emperors in Sicily might have preferred to make Rome itself once again the imperial capital as soon as possible. In that case it is likely that the local Roman dialect — utterly despised by Dante! — would have been favored, perhaps in anticipation of a Petrarchian-Erasmian revival of classical Latin. Unfortunately for Dante's political hopes, but fortunately for his language, the Hohenstaufen dream of true empire failed to materialize. Palermo ceased to be an imperial capital, Rome remained in the hands of the Popes, and Italy was quickly transformed into that marvelous land of many linguistic-cultural centers of relatively equal status which Dante so ably surveys for us in his treatise on vernacular eloquence.

British India experienced a comparably decisive time in 1911-1912, just a year before Rabindranath Tagore's Nobel Prize. At that time, the British decided to move their capital some 900 miles inland, from Calcutta to old Delhi in the heart of populous Urdu-Hindi-speaking Hindustan. Next to that old

Delhi, the British, when they made their move, immediately began to build a New Delhi of magnificent marble. That New Delhi, they said, was to serve them as a permanent memorial of their rule, even as it could later serve an independent India as a much more centrally located, and therefore much more truly national capital.

That shift proved to be a terrible blow to the Bengali intelligentsia, for it soon brought an end to all imperial support of Bengali as against the Hindi-Urdu versions of Hindustani. Just then, too, it was that mighty Gandhi made his appearance, to crusade for the ouster of the British, for the immediate abolition of untouchability among the Hindus, and for the adoption of Hindustani in both scripts as the national language of independence — the only language capable, in his view, of holding Muslim-Hindu India together as one nation. But, while he favored a solution to India's language problem on the Norman-English model, the always half-naked but highly so-phisticated Indian nation-builder went about defending his language proposals with a zeal and wit and thoroughness worthy of comparison with the best labors of Dante in the *De Vulgari Eloquentia.*

When Gandhi started his crusade for Hindustani, Grierson's *Linguistic Survey of India,* cited earlier, was more than half-way completed. What it provided was a view of the linguistic condition of India quite like Dante's view of the linguistic situation of Italy at the start of the fourteenth century. India and Italy are both continental peninsulas. Italy is slender; India is broad. India's main geographical divisions run mostly east and west, setting off a mountainous Himalayan region in the north, a great Indo-Gangetic plain in the center, and a vast Peninsula proper extending far to the south. Italy's main physical division runs generally north-south; so that while there is an Alpine region corresponding to the Himalayas in the north, the slender peninsula itself is divided so as to set off eastern and western halves. "And if someone should ask what the line of division is," Dante writes, "I would answer, in a word, the ridge of the Apennines, which, in the manner of a tile roof . . . drains Italy's waters into the Tyrrhenian sea on the right and into the Adriatic on the left."

The peninsula proper, Dante goes on to say, has five distinguishable regions and peoples on each side of its central ridge, making ten in all, with two islands, Sicily and Sardinia, to the west, which he assigns to the western half, and two extra-peninsular regions to the north-east, Friuli and Istria, which are assigned to the eastern half. And then he gives this marvelous summary of his survey, which, simply with the substitution of Indian for Italian names of places and peoples, can stand as a statistically accurate summation of the Grierson *Survey* as updated in the latest India census reports. "From this," writes Dante,

> it appears that Italy alone is divided into at least fourteen vernaculars, And all of these vernaculars are further divided within themselves, so that in Tuscany, for instance, the language of the Sienese differs from that of Arezzo, and in Lombardy, that of Ferrara from that of Piacenza. And we may even observe certain differences within a single city, as I remarked above. And so if I were to add up the primary, secondary, and subsidiary differences in the vernaculars of Italy, I would not just approach a figure like one thousand different dialects in this, the smallest corner of the world, but would even exceed this figure. ([5] 126)

Like Dante's, Grierson's survey gives us "at least fourteen" major vernaculars, and the latest census reports for India, Pakistan, and Bangladesh give us, indeed, more than a thousand dialects in all. Yet, far more striking than this statistical parallel is the parallel between Gandhi's approach and Dante's to the problem of identifying what sort of vernacular, out of so many vernaculars, could properly qualify as a popular national language. We must remind ourselves that Gandhi's chief concern was to hold all Indians together in a single nation-state, to prevent, in other words, their division into a Hindi-using Union of India, an Urdu-using Pakistan, and a Bengali-using Bangladesh, etc. We know the criteria Dante laid down for a worthy Italian national vernacular. To qualify, he said, it would have to be *illustre, cardinale, aulicum,* and *curiale.* The English cognates — illustrious, cardinal, aulic, and curial — will do, or almost do, for some of the original terms, though not for all.

Illustrious means luminous in itself, he says, but also capable of giving the power of illuminating to others; cardinal means hinge-like, suggesting a vernacular capable of carrying all the other vernaculars around with it, as on a turning door; aulic means courtly in the royal sense, suggesting the sort of language people would use at a national monarchic capital, like London or Paris; and curial, finally, means courtly in the juridical sense, suggesting a language that is "fair to all," giving all the other vernaculars their due, or justice, like a true court of law.

With those we can compare Gandhi's four principal criteria for a national vernacular: "1. It should be easy to learn for government officials. 2. It should be capable of serving as a medium of religious, economic, and political intercourse throughout India. 3. It should be the speech of the majority of the inhabitants of India. 4. It should be easy to learn for the whole country." A moment's reflection suffices to see that the first of these matches Dante's aulic, the second his illustrious, the third his cardinal, and the fourth his curial. Gandhi concludes that only two of India's vernaculars could possibly qualify. And they are, to be sure, the two Gilchrist and Carey fought over at the College of Fort William. Gandhi comes down heavily in favor of Gilchrist's Hindustani in the two scripts. It alone, he says, can hold the Indian Hindu and Muslim communities together; it alone is humble enough, and simple and utilitarian enough, to be easily learned by all; and it alone, precisely because it has developed as a hybrid *lingua franca, is* already known in most regions of India, north and south, east and west. Of course, in his aversion to anything associated in any way with the departing British, Gandhi flatly rejected the idea of a shift to "neutral" Roman characters, though that alone could have made Hindustani acceptable.

In any event, as independence day approached for India at the start of World War II, an Indian equivalent of what had been for Italy a linguistic-literary preparation extended over five and a half centuries, had suddenly to be compressed, as we have suggested, into five and a half years. There was no time in India, after Tagore's death in 1941, for the sort of free competition that finally raised Dante's native tongue to undisputed primacy over all other competing dialects in Italy. Once it was clear that England would indeed "quit India" as soon as possible after the war, language choices simply could not be delayed. Gandhi, as we said, fought hard for Hindustani in the two scripts. And, in a sense, that is what prevailed: to be imposed, however, not by one, but by two separate Indian governments. In the traditional Nagari script, and called Hindi, it was declared the official language of the predominately Hindu Union of India. In its Arabic script, and called Urdu, it became the official language of predominantly Muslim Pakistan. Yet Carey's Bengali, too, has had its political innings of sorts. With the separation of East Pakistan from West Pakistan, we now have an independent Bangladesh. It is predominantly Muslim, and would therefore not have been to Carey's liking. But its language is a Muslimized Bengali, not Urdu.

Over the three Indias today a great-hearted spirit hovers, pleading for tolerance. It is the spirit of Gandhi, who, we should note, has been called India's spiritual banyan, touching the ground everywhere and taking root everywhere. With that we can permit ourselves to return to the great image for linguistic diversity in unity with which we started. I ought perhaps to have noted earlier that when Milton first learned of India's great figtree, he was so impressed that he at once planted it in his poetic Eden for our first parents to make use of in hiding their new-found nakedness. "They chose," Milton writes,

> The fig-tree; not that kind for fruit renown'd,
> But such as at this day, to Indians known,
> In Malabar or Deccan spreads her arms
> Branching so broad and long, that in the ground
> The bended twigs take root, and daughters grow
> About the mother tree, a pillar'd shade
> High over-arch'd, and echoing walks between;
> There oft the Indian herdsman

[and we might there substitute the modern linguistic-literary comparatist!]

> . . . shunning heat
> Shelters in cool, and tends his pasturing herds
> At loopholes cut through thickest shade . . . . (*P.L*, IX, 1100-1111)

There are many linguistic banyans in our world today. The current writing in English in many lands around the world certainly constitutes, as we noted at the beginning, such a banyan. And strange to say, one of the branches of that English banyan has long-since extended itself over India, to be grafted into the native banyan that started its literary growth with the Vedas. But now, that grafted branch too has put down roots and a trunk of its own there, and is fast becoming, before our very eyes, something as much native Indian, they say, as it is English. But, philologists or not, we know the rule: *Quot rami tot arbores.*

NOTES

[Where sources are identified in the text, page references are inserted after passages quoted; and, after the first numbered reference to sources identified in the notes below, subsequent page references appear parenthetically in the text, with the note number in square brackets, followed by the page ([no] p.).]

1. T. S. Eliot, *To Criticize the Critic* (New York, 1965), pp. 43-60.

2. In G. T. Garratt, ed., *The Legacy of India* (Oxford, 1967).

3. E. C. Dimock *et al.*, eds., *The Literatures of India* (Chicago, 1974), p. 13.

4. Sir Walter Scott, *Ivanhoe* (Everyman's Library, London, 1967), pp. 26-27.

5. Anne Paolucci, ed., *Review of National Literatures*, Vol. 10, special issue on *India* (New York, 1980), p. 92.

MACHIAVELLI'S *MANDRAGOLA*

Machiavelli's *Mandragola*, for centuries half-hidden from view in the shadow of *The Prince*, has only lately begun to receive adequate recognition as what it unquestionably is: the unrivaled masterpiece of the Italian comic theater. Carlo Goldoni, the eighteenth-century author traditionally honored as Italy's foremost comic playwright, will, no doubt, because of the mere quantity of good work he produced, continue to be so honored; nevertheless, the best Italian critics today are inclined to uphold the judgment of T. B. Macaulay that the *Mandragola* "is superior to the best of Goldoni and inferior only to the best of Molière."[1] They agree that no one work of Goldoni rises to the level of dramatic perfection of the *Mandragola*. They recognize also that precisely where Goldoni's art seems weakest as compared with Molière's — in intellectual fiber and depth of characterization —Machiavelli's art is exceptionally strong; and some critics press the advantage even further, noting that Machiavelli displays technical mastery also in the one phase of dramatic art wherein Molière himself was admittedly weak, namely, in the architectural design of the action, in the unraveling of the plot, which, as Voltaire observed, is often brought on in Molière with too little preparation and in an improbable manner. Voltaire, incidentally, is said to have asserted that the *Mandragola* was "worth more than all the comedies of Aristophanes."[2] One might more justly assert, rather, that had Machiavelli been willing to divert himself with writing a few more plays of comparable merit, and had he not written *The Prince* and the *Discourses*, he would long ago have been acclaimed a master of comedy to be ranked as

[From *Machiavelli's "Mandragola."* Original translation. Macmillan Publishing, New York, and Collier Macmillan Publishing London. First printed in 1957.]

the equal of Aristophanes and Molière.

Two other comedies, both typical products of the Renaissance theater, have come to us from the pen of Machiavelli: *Andria*, translated from Terence, and *Clizia*, an imitation of Plautus. But in the *Mandragola*, written sometime between 1512 and 1520, Machiavelli rose above the Renaissance ideal, abandoning translation and imitation for pure invention. Spectators at its earliest performances (one of the first took place in the year 1520 in the presence of Pope Leo X) judged the play to be something distinctly new — and modern literary scholars generally have concurred in that judgment.

The theme of the play, sexual seduction, is, of course, not new. A love-sick young man enlists the aid of servants, friends, and rogues that he may gratify an inordinate desire to possess the beautiful wife of an old "doctor"; obstacles are encountered; plans to overcome them are devised and revised. At last, after a series of humorous turns, the desired end is attained. All this belongs to comic tradition. Machiavelli, however, introduces an element that makes a fundamental difference. He represents the beautiful wife as an evidently virtuous woman who would not under any circumstances invite amorous advances and who has not the least intention of betraying her husband. Remarking the novelty of this representation of the wife, Professor D. C. Stuart, in the *Development of Dramatic Art*, observes that as a consequence "scenes and situations unknown in Latin comedy are introduced."[3] But this novel characterization is by no means accidental. It is, itself, a consequence of Machiavelli's wholly original conception of the basic action of the play. With the genius of purest comedy evidently guiding him, he boldly manipulates the commonplace amorous intrigue, which is his theme as if it were a problem in international diplomacy. From the outset, the young hero of the play seems as ardently concerned to secure emotional health for himself as some fiery statesman might well be to secure the *salus republica*. He represents himself as caught in a situation of clear and present danger; he must attain his end or be destroyed. And with very life at issue, the voice of reason itself, he tells us, dictates that he must be willing to do whatever necessity indicates to secure victory and, with victory, the enjoyment of that hallowed peace and happiness which is the goal of all human endeavor.

In pursuit of such happiness the young hero enters, conditionally, upon an alliance with a known ruffian who performs his services with the aplomb of an experienced official of the diplomatic corps. The ruffian warns against shortsightedness, against unnecessary violence, against the allurements of easy but merely temporary success; and he advises a definition of policy such that everyone involved may anticipate from its successful execution some real or apparent benefit. The task, thereafter, is merely to negotiate with all parties, pointing out to each the nature of the advantage to be derived, beginning with those whose advantage is most obvious (even if only apparent) and, with their support, proceeding to the persuasion of the one person who, seemingly at least, stands to lose something precious in the transaction. Bluntly stated, the immediate object is to enlist the aid of husband, mother, and father-confessor in persuading a virtuous wife that she shall have performed a faithful act of conjugal obedience while admitting an utter stranger to the enjoyments of her bed. Such is the immediate object; the ultimate object is to effect in the wife a fundamental "transvaluation of values."

The attainment of these two objects involves the chief personages of the play in a series of actions which prompts Professor Stuart to remark: "Of the cynical immorality of these situations the less said the better; but nevertheless these scenes strike a note never heard even in Plautus. They give an opportunity for dramatic progression."[4] And even the great Francesco de Sanctis, who otherwise judges the *Mandragola* very severely on moral grounds, is constrained to acknowledge that in the closing scenes Machiavelli rises to a display of "comic power and originality matched by little in the ancient or modern theater."[5]

The chief personages of the play — the Prologue informs us — are four: a low-designing lover, a leech or ruffian who is "deceit's own child," an absurdly pompous old "doctor," and a monk who has lived ill. We have already considered briefly the characterizations of the young lover and his ruffian adviser. The old "doctor" is, of course, the butt of the farcical intrigue.

A scrawny old pigeon of a man, he struts and cackles among women and servants, bows and scrapes before his betters, and scurries out of sight at the mere suggestion of real danger. He is vulgar, stupid, impotent, shameless; but Machiavelli masterfully elevates him to the level of high comedy by arming him with the proverbial wisdom of the common people. His speech is a *vade mecum* of popular sagacity. His every decision, his every deed has the sanction of some traditional Florentine proverb, so that the old fool has the satisfaction of thinking himself a veritable fox as he leads himself by the nose whither others want him to go.

The fourth chief personage, the monk who has lived ill, makes his appearance very late in the play. The Prologue warns us that we may miss him if we hurry away too soon. And yet his is unmistakably the most important personality, so profoundly complex that there have been almost as many diverse interpretations of his character and of the significance of his part in the play as there have been critics. In the judgment of some he is a cheap hypocrite, a deceitful casuist and simoniac trading for a pittance the spiritual goods entrusted to his care, a lecherous corrupter of womanhood, of family, of society. For others he is a delightfully Boccaccesque personality, by some quirk of fate thrust into a monkish order, conducting himself as well as one can under the circumstances and consenting, when he cannot graciously do otherwise, to spice our enjoyment of the venereal suggestiveness of the play with a touch of clerical wit. Still other critics have seen in him a frank spokesman for Machiavelli's own profoundest sentiments regarding the nature of man and the motives underlying the normal conduct of human affairs.

He is, indeed, as some of the best critics have suggested, exactly the same sort of enigmatic personality that Machiavelli's prince is. The latter, too, has been variously appraised, being most frequently denounced as the embodiment of absolute immorality, yet almost as often admired for his unwavering pragmatism, and sometimes even quite earnestly acclaimed as the only conceivable instrument of temporal salvation for a politically depressed people. Each of these diverse interpretations, of the monk as of the prince, contains a large measure of truth; each is the result of appraising a singularly rich personality from a different point of view. The fact that Machiavelli, with the instinct of a dramatist, declines to impose upon his readers any single point of view is, perhaps, a defect in *The Prince*, for it renders equivocal the meaning of a work that may have been intended to be clear and unambiguous. But it is no defect in the *Mandragola* and, indeed, no defect in *The Prince* either, if the latter be judged from a purely literary standpoint. So judged *The Prince* becomes a grand tragedy — a play, rather than a treatise, offering a tragic view of the same world of which the *Mandragola* is the comedy.

Machiavelli, it would seem, was incapable of delineating an unequivocal representation of the world underlying his literary masterpieces. At any rate, one looks in vain through the entire corpus of his writings for such a picture. Here and there, especially in the *Discourses*, in the lesser tracts, and in the *Florentine Histories*, profoundly suggestive indications are given, but always in a fragmentary, and frequently in a self-contradictory or, rather, paradoxical manner. Yet the indications are sufficient to enable a serious student of political philosophy to recognize their compatibility with that grand conception of ethics and politics, and of the interrelation of the two in history, which had its foundation in Aristotle and which has received its most systematic exposition, from a secular point of view, in the *Philosophy of Law* of Hegel. Its equivalent in traditional Christianity is to be found in St. Augustine's elaborate conception of the *civitas terrena*.

The world of the *Mandragola* and of *The Prince* is a world of men, women, and children all earnestly pursuing peace and happiness, yet unfortunately pursuing these wonderful ends in such a way that the satisfaction of one person often, if not always, involves the frustration of another. Conflicts of interest inevitably arise — between the crying infant and its mother, between children, youths, adults, families, clans; and in these conflicts either both parties are frustrated or one party emerges as victor and the other as vanquished. No doubt there have always been some human beings who would rather die than submit to the will of another, but these have, in fact, been such rarities that all peoples, at all times, have looked upon them with wonderment. The majority of human beings easily learn to accommodate themselves in defeat, submitting their wills, gradually, as well as their bodies to the guidance of their conquerors. Thus emerges that "consent of the governed," that common will, which transforms the relations of victor and vanquished into that of ruler and ruled. The institution of law and education is then possible, the latter implementing the former by training youths, from the earliest possible moment, to conduct themselves habitually in accordance with the common will. The product of the common will is the commonwealth, or *res publica*.

A people with a *res publica* are able to enjoy much peace and happiness among themselves — provided they can secure their commonwealth against the inevitable aggressions of their richer and poorer neighbors. If they can, they will no doubt continue to prosper, augmenting their commonwealth, insuring domestic tranquillity, and providing for the common defense first by merely thrusting back aggressors who invade their peaceful land, later, with more prudence, going forth to meet and stop aggressors before they actually invade, and finally, with maximum prudence, streaming outward themselves in full force to make the world utterly and forever safe, so that they who have proved most willing to fight for freedom may thereafter live comfortably in the peaceful pursuit of happiness.

So, according to the basic pattern glimpsed by Machiavelli, runs the course of the world's pursuit of happiness. Aristotle, in his *Politics*, concentrated his attention on the phase of this process which culminates in the establishment of a republic with sufficient means to facilitate among its free citizens the pursuit of knowledge and happiness. The Roman political and juridical thinkers concentrated on the problem of establishing the habits of peace throughout the word, putting an end to the aggressions of haughty people and helping backward areas to help themselves. St. Augustine, called upon to explain the sack of Rome in 410, chose to assess the colossal misery involved in the whole process, especially in its culminating stage — the establishing of an enforceable world peace.

In *The Prince* Machiavelli restricted himself to an analysis of the problem of releasing a vanquished people from the bondage of factional disunity imposed upon them by powerful neighbors. This is perhaps the ugliest phase of the process, especially from the point of view of the citizens of nations that have long ago solved the problem in question, and whose statesmen are masters of the high art of preventing other peoples form doing so. But in whatever phase men and societies may find themselves, the fundamental human nature, the underlying natural impulses, Machiavelli, insists, remain the same. His view of human nature, pessimistic as it may seem, accords exactly with that of Aristotle, who observed that, apart from the restraints of politically constituted society, men are apt to behave toward one another worse than the most savage beasts; and it accords also with the traditional doctrine of Christianity on human nature, especially as articulated by St. Augustine. One should not forget however, that in St. Augustine's view nature is not the sole force operating in human history. According to the great African bishop, Divine Grace also operates, sustaining, in the midst of the *civitas terrena*, a pilgrim portion of the City of God.

Of Divine Grace operating in the world, Machiavelli, needless to say, saw nothing. From a Christian point of view, therefore, one may say that his unpleasant doctrine is not the whole story. But, as T. S. Eliot has very emphatically observed in his short essay on the subject, from no other point of view can one fairly make this restriction.[6] Against modern readers who find themselves revolted by the immorality of the world of *The Prince* and the *Mandragola* and who, on that account, repudiate Machiavelli's representation of human nature as unrealistic or perhaps true only for Italians of his own time, T. S. Eliot has written significantly: "Machiavelli was no fanatic; he merely observed the truth about humanity without the addition of superhuman Grace." His view, Eliot continues, "is therefore tolerable only to persons who have also a definite religious belief; to the effort of the last three centuries to supply religious belief by belief in Humanity the creed of Machiavelli is insupportable." All that the author of *The Prince* and of the *Mandragola* failed to see about human nature, Eliot concludes, is "the myth of human goodness which for liberal thought replaces the belief in Divine Grace."

With the foregoing representation of the historical pattern of the earthly pursuit of happiness to serve as a background, it is perhaps easier to see why, judged from a purely literary standpoint, *The Prince* is indeed a tragedy and the *Mandragola* a comedy. *The Prince* represents a desperate, utterly frustrate attempt to salvage some genuine happiness out of a wretched national situation; the *Mandragola*, on the other hand, represents a mere prank whereby an audience is invited, for its recreation, to observe how, even in the tragic land of *The Prince*, some small measure of delight may be secured by deception worked so cunningly and with so little violence as to inflict as little pain as possible upon those who are being deceived. The spectacle of this cunningly worked deception may be enjoyed, on a thoughtless level, simply for its own sake. But appreciation of the element of greatness in the play requires that a picture of the tragic world of *The Prince* be ever kept at least faintly in mind. And Machiavelli is able to force upon this audience repeated reminders of the presence of that world primarily through his characterization of the monk, Fra Timoteo, to whom he has given that "inexplicable touch of infinity" — as A. C. Bradley calls it — which is the mark of true greatness in dramatic creation.

NOTES

1. Thomas Babington Macaulay, "Machiavelli," in *Macaulay, Prose and Poetry*, selected by G. M. Young (Cambridge, Mass., 1952), p. 252. The essay was originally printed in the *Edinbough Reveiw*, March, 1827.

2. See preface by I. D. Levine in Niccolò Machiavelli, *Mandragola*, tr. Stark Young (New York, 1927), pp. 8-9.

3. Donald Clive Stuart, *Development of Dramatic Art* (New York and London, 1928), p. 286.

4. *Ibid.*

5. Francesco de Sanctis, *Storia della letteratura italiana* (Milano, 1928), II, 89.

6. T. S. Eliot, "Niccolo Machiavelli," in *For Lancelot Andrews* (Garden City, N. Y., 1929), pp. 62-63.

THE POETICS OF
ARISTOTLE AND HEGEL

Hegel's poetics, like Aristotle's, is based on the comparative study of individual works of art; but whereas Aristotle's is limited to a single literature, Hegel's is comparative in the modern sense, ranging beyond ancient classical poetry to comprehend also the symbolic poetry of the Far and Near East and the romantic poetry of medieval Christendom and the modern Western nations.

Aristotle's *Poetics* is, of course, the earliest example of systematic literary criticism in any literature; and not until Longinus produced his treatise *On the Sublime* many centuries later was there a second example at all worthy of comparison with it. Its unadorned style, the rigor of its method, even its fragmentary brevity which emphasizes its main points by isolating them, have made it the most readable and by far the most influential philosophical work of its kind in the Western tradition. W. D. Ross, editor of the great Oxford translation of Aristotle's works, summed up the scholarly opinion of his age when he said of the brief treatise that it contains "a greater number of pregnant ideas on art than any other book."[1]

Nevertheless it is a fact that Aristotle's theory of poetry has survived only as a patched remnant of what it originally must have been. We have no general aesthetics from him – no philosophy of fine art embracing architecture, sculpture, painting, and music, as well as poetry (though in Book VIII of his *Politics* Aristotle says much that is aesthetically very suggestive about the power of music); and in the *Poetics* itself, only the doctrine on tragedy approaches completeness, there being no discussion of lyric poetry, the bare promise of a theory of

[From *Hegel in Comparative Literature, Review of National Literatures*, Vol. I, No. 2, St. John's University, New York, 1970.]

comedy, and only a few pregnant paragraphs on the art of the epic. Hegel's poetics, on the other hand, is the culmination of an aesthetics that is elab-orated through three large volumes of his complete works; and it treats equally of epic, lyric, and dramatic poetry, supplying what is missing in Aristotle's treatise with respect to Greek literature, at the same time that it reinterprets the Aristotelian insights in the light of the literary experience of other peoples.

In this paper we mean to approach the study of Hegel's poetics through Aristotle, emphasizing the extraordinary continuity of thought that may be traced from one to the other across two and a half millennia of literary history. That Hegel's view of tragedy can be profitably studied as an extension of the Aristotelian doctrine has often been acknowledged by competent scholars. In his *Oxford Lectures on Poetry*, the eminent Shakespearean critic A. C. Bradley, for instance, thus links the two with the highest possible praise: "Since Aristotle dealt with tragedy and, as usual, drew the main features of his subject with those sure and simple strokes which no later hand has rivaled, the only philosopher who has treated it in a manner both original and searching is Hegel."[2]

One object of the following pages is to suggest that what Hegel has to say about the symbolic, classical, and romantic types of poetic intuition, about verbal imagery and versification, and about the masterpieces of dramatic comedy as well as the epic and lyric genres, is no less original and searching than his treatment of tragedy. A corollary object is to suggest that, precisely because adequate Aristotelian counterparts of so much of it do not exist and perhaps never have existed, the whole of Hegel's poetics deserves to be more widely studied that it is today.

1. Aristotle's Ideal of Mimesis: Its Validity and Limitations

In an early chapter of the *Poetics*, Aristotle traces the origins of poetry back to man's natural sense of harmony and rhythm and his equally natural impulse to make imitations, to learn by imitating, and to take delight in imitations even when the things themselves are perhaps painful to look at. But the origins of poetry are not, of course, to be confounded with poetry in its true form: for, as Aristotle explains, "starting with natural aptitude, men very gradually made a series of improvements on their first efforts, till finally their rude improvisations gave birth to poetry."[3]

What distinguishes all genuine art from its crude beginnings in imitative making (*poiesis mimetikós*) is the wonder its finished products are able to inspire. Wonder, Aristotle says, intensifies our sense of ignorance and "implies the desire of learning, so that the object of wonder is an object of desire."[4] In an often cited passage of the *Metaphysics*, where he links the origins of philosophy with poetry, Aristotle observes that the desire to know is first keenly aroused in men only after their other more immediate needs have been satisfied and they can be at leisure to contemplate the "phenomena of the moon and of the sun and the stars" and, more particularly, to wonder "about the genesis of the universe." And it is then not merely the phenomena themselves that inspire wonder but also the inherited myths about them. "Whence even the lover of myth," Aristotle concludes, "is in a sense the lover of Wisdom, for the myth is composed of wonders."[5]

In the *Poetics*, explaining why men seem to take delight even in the crudest forms of imitations, Aristotle says more explicitly:

> To be learning something is the greatest of pleasures not only to the philosopher but also to the rest of mankind, however small their capacity for it; the reason of the delight in seeing the representation is that one is at the same time learning — gathering the meaning of things, e.g. that the man represented is so and so or of such kind: for if one has not seen the object before, one's pleasure will not be in the picture as an imitation of it, but will be due to the execution or coloring or some similar cause.[6]

Later in the treatise, this line of reasoning leads to Aristotle's grand defense of poetry against Plato's notorious condemnation of it in Book X of the *Republic*, where Plato's spokesman argues that poetry at its best gives us only imitations of imitations, or lies about lies, twice removed from reality. In Chapter 9 of the *Poetics* — rejecting Plato's view without citing his name — Aristotle writes what is certainly the most "Hegelian" page of the treatise. Comparing the poet's grasp of the truth of things with that of the historian who aspires to report events as they really happened, Aristotle concludes that imitative poetry can bring us much closer to the highest level of truth than even the best prose of history can. The distinction between historian and poet, he writes,

> is not in the writing prose and the other verse — you might put the work of Herodotus into verse, and it would still be a species of history; it consists really in this, that the one describes the thing that has been, and the other a kind of thing that might be. Hence poetry is something more philosophic and of graver import than history, since its statements are of the nature rather of universals, whereas those of history are singulars. By a universal statement I mean one as to what such and such a kind of man will probably or necessarily do — which is the aim of poetry, though it affixes proper names to the characters. By a singular statement, I mean one as to what, say, Alcibiades did, or had done to him. In Comedy this has become quite clear in our time; it is only when their plot is already made up of probable incidents that they give it a basis of proper names, choosing for the purpose any names that may occur to them, instead of writing like the old iambic poets about particular persons. In Tragedy, however, they still adhere to the historic names; and for this reason: what convinces is the possible; and while we cannot be sure of the possibility of what has not yet happened, that which has already happened is manifestly possible . . . . But even in Tragedy there are some plays with but one or two known names, the rest being inventions.[7]

To grasp the profundity of Aristotle's argument here — an argument which says that poetry, like philosophy, transcends the flux of history, and may thus be regarded as what Hegel will later call an "absolute moment of spirit" — one must, however, at least briefly recall its basis in the general Aristotelian criticism of Plato's theory of ideas. Needless to say, Plato's condemnation of poetry was no passing whim but an essential part of his nature, but all sensory things, natural as well as artificial, are like flitting shadows, devoid of reality and therefore of truth.

And Aristotle, who had been Plato's disciple for twenty years, fully understood the force of the arguments that had led Plato to assume such a view and thus to condemn poetry as he did.

As Aristotle explains in the *Metaphysics*: "The supporters of the theory of ideas were led to it because on the question of truth they accepted the Heraclitean sayings which describe all sensible things as ever in flux: so that if knowledge or thought is to have a valid object, there must be some other and permanent entities apart from those which are sensible; for there can be no knowledge of things which are in a state of flux.[8] The Pythagorians, much earlier, had for the same reason claimed that numbers were the abiding reality. The trouble with such theories, according to Aristotle (as also according to Hegel), is that while they are introduced at first to make the flux of sensory experience intelligible, they somehow always fail in the end to enlighten us as to what connection their abiding realities can conceivably have with the transient things they are supposed to explain. In a passage of great relevance for his theory of poetry, Aristotle writes: "The Pythagorians say that sensory things exist by 'imitation' of numbers, and Plato says that they exist also by participation, changing the name. But what the participation or the imitation of the forms could be they have left an open question.[9] . . . For to say that they are patterns and that sensory things share in them is to use empty words and poetical metaphors."[10]

Aristotle's entire system of thought, including his *Poetics*, is his answer to that open question — an answer that sympathetically salvages all it can of the Platonic doctrine, filling empty words with scientific meaning and translating poetical metaphors into the logic of genuinely philosophic prose. As Hegel reminds us in his *History of Philosophy*, it is surely one of the supreme ironies of that history that Plato, the most poetic of philosophers, should have condemned poetry so vehemently, while Aristotle, who first displayed the possibilities of strictly scientific prose, should have undertaken to defend Homer and the great tragedians by suggesting that the Platonic theory of ideas is itself a wondrous myth that compels us to philosophize: a myth that must excite our imaginations before it can begin to gratify our intellects with its representations of the soul as an unruly two-horsed chariot, of our sensory environment as a cave, of the shaper of natural things as a demiurge who gives to airy nothing a local habitation and a name, or of that remarkable tribe of two-headed and eight-limbed men, women, and androgenes who have long since been split in two.[11]

For all his sympathy and understanding, Aristotle is able finally to salvage only one of the supersensory Platonic ideas. But that, fortunately, is the only one the great poet-philosopher really took seriously: his Idea of Ideas, or Highest Good (*tó agathón*). Framing a working hypothesis for his inquiry into the possible significance of "imitation" and "participation" as used by the Platonists, Aristotle writes: "We must consider, first of all, in which of two ways the nature of the universe can contain the good, or the highest good, whether as something separate and by itself, or as the order of the parts." He proposes to assume the most general hypothesis, namely, that the good is present in both ways, as in an army, where the order is present in the whole but also in the commanding general, and "more in the latter, since he does not depend on the order but it depends on him." The natural universe, Aristotle continues, is probably like a vast army, with each of its parts under specific orders to act as it has been trained to act. "The truth is," he writes, "that all things in nature are ordered together somehow, but not all alike — both fishes, and fowls, and plants . . . . All are ordered to one end, but each differently."[12]

Using Platonic terms, one might say that it is the *idea* of a stone, for instance, to fall toward the center of the earth, or of an acorn to grow into an oak. But Aristotle prefers the term *nature* (*physis*), which literally means "principle of motion," and of change generally, as well as of rest. It is the characteristic act of the stone in falling and of the acorn in growing that constitutes the nature, or moving principle of each — a principle that "draws" each of them into the general order of the universe the way metal filings are drawn into place in the field of a magnet. The natural universe as Aristotle conceives it is indeed just such a magnetic field, with Plato's Idea of Ideas at its center. Each natural thing "imitates" or "participates in" that supreme Idea, responding to its gravitational pull even as the diversely qualified units of an army — crates and donkeys, privates and captains — respond differently but coordinately to the same general command. Most typical of the natural process in this Aristotelian sense is the characteristic act of a seed, which is, as he explains, "productive in the same way as the principle of art; for like the artist, the seed contains the form of the thing potentially.[13]

The characteristic act of man that links him into the general order of the universe is, of course, his rationality. Man has much in common with inorganic things as well as with plants and other animals. But what distinguishes him is his natural drive to rationalize every aspect of his being. By nature, says Aristotle, all men desire to know, to be happy, and to make for themselves whatever means their instinctive reason may require for their successful pursuit of knowledge and happiness. These are the three all-comprehending natural activities of man — theoretic, practical, and productive — which are rooted in his intellect, will, and generative love. In primitive circumstances, as also in childhood, the three tend to pursue distinct lines of development; but gradually, as Aristotle explains, under the discipline of reason, they begin to converge on one another, like terrestrial meridians drawn up from the equator to the pole. It is the awakening of wonder that makes them converge — for the desire aroused by wonder excites man irresistibly to pursue the highest possible satisfaction of all his potentialities in a single object, the experience of which Aristotle calls *sophía*. And with this we reach the crowning height of Aristotle's defense of poetry; for he holds that productive activity, in the form of poetic mimesis, not less than philosophical *theoría* and ethical *prāxix*, can bring man within sight of the ultimate goal.[14]

In imitative art, therefore, as distinguished from utilitarian making, the satisfactions of intellect, will, and generative love are combined; and, according to Aristotle, the more perfect the combination, the higher the level of artistic achievement. He does not speak of architecture as an imitative art (for reasons we must explore later) and does not classify sculpture or painting in terms of their diverse capacities to gratify man's natural desires. But he does so classify "epic poetry, tragedy, comedy, dithyrambic poetry and the music of the flute and lyre," and his conclusion is that tragic drama is the most perfect of all imitative arts because, from its best examples, we learn the highest truths about human conduct at the same time that we are made happy in an ethical sense by the catharsis of emotions its special kind of imitation provides.[15]

That, in bare outline, is Aristotle's defense of the ideal of poetic mimesis as it relates to his entire system of philosophy. That ideal was destined to prevail in the Western philosophic tradition for at least two thousand years, though not without intervals when, for Christian or Judaic as well as Platonic reasons, sages rejected it as unworthy of man's serious concern. Virgil, Dante, Shakespeare, Milton, Corneille, Racine, and even Dryden and Pope willingly accepted the designation of their art as "imitation of nature." But, by Hegel's time, the tide of thought and fashion had turned very strongly against the concept. In the "romantic era" — for reasons Hegel himself helps to clarify with his distinctions between symbolic, classical, and romantic art — the term "imitation" suddenly ceased to convey with any fair measure of accuracy the average practicing poet's estimate of his art, not even when his so-called *creations* were manifestly inferior to the imitation of old. Today, of course, the term is so far out of fashion in literary criticism that if Erich Auerbach had translated the title of his renowned *Mimesis* into plain English, the work would probably have gathered dust in a publisher's warehouse or never been published at all.

Hegel in his *Aesthetics* defends the concept but does not insist on the term. Or rather, he acknowledges that, from a philosophical point of view, the doctrine of art as *poíesis mimetikós* is magnificently adequate to account for the glorious artistic achievements of the Periclean Greeks and some of the great masters of the Italian renaissance: but he holds also that, precisely because it so adequately accounts for the perfection of such *classical* art, the concept tends to be altogether misleading when applied to evaluate the artistic labors of the *symbolic* East, and all primitive peoples, as well as of the *romantic* Judeo-Christianized West.

Even more obviously than Aristotle's, Hegel's theory of poetry is an integral part of a philosophical whole, the organic unity of which is manifest in each of its parts. With good reason, therefore, in his Oxford lecture on "Hegel's Theory of Tragedy," A. C. Bradley speaks apologetically of having to "tear" the theory "from its connections with the author's general view of poetry, and with the rest of his philosophy." The Hegelian view of tragedy, Bradley notes, is in its profoundest significance inextricably linked "with his view of the function of negation in the universe" so that "no statement which ignores his metaphysics and his philosophy of religion can be more than a fragmentary account of that theory."[16]

Bradley's admonition is a reminder that the theoretical, practical, and productive spheres — which are, for Hegel, metaphysics, religion, and art — ultimately converge upon one another in Hegel's system even as they do in Aristotle's. Of course, for the Greeks of Aristotle's time, *prāxis* had long ceased to be a matter of religion and had evolved instead into a system of rational ethics and politics that acknowledged no divine imperatives other than those dictated by the *daimon* of natural reason. On the other hand, what the Greeks had experienced as religion had been very early confounded with art; and it was as art, particularly in the form of tragic poetry, that their originally distinct religious and aesthetic experiences finally converged with rational ethics and metaphysics in the high speculative thought of Aristotle.

According to Hegel — and here we begin to define from his point of view the limitations of the ideal of *mímesis* — the Greek experience in this respect had been unique. Among no other people, before or since, has art so completely absorbed religion. Nor has there ever been another people among whom artistic beauty, particularly in the plastic and poetic representation of the human form, has been so exalted as to make it a thoroughly adequate expression of a spiritual religion. Hegel agrees with the saying of Herodotus that Homer and Hesiod "fashioned their gods for the Greeks."[17] By that he means, however, not that the Greek gods were "made up" like works of fiction, but rather that the poetic myth-makers, taking primitive Greek religious experience for their content, so fully expressed its meaning in adequate imagery that, by the time of Phideas, there was nothing left for religious worship to claim as its exclusive object beyond the limits of artistic beauty. "The Greek nation," Hegel writes, "made its spirit visible for its intuition and imaginative consciousness through the representation of its gods, giving them by means of art a well-defined existence that accords with its true content. By virtue of this complete adequacy of form, which characterizes Greek art in its essential concept, as well as Greek mythology, art became in Greece the highest expression for the Absolute, and Greek religion is the religion of art itself."[18]

The great sculptors and poets of Greece, Hegel explains, were able to absorb the entire content of their inherited religion in their art because — unlike their counterparts in the ancient East and in the modern Christian West — they were persuaded that intelligence, will, and generative love, divine or human, can be adequately expressed only in configurations of stones, metals, colors, sounds, or words that imitate aspects of the inward or outward life of man. Having very early attained an adequate idea of what the natural and spiritual divinities really were in themselves, the Greeks finally succeeded in giving them wholly adequate expression in idealized representations of idealized human nature and conduct. Defending this classical ideal of imitative making, yet anticipating what he will say about the limitations of its validity as a characteristic principle of all art, Hegel writes: "Personification and anthropomorphism have often been decried as a degradation of the spiritual; but art, insofar as its end is to bring before perception the spiritual in sensuous form, must advance to such anthropomorphism, as it is only in its proper body that mind is adequately revealed to sense."[19]

Hegel reminds us that even in their loftiest conception of divinity, as we find it in the pages of Aristotle, there is always among the Greeks an insistence on the total assimilation of the divine and human. Aristotle's divinity is by no means a humanized god in the sense that the Olympian gods of Homer are humanized. The God of the *De Anima, Ethics,* and *Metaphysics* is an act of purest thought, indeed of thought thinking thought — *nóesis noéseos nóesis*; but, even so, the divine and the human are to be assimilated; for man's perfection consists, says Aristotle, in being raised by God, as the ultimate object of his natural desires, to full participation in the eternal actuality of divine thought. Of that experience, Aristotle writes: "Not in virtue of his humanity will a man achieve it, but in virtue of something in him that is divine; and by as much as this something is superior to his composite nature by so much is its activity superior to the exercise of the other forms of virtue . . . . Nor ought we to obey those who enjoin that a man should have man's thoughts and a mortal the thoughts of mortality, but we ought so far as possible to achieve immortality, and do all that man may to live in accordance with the highest thing in him; for though this be small in bulk, in power and value it far surpasses all the rest."[20]

To represent by poetic mimesis the power and value of the highest thing in human nature was thus for Aristotle to represent adequately the life of God — conceived as the source of all being, all beauty, all goodness, all truth. Aristotle saw it accomplished in the poetry of tragic drama; and the Greeks generally saw it in the literally countless pieces of sculpture that embellished every inhabited corner of their world. Of the wealth of statuary produced by the Greek people, Hegel writes:

> A more spiritual religion can rest satisfied with the contemplation and devotion of the soul, so that the works of sculpture pass for it simply as so much luxury and superfluity. A religion so dependent on the sense vision as the Greek was must necessarily continue to create, inasmuch as for it this artistic production and invention is itself a religious activity and satisfaction, and for the people the sight of such works is not merely sight-seeing but is part of their religion and spiritual life . . . . Only on grounds such as these can we find a rational explanation, if we consider the great difficulties which the technique of sculpture implies, for the host of sculptured figures, this forest of statues of every kind, which in their thousands upon thousands were to be met with even in any one city, in Elis, in Athens, in Corinth, and even in towns of lesser importance, as also in the greater Greece beyond and the Islands of the Cyclades.[21]

In the best poetry of a people that sees divinity so plainly in human nature, beauty is truth, truth is beauty — that is all they know on earth, and all they need to know. But it has been quite otherwise, says Hegel, for the non-Greek peoples of the ancient Far and Near East whose religious experience, however vague it may have been, always transcended the expressive powers of their art; and it has been otherwise also for all peoples almost everywhere since the end of the Greco-Roman era, not only in the East, but also in the West, where the Hellenic heritage of artistic beauty, eudemonistic ethics, and speculative philosophy has been orientalized or, more precisely, Hebraicized in the faith of Christianity.

Putting it another way: Among people for whom God is unfathomable mystery or annihilating necessity or outpouring love, artistic expression must of necessity — according to Hegel — either fall short of or transcend the perfection of mimesis in Aristotle's sense. Falling short of that *classical* ideal, in which intuition and expression, content and form, are reciprocally adequate, art is and remains primitively *symbolic*, regardless of the level of skill attained by the artist or the medium of expression used; transcending that ideal, art becomes *romantic*, expressing more, and somehow expressing it better than the medium and manner or artistic expression would seem to allow, so that the result is art indeed, but art on the point of transcending itself.

2. Symbolic Origins, Classical Perfection, and Romantic Transcendence

The terms "symbolic," "classical," and "romantic" serve in Hegel's *Aesthetics* as the basis for a complex, or at least many-faceted system of comparative study and classification. They are used, first of all, as broad designations for types of artistic expression, distinguished, as we have already suggested, according to the diverse relationships that may obtain between artistic content and form. On the other hand, they serve also to characterize the several arts in their particularity, based on the distinctive material qualities of the various media, each of which appears to be inherently better suited for one type of artistic expression rather than another.

Painting, music, and poetry, for instance, which use the relatively subjective media of colors, sounds, and words, are classified by Hegel as the typically romantic arts in which there is always a more or less latent yearning to say more than art can adequately say. By extension of the same line of reasoning, sculpture, which adequately *fills* space, and architecture which suggestively but never quite adequately *encloses* it for the expression of meaning, are classified respectively as the classical and symbolic arts par excellence. In the case of poetry, however, there is the added complication that, within the range of its several genres — epic, lyric, and dramatic — the medium of words is able to call into being for the human consciousness imaginative equivalents of all the impressions the other arts can make, so that what is said of symbolic architecture and classical sculpture, as also about romantic painting and music, applies equally, in all but material respects, to poetry, and must therefore be considered an essential part of the Hegelian poetics. In a wider perspective, finally, symbolic, classical, and romantic serve to designate entire epochs of art history, as also, in some instances, the complete artistic legacy of one or another of the peoples among whom art has flourished.

Needless to say, none of the terms under consideration here is an Hegelian invention; and his use of them throughout the *Aesthetics* is, moreover, scrupulously respectful of the wealth and complexity of meanings each of them had acquired in the European cultural milieu. Suggestive of that wealth and its attendant ambiguities is the controversy that surfaced after publication of the massive *Symbolik* by the eminent classicist Georg Friedrich Creuzer, whose *symbolic* interpretations of the *classical* myths of Greece and Rome were vehemently criticized in some quarters for their romantic novelty and bias. What is truly remarkable about Hegel's use of the terms is how he manages to avail himself of the complexities and even ambiguities of meaning to build a system of analysis and classification organically pliant enough to accommodate the seemingly infinite multiplicity of details that makes up the historical legacy of fine art.[22]

When one plunges into the *Aesthetics* it is, as someone recently remarked, like breaking in upon a grand intellectual parliament in full session. One soon becomes aware that issues of long standing are being heatedly debated, old business is being resuscitated or tabled for later discussion, while new business is constantly being proposed. Most of the voices heard are eloquently partisan: proud artists of other times and places defending their works against the ever impatient claims of the present; critical theoreticians exploring the difference between natural and artificial beauty, utilitarian and genuinely free art, artistic inspiration and the disciplines of *ars* and *usus*, without which *ingenium* can never hope to soar; champions of the several media debating the virtues and limitations of each; and, perhaps most important of all, eloquent representatives of the other major intellectual disciplines — politics, history, psychology, phenomenology, natural science, law, mathematics, ethics, rhetoric, and even economics, as well as religion and philosophy — that have or claim to have a legitimate interest in aesthetic theory. Something of the same effect is produced by Aristotle's' *Poetics*, though there, of course, it is only the Greek people who speak their mind, whereas in Hegel's *Aesthetics* where the Greek mind is very powerfully represented at all times, we have, nevertheless, a parliament which is genuinely of many nations.

But from a methodological point of view, the debt to Aristotle here as elsewhere in the corpus of Hegelian writings is enormous and unmistakable. No earlier scheme for the classification of works of art can have influenced Hegel or stimulated him more than the one that Aristotle himself has hurriedly sketched for us in the first three chapters of the *Poetics*. The three basic designations, *symbolic*, *classical*, and *romantic*, are of course lacking in that early sketch; but that the key to scientific classification is to be sought in relationships of content, form, and medium, is very emphatically indicated. The arts that may be grouped together as modes of imitation, Aristotle tells us, "differ from one another in three ways: either by a difference in the means [medium], or by differences in the objects [contents], or in the manner [form] of their imitations."[23] As to means, those most frequently used, he explains, are shape, colors, and sounds of the human voice; and it is remarkable, he adds, "what things some persons are able to imitate or portray by their aid, whether through art or constant practice." In the case of the imitative arts that particularly concern him in the *Poetics* – namely, "epic poetry and tragedy, as also comedy, dithyrambic poetry, and most flute-playing and lyre-playing" – the "means with them as a whole," he writes, "are rhythm, language, and harmony – used, however, either singly or in certain combinations."[24]

Turning from the means to consider the objects of imitation, Aristotle observes that what painters, musicians, choreographers, and poets usually choose to imitate are "the characters of men, as well as what they do and suffer," which characters can be represented as "either above our own level, or beneath it, or just such as we are." Illustrating his meaning from the practice of Greek painters, he notes how "the personages of Polygnotus are better than we are, those of Pauson worse, and those of Dionysius just like ourselves." But "even in dancing, flute-playing, and lyre-playing," he generalizes, "such diversities are possible"; and it is, of course, by "representing objects with this point of difference" that tragedy and comedy, as well as epic and mock-epic narratives, are distinguished from one another.[25]

Taking up, finally, the question of how the arts may be distinguished according to the "manner in which each kind of object is represented," Aristotle suddenly narrows his perspective to focus exclusively on poetry and its subdivisions. "Given the same means and the same kind of object of imitation," he writes, "one may either: (1) speak at one moment in narrative and at another moment in an assumed character, as Homer does; or (2) remain the same throughout, without such change; or (3) represent the whole story dramatically, as though its characters were actually doing the things represented."[26]

There can be no doubt that what Aristotle distinguishes here, with such marvelous brevity and precision, are poetry's so-called three voices – epic, lyric, and dramatic – which we mean to take up in the last section of this paper. But what is of more immediate interest, from an Hegelian point of view, is the implication of Aristotle's discussion of manner for a study of the relations of poetry to the plastic arts and music. Aristotle clearly indicates that not only poetry but the other arts also will admit of differences of manner, given the same means and objects of imitation. And the inevitable question is, of course:

What could conceivably be the equivalents of the points of view of epic, lyric, and dramatic poetry in architecture, sculpture, painting, or music? Aristotle offers no explicit answer. But Hegel, developing the Aristotelian hints, certainly does; and what comes out of it is the fundamental notion of symbolic origins, classical perfection, and romantic transcendence which is the nerve center of the entire Hegelian aesthetics.

According to Hegel, the general spectrum of the arts consists of a progression which is paralleled in poetry by the progression from epic to lyric to dramatic points of view. As he says when he finally comes to focus on the subject in the last quarter of the *Aesthetics*, the art of speech, in its three distinct genres, "is the final step, the *totality* which unites and embraces in a yet higher sphere, in the sphere of the very life of spirit itself, the two extremes of the plastic arts and music."[27] Because it is the truly universal art, constituting an "organic whole no longer referred exclusively to any specific type of execution on account of the one-sided character of its medium, the art of poetry comprehends in itself the various types of artistic production"; from which it follows, Hegel explains, that the "*criteria* of our classification of its genres or species" must be borrowed "from the general concepts of artistic production" previously explored in tracing the organic interrelationships of the plastic arts and music from their remotest origins up to the threshold of poetry itself.[28] Again and again in the long section on poetry, Hegel refers us back to earlier parts of the *Aesthetics* for full discussions of methods and principles of analysis that apply no less directly to poetry than to the other arts in connection with which they were originally introduced. For that reason, before presuming to examine Hegel's searchingly original treatment of epic and lyric as well as dramatic poetry we must at least cursorily review the main lines of his "progression of the arts," which is not only an indispensible introduction to his general poetics but also an integral part of it.

Literally echoing Aristotle's words, Hegel observes that "the artistic consciousness, no less than the religious . . . and we may even include the impulse of scientific inquiry, have originated in *wonder*.[29] He agrees with Aristotle that, in the birth-pangs of wonder, nature ceases to appear to man as it did in his original condition of physical dependence. It appears to him, instead, as a vast other-than-himself pervaded by a "mighty presence," in which he vaguely discerns, or tries to discern, a willful consciousness like his own. What he manages to perceive simultaneously attracts and repels, excites and frustrates him; and, according to Hegel, it is in the dialectic of such alternating excitement and frustration that primitive art as well as religion and philosophy discover their common source.

Yet in that first awakening, it is art rather than religion or philosophy — the productive rather than the practical or theoretic impulse — that first provides what all three kinds of experience initially require. Nothing less will do than a vivid apprehension of nature's all-pervading spirit in a form that is, on the one hand, completely objective to sense and, on the other, immediately recognizable as an expression or product of mind. In this sense art is, writes Hegel, "by virtue of its power to create forms cognate with its own substance, the first interpreter of religious consciousness."[30]

Yet that first wondrous apprehension is so vague that it can receive at best only the vaguest form of artistic representation. In Aristotelian terms, one would say that the *object* to be imitated is initially so inadequately conceived that the usual *means* of imitation must either be distorted into monstrous shapes or used in such a *manner* as to charge their commonplace forms with an unnatural suggestiveness. In either case, intuition and expression, objective content and artistic form, remain reciprocally inadequate. And a relationship of reciprocal inadequacy is, as we have seen, what defines the symbolic type of art, best exemplified in the architecture, but also in the sculpture, painting, music, and poetry of the ancient Far and Near East. At its worst, it is an art of unnatural shapes, confusions of color, weird sounds, and hieroglyphs, while at its best it is, as Hegel observes, awe-inspiring in its "aspirations, its disquiet, its mystery, and its sublimity."[31]

Of awe-inspiring art, Aristotle in his *Poetics* has virtually nothing to say. Though he was aware of the pyramids and cliff-tombs of Egypt and the towering ziggurats of Mesopotamia, he says nothing about them. For from his classical point of view, all such works of the Eastern spirit could represent at best only a prolonged anticipation of what art ought to be. Merely to serve as fitting environments for genuine artistic expression in the classical sense, the pyramids, for instance, would have to be struck by a lightning bolt of spirituality, capable of vivifying the mummified bodies encased in them, even as the art of Phideas was able to strike artistic life into figures of marble or bronze.

What the classical Greeks were apparently unable to see, and what Hegel helps us to see, is that, at its best, the symbolism of architecture actually calls upon itself that vivifying lightning bolt. When the builder's art, limited by the mechanical qualities of its means, has advanced to the state where it can "level a space" for celebration of the rites of spirit — which is to say, when it has provided a *templum*, in the root sense of the word, which stands before us as a "fit place for the concentration of spirit, and for its direction toward the mind's absolute objects" — the divinity whose rites are celebrated must sooner or later make a sensory appearance.[32] The sculptor's art is thus summoned into being by architecture's symbolism. And it comes, Hegel writes, "in a lightning flash of individuality that smites its way into the inert mass" of its material medium, bringing to focus on a single point all the living intelligence that gives to architecture its many faceted symmetry.[33] The sculptured gods of Greece appear to us at a glance to have an organic center of life in them, for only a spiritual concentration of mind could have fashioned them as they are. In their perfect adequacy of content and form the classical type of art attained, Hegel asserts, "the highest excellence of which the sensuous embodiment of art is capable."[34]

Yet, the impulse of art can aim higher: just as the Homeric-Phidean Zeus which animates the temple of classical architecture is a far more adequate expression of spirit than any mummy in the symbolic pyramids of Egypt, so, on the other hand, according to Hegel, is the spirit of the consecrated host in Christianity's soaring cathedral utterly beyond the range of expressiveness of classical sculpture. The prolific statuary of the Greek religion of art had had — Hegel reminds us — a long preparation in the symbolic configurations of the Eastern artistic consciousness which expressed itself most suggestively in the sphinxes of Egypt; but he reminds us further that it has also had a prolonged aftermath of romantic longing to transcend itself, not only in the tormented shapes of penitent sinners and martyred saints that fill the niches, frame the portals, and embellish the walls of Gothic cathedrals, but also in the works of some of the Renaissance masters who deliberately tortured sculpture's objectivity to reveal a subjective content which can never be adequately expressed by means of stone or bronze.

Even the most god-like figures of Greek or Renaissance sculpture, Hegel observes, have vacant, expressionless eyes. Try as he may, the conscious beholder cannot look *into* those figures as into a conscious soul, for their eyes lack the light-focus, the spiritual glance, of inward life. To express the inner life of self-consciousness — or, rather, to attempt to express it — is the task of romantic art.

Romantic art, Hegel explains, "destroys the completed union of the Idea and its reality" attained in the classical type and renews on a higher level the tension between content and form, "which was left unvanquished by symbolic art."[35] Its new content has a "significance which goes beyond the classical mode of expression." Indeed, it finds the materials of three-dimensional space, as they present themselves objectively to consciousness, altogether inadequate, and attempts, therefore, to strip them of their "immediate material guise," so that they may be used to reveal rather than embody the higher spiritual content. In such art, Hegel writes, the solidity of sculpture is cracked open, and the rich interior life of spirit, with its perception, feeling, and thought, is revealed to human consciousness by means of color, sound, and, finally, the spoken or written word, used as "the mere indication of inward perceptions and ideas." To the extent that it succeeds in dematerializing its means of expression, romantic art "must be considered as art transcending itself."[36]

Painting, the transitional romantic art, makes use of material substances for its expression, but its true medium is reflected light, or color, which it attempts to separate as much as possible from the mechanical and spatial qualities of external existence. By compressing the three dimensions of space into a plane surface, it provides a "mirrored" view of the sensory world — a view that comprehends within its relatively small frame the broad expanse of land and sea and sky; the shapes and aspects of man in every posture and mood; animals, plants, inanimate objects, the world of human art, as well as abstract associations of color and line. "All this diversity of material," Hegel writes, "is capable of entering into the varied content of painting . . . if only some allusion to an element of mind endows it with affinity to thought and feeling."[37]

But the content best suited for expression in painting, according to Hegel, is the emotion of love. And of the many varieties of love, ranging from the crudest carnal *éros* to the sublimest spirituality of *agápe*, the most challenging to art is that which Christian faith holds to have been embodied in the womb of the Virgin Mary, mother of the incarnate God of Abraham, Isaac, and Jacob. For the Jews, Hegel reminds us, that all-mighty God has remained unutterable even in name, though the whole of creation is deemed to be His utterance. But in the great moments of the Christian drama of the Word made flesh, it is otherwise. Those moments are, first of all, the Annunciation, where the burning seraph, aflame with divine love, says: "Hail, full of grace!"; then come the moments of the new-born child in the manger and of the infant in his mother's arms; and finally the crucifixion, burial, and resurrection. From the point of view of the painter's art, the best of these moments are, says Hegel, those of Mary's love in all her relationships to the Christ, and also those of the rending human passion (*Zerrissenheit*) of the cross. In one remarkable paragraph, the Lutheran Hegel does not hesitate to write:

> We therefore find that religious love is set forth in its fullest and most ideal human form, not in that for Christ amid his trials, nor in His resurrection, nor as He delays His departure among His friends, but in the emotional nature of a woman, Mary. Her entire soul and life is human love for the Child, which she calls her own, and, along with it, adoration and love of God with whom she feels herself united. She is humble before God, and yet is steeped in the infinite exaltation that she is the single one among maidens who is above all blessed. Not alone and apart, but only in her Child is she made perfect in God; but

in that, whether it be by the cradle or as queen of heaven, she is entirely content and blessed, without passion and yearning, with no other want, with no other aim to have or possess anything but that which she possesses.[38]

Hegel dwells at great length on the qualities of color as the artistic medium of painting; and it is only after he has explored all its capacities to express the subjectivity of human feeling that be turns finally to consider its limitations. His conclusion is that, "however much painting is evolved in the direction of a more ideal independence . . . no longer attached materially to shape as such, and is permitted to pass spontaneously into its own proper element, that is, into the play of visibility and reflection, into all the mysteries of chiaroscuro, yet this magic of color is still throughout a spatial mode; it is an appearance growing out of juxtaposition on a flat surface, and consequently a subsistent appearance."[39]

In music, the second romantic art, the dimensions of space are dissolved into tones that have only temporal extension. Music puts aside the perspective and coloring of human perception in order to express the rhythm and stress of inward life, finding "utterance in its tones for the heart with its whole gamut of feelings and passions."[40] It has content, but not in the sense that the plastic arts have. Externally, it conforms, like architecture, to quantitative laws that strictly regulate the conjunction and succession of tones, yet it does not present an enduring form for the conscious mind to contemplate from without. The swiftly evanescent world of tones, writes Hegel, "directly penetrates through the ears of man to the depths of his soul, attuning the same in concordant emotional sympathy.[41] Music is, in essence, the most subjective, the most inward of the arts, and, therefore, the most romantic.

Hegel reminds us that music, in the broadest etymological sense — embracing for the Greeks all that pertained to a higher intellectual as well as artistic education — was the source of both music and poetry as we distinguish them today. It was not until long after Aristotle wrote his *Poetics* that musical composition, which had always been a part of the poet's art, finally began to raise itself to a position of independence; though it is perhaps no less true to say that it was rather poetry that made the final separation, bringing to completion romantic art's last phase of "dematerialization." On the musical qualities of the human voice, Hegel wrote:

> With respect to the tones emitted, it may be regarded as the most complete instrument of all. It unites in itself the characteristics of both wind instrument and string. That is to say we have here in one aspect of it a column of air which vibrates, and, further, by virtue of the muscles, the principle of a string under tension. just as we saw that in the color inherent in the human skin, we had the most perfected presentment of color, so, too, we may affirm of the human voice that it contains the ideal compass of sound, all that in other instruments is differentiated into its several composite parts. We have here the perfect tone which is capable of blending in the most facile and beautiful way with all other instruments. Add to this that the human voice . . . expresses the ideal character of the inner life, and most immediately directs such expression. In the case of all other instruments on the contrary we find that a material thing is set in vibration, which, in the use that is made of it, is placed in a relation of indifference to and outside of the soul and its emotions. In the human song, however, it is the human body itself from which the soul breaks into utterance.[42]

It is, of course, with words, in the art of speech, that the human voice best sings its songs. But that art can build, and mold, and paint as well as sing, for as we have already seen, it unites in itself the characteristics of all the other arts. Separated from music in the narrow sense, the art of speech still uses sounds, but not as fixed tonal qualities. The sounds of poetry, like its written letters, are conventional signs that can communicate artistic impressions only when correctly interpreted. Indeed, poetry's grandest utterances can be and have been *translated*, so that while not a single sound of the original remains what it was, yet the essential poetry somehow unmistakably survives — still Homer, still Dante, still Shakespeare.[43] Poetry is thus the least dependent of all the arts on external, sensuous means of expression; yet in the universalized space of the imagination, it can represent "an objective world in which the determinateness of sculpture and painting is not altogether absent, and is capable of unfolding all the conditions of an event, a succession or interchange of emotional states, passions, conceptions and the settled course of human conduct with more thoroughness than any other art."[44] For the inner eye, it can present a canvas of color and line richer than that of any painting. For the inner ear it can sing melodies that are sweeter than the finest known to the sensual ear. And, finally, on its highest level, it can call the very world of architecture into objective existence before us and people it with figures of living flesh whose gestures and movements are animated painting and whose cadenced speech is the sublimest song of thought and feeling.

3. The Three Voices of Poetry

"We find it difficult," Hegel observes, "to recall a single author among all who have written on the subject of poetry who has not evaded the attempt to describe what is poetical let alone to provide a clear definition." Hegel's point is that poetry, as the universal art, includes so much of what characterizes the other arts, generally and specifically, that, without having studied what is architectural, sculptural, pictorial, and musical, we can hardly hope "to determine where we must look for that in which the essential character of poetry consists."[45]

Poetry, as we have noted, completes the process of art's gradual dematerialization of its means of expression. Indeed, according to Hegel, its "supreme characteristic consists in the power with which it subjects to the mind and its ideas the sensuous element from which painting and music began to liberate art."[46] Yet with the passage from the *sound* of music to the *word* of poetry, there occurs an abrupt qualitative reversal, as if the progression of the arts had suddenly been pulled inside out. The word of poetry is, for the artistic consciousness as a whole, what the focal point of sight is for the physical eye. The cone of lines brought to focus upon it from the outside passes through that point of no dimension to be re-projected inwardly; and while we are easily persuaded that those lines have brought their temporal and spatial characteristics with them, from the outside, it is really only as they are re-projected inwardly that we consciously experience them. All that we actually perceive of the art-products of architecture, sculpture, painting, and music — Hegel reminds us — is their focused reprojection in the inner space and inner time of our imaginative consciousness. And poetry enters that inner space and time most directly precisely because it is not burdened with the external spatial and temporal dimensionality of stones, colors, or sounds. Once it is admitted that the words of poetry, like those of prose, are mere signs for the mind, wholly unsubstantial in themselves, one can hardly resist concluding with Hegel "that the proper medium of poetical representation is the poetical imagination and intellectual portrayal itself." And inasmuch as all the other arts, for all their spatial and temporal substantiality, must finally register their impressions in this same element, it follows, writes Hegel, "that poetry runs through them all and develops itself independently in each."[47]

The danger with poetry is that it is always tempted to neglect its architectural, sculptural, pictorial, and musical powers; just as architecture, at the opposite extreme of art's vast spectrum, is never quite able "to subordinate its external matter to the ideal content sufficiently to clothe it in a form adequate to mind," so "poetry on the other hand carries the process of negating its sensuous medium so far that . . . it comes dangerously near to bidding goodbye to the region of sense altogether, remaining wholly absorbed in that of ideality."[48] The art of poetry, as distinguished from the innate talent and inspiration of the poet, consists therefore in the discipline of language, to prevent it from stripping poetic intuitions of their sensory or imaginative individuality while at the same time preserving and enhancing their universal suggestiveness — so that poetry can continue to be what Hegel says it has always been: "the most universal and cosmopolitan instructor of the human race."[49]

Hegel, like Aristotle, explores in great detail the discipline of poetic language. Several hundred pages of the *Aesthetics* are given over to detailed analyses of figures of speech, clarity of expression, and versification, amply illustrated with examples from the best poets of all times. And René Wellek, who is usually very sparing with such praise, has observed admiringly:

Hegel shows a remarkable grasp of the role of linguistic features (diction, word order, sentence structure) in poetry and eloquently expounds the effects and charms of versification and rhyme. He makes the true observation that a "genuine artistic talent moves in his sensuous materials as in his most proper native element, which lifts and carries it rather than hinders and oppresses." He suggests that verse is implicated in the rhythm of the ideas, that it is a "music which, though in a distant way, echoes the dark yet definite course and character of the representations." He asserts the need for rhythm but not for exact measure in poetry and describes well the clash between the metrical pattern and the rhythm of prose which "gives the whole a new peculiar life."[50]

It is thus only when he has thoroughly explored what Aristotle calls the means of poetic imitation, which are "rhythm, language, and harmony," as well as its most suitable objects, which are the ethically significant actions of men, that Hegel turns finally from analysis to synthesis, from the parts to the whole of poetry as it has come to utter itself, actually, in its epic, lyric, and dramatic "voices."

In an essay published in 1953, bearing the title we have appropriated for this section of our paper, T.S. Eliot reminded our age that poetry does indeed have three distinguishable voices. He confessed there that, before 1938, be himself had heard only two of those voices: "that of the poet talking to himself — or to nobody," and "that of the poet addressing an audience, whether large or small." He had heard those two voices in that sequence, he says, in the course of his own poetic growth; that there was a third, he did not realize until he had twice tried and failed to write poetry suitable for the stage. Only *after* he had written *Murder in the Cathedral*, did the dramatic voice finally "force itself," as he says, "upon my ear." The dramatic voice, he explains, is that of the poet "when he is saying, not what he would say in his own person, but only what he can say within the limits of one imaginary character addressing another imaginary character."[51]

Except for his reversal of the order of the first two voices, all that Eliot says here is quite Hegelian, and most Hegelian of all is his conclusion that, in the case of dramatic poetry,

if it is a great play, and you do not try too hard to hear
them, you may discern the other voices too. For the work
of a great poetic dramatist, like Shakespeare, constitutes
a world. Each character speaks for himself, but no other
poet could have found those words for him to speak. If you
seek for Shakespeare you will have to find him only in the
characters he created; for the one thing in common
between the characters is that no one but Shakespeare
could have created them. The world of a great poetic
dramatist is a world in which the creator is everywhere
present, and everywhere hidden.[52]

The statement is so Hegelian in detail and emphasis that it
argues strongly for some kind of direct or indirect influence.
Yet all we have that suggests a possibility of such influence is
Eliot's acknowledgment, made shortly before the third voice
forced itself upon him, that he regretted not having studied
Hegel sooner. With what uncharitable critics have described as
his usual infinite lack of charity, Eliot had written in 1935: "I
wish that I had taken Hegel more seriously in my youth, but like
many people, I was caught napping; I never expected that
Hegel, having been inverted by a Jewish economist for his own
purposes, should come back in favor."[53]

As we have noted, in his long treatment of the subject,
Hegel reverses the order of the first two voices distinguished by
Eliot — or, rather, holds to the traditional sequence derived
from Aristotle and validated, moreover, by the historical experience of most nations, in which the narrative or epic voice is
heard first, followed by the subjective or lyric voice, and, finally,
by the dramatic, which is a synthesis of the two.

The poetic voice of narration (which Aristotle distinguishes
as Homer's manner) has a wide range. It includes, says Hegel,
the ancient epigrams and gnomes, the cosmogonies and
theogonies, as also the romances, ballads, idylls, and didactic
nature poems of latter times, to which we must add, finally, the
verseless, but nonetheless poetic modern novel. But its richest,
culminating form has always been and remains the Epos. As a
sort of germ of the Epos, Hegel points to the epigrammatic
"distich which we read in Herodotus referring to the slain
heroes of Thermopolyae." The words merely report a fact. On
a certain spot at a certain time "four thousand Peloponnesians

fought against three hundred myriads." But its purpose, which is to commemorate the heroic event with an inscription, makes that statement poetical in the epic sense. The language respects the objective simplicity of the fact; but to distinguish it from ordinary speech and enhance its value, we have, as Hegel observes, the abruptness of "a distich in lieu of a sentence."[54]

Of course, in the true Epos, what we have set before us is no mere inscription but the full compass of a grand action, enriched by "association with the organically complete world of a nation and an age."[55] All the great epic poems that have come down to us have been national bibles; still, as Hegel notes, "it is not every national bible that can claim the poetic form of the epopoeia; nor do all nations which have embodied their most sacred memorials . . . in the form of comprehensive compositions of the epic type, possess religious books." The Old Testament, for instance, has much epic narrative in it, yet, as a whole, it is not a work of art; and neither is the New Testament or the Koran. Conversely, while the Greeks have their Homeric epics, they are "without ancient religious books" such as the Hindus and Parsees as well as the Hebrews possess.[56]

The ancient Chinese, for reasons that Hegel explores at length in his *Philosophy of Religion* and *History of Philosophy*, had no genuine Epos; whereas the imaginative, infinitely less prosaic Hindus had two of great poetic value: the *Ramajana* and the *Maha-Bharata*, which together place before us "the entire world-outlook of the Hindu race in all its splendor and glory, its confusion, fantastical absurdity and dissolution, as also in the contrasting exuberant liveliness and fine traits of heart and emotion, which characterizes the profuse vegetation of its spiritual growth."[57]

The Hebrews, Hegel observes, have sung their best verses in the second, lyrical voice rather than in the first. "In its conception of the Creation, in the histories of the Patriarchs, the wandering in the wilderness, the conquest of Canaan, and in the further historical course of national events," he writes, "the sublimity of the Jewish imagination no doubt possesses many elements of primitive epic poetry"; but the religious interest, on the one hand, and the historical, on the other, are

so strong throughout as to overwhelm any purely artistic
impulse that might have given the whole an epic, poetic unity.[58]
The Arabs too, despite their heroic exploits in the great days of
Mohammedanism, have never sung a genuinely epic song; and
where an epic voice was raised among the peoples forcibly
converted to Mohammedanism, as in the case of the great
Persian Firdusi, the indispensable element of national spirit
had long since been silenced in defeat.[59]

One cannot sum up what Hegel has to say about the
Homeric epics. He confirms in detail Aristotle's judgment of
them, and, in a tour de force of *comparative* literature, uses them
to illustrate his appraisals of all other narrative poems before
and since. He rejects entirely the thesis of Friedrich August
Wolf, founder of modern philology, who suggested that the
Homeric poems might be of composite origin. With sharpness,
Hegel remarks that, while Wolf's thesis is entertained "by men
of talent and learning . . . it remains none the less a crude and
illiterate view. It in fact amounts to nothing less than excluding
from the finest ethic compositions any genuine character of
artistic composition."[60] Elsewhere, on the same theme, Hegel
writes:

> However much an epic may express the affairs of the
> entire nation, it remains the fact that the individual is the
> poet, not the nation as a whole. The spirit of an age, of a
> people, is no doubt the essential operative cause; but the
> realization is only secured in the work of art as conceived
> by the constructive genius of a particular poet, who brings
> before our vision and reproduces this universal spirit and
> its content as his own experience and his own product.
> Poetical composition is a real spiritual birth, and spirit or
> intelligence only exist as this or that actual and individual
> conscious and self-conscious life . . . . And as for the Iliad
> and the Odyssey . . . the notion that they are conglomer-
> ates without essential unity, patched together of various
> rhapsodies composed in a similar strain, is a thoroughly
> barbaric and un-artistic idea. Of course, if such a view
> merely amounts to this, that the poet, in his bare individu-
> ality, vanishes in his creation, it is the highest form of
> praise. This is merely a statement that we are unable to
> recognize any positive traces of wholly personal opinions
> and feeling.[61]

Homer's voice is certainly the voice of a nation; but it is a voice supplied by the heart and soul of the *unique* genius of the creator of the poems.

Virgil, according to Hegel, is far less absorbed in his epic song. "The level of education from which the Homeric poems originated," he remarks, "still continues in a fair harmony with the poetic subject matter," whereas in Virgil, "we are reminded by every single hexameter that the general outlook of the poet is totally different from the world which it is his endeavor to depict . . . . Throughout the whole of the Virgillian Epic we feel ourselves in the atmosphere of ordinary life; the old tradition, the saga, the fairyland of poetry enters with prosaic distinctness into the frame of our common-sense faculties."[62] And the same is true of Milton's *Paradise Lost*, Klopstock's *Messias*, Voltaire's *Henriad*, and many others. "In all these poems," Hegel continues, "we cannot fail to detect a real cleft between the content and the reflection of the poet which modifies his description of the events, characters, and circumstances."[63]

There is no such cleft in the primitive epic cycles of the Germanic pagan and medieval Christian world. But, according to Hegel, the materials of those cycles and the poems themselves represent a state of culture corresponding to the pre-Homeric period of Greece, so that for genuine artistic fulfillment these materials must await the appearance of Dante and later poets. As for the *Divine Comedy*, Hegel's appraisal of it in the *Aesthetics* is most extraordinary and worthy of a special essay in itself. The depth of its influence on the first-ranking Italian literary critic, Francesco De Sanctis, is explored elsewhere in these pages by Professor Kouzel. But we should at least note here that Erich Auerbach, in his classic *Mimesis*, refers to it as "one of the most beautiful passages ever written on Dante."[64] Auerbach acknowledges also that his own book-length study of Dante's realism, *Dante als Dichter der irdischen Welt,* had for its basis the insights of Hegel's analysis.[65]

Hegel's pages on the epic genius of Ariosto, whose comic perspective he links with that of Cervantes (as also with that of Shakespeare in the comic episodes of the tragedies and histories as well as in the comedies) appear to have exerted considerable influence, though not always openly acknowledged, among Spanish as well as Italian literary critics. In *Orlando Furioso* and *Don Quixote*, as in Shakespeare's Falstaff, the "self-dissolution of Chivalry" is set before us — Hegel asserts — with "unsurpassed adequacy."[66] The heroes of Ariosto's tale "are seriously engaged in what is often unadulterated folly and the wildest eccentricity." On the negative side, we find that "love is frequently degraded from the Divine love of Dante, or the romantic tenderness of Petrarch, to sensuous tales and ludicrous collisions; or heroism appears to be screwed up to a pitch that is so incredible it ceases to amaze, and excites a smile over the fabulousness of such exploits." And yet, through all his fantastic surprises, and despite his ludicrous treatment of the subject, Ariosto is able, according to Hegel, "to secure and display for us the true nobility and greatness of chivalry in the exhibition of courage, love, honor, and bravery, as he can also on occasion excellently depict other passions, as for instance, cunning, subtlety, and presence of mind." Then comes the penetrating and much-admired tribute to the genius of Cervantes:

> Just as Ariosto inclines more to the *fabulous* element in this spirit of adventure, Cervantes develops that aspect in which it is appropriate to *romantic* fiction. We find in his Don Quixote a noble nature in whose adventures chivalry goes mad, the substance of such adventures being placed at the center of a stable and well-defined state of things whose external character is copied with exactness from nature. This produces the humorous contradiction of a rationally constituted world on the one hand, and an isolated soul on the other, which seeks to create the same order and stability through its own exertions and the knight errantry which could only destroy such order. Despite this ludicrous confusion, however, we still have in Don Quixote that which we have eulogized in Shakespeare. Cervantes has created in his hero an original figure of noble nature . . . . In all the madness of his mind and his enterprise, he is a completely consistent soul, or rather his madness lies in this, that he is and remains securely rooted in himself and his enterprise. Without this unreflecting equanimity respectively to the content and result of his actions he would fail to be a truly romantic figure; and this

self-assuredness, if we look at the substantive character of his opinions, is throughout great and indicative of his genius, adorned as it is with the finest traits of character . . . . From another point of view, however, the exploits of Don Quixote are merely the central thread around which a succession of genuinely romantic tales are intertwined in the most charming way, in order to unfold the true worth of that which the romance in other respects scatters to the winds with the genius of comedy.[67]

Returning to the romantic epic in the stricter sense, Hegel praises the *Lusiads* of Camoens, remarking, however, that there is a "real barrier between the subject that is national and an artistic culture that is borrowed from the ancients and the Italians." Milton's *Paradise Lost* and Klopstock's *Messias* represent for him an "autumnal blossoming of the religious Epopoeia," embodying the principles of the Reformation. Milton, according to Hegel, is certainly "an admirable master of his age," both in breadth of culture gained through study of the ancients, and in refinement of language. Still, as epic poetry, his masterpiece falls far short of the heights of Homer or Dante: "For not only does the conflict and catastrophe of *Paradise Lost* take a direction which is contrary to its dramatic character, but it is, in a unique way, supported by a lyric impulse and ethical and didactic predilections which hardly accord with the subject as we have it in its original [Biblical] version."[68]

Hegel concludes his treatment of epic poetry with the observation that its future lies with the romantic novel: that "true Epopoeia" of modern society which "presupposes a basis of reality already organized in its prosaic form, upon which it then attempts . . . to make good once more the banished claims of poetical vision."[69] Predicting that its basic theme for a long time to come will be what we now call the "generation gap," Hegel observes that, in its total effect, what the modern novel gives us is the spirit of Ariosto and Cervantes in reverse. The spirit of chivalry, he says, is "once more taken seriously and receives a new content." The difference is that, given the advanced development of modern civic society, the "chimerical objects which the knight of chivalry proposed for himself" in Ariosto and Cervantes are replaced by obstacles in the form of "police administration, tribunals of justice, the army, and political government generally." In a paragraph that perhaps seems much more relevant now than when it was written, Hegel concludes:

> Confronted by the existing order and the ordinary prose of life [the characters of modern novels] appear before us as individuals with personal aims of love, honor, ambition, ideals of world reform, ideals in the path of which that order presents obstacles on every side. The result is that personal desires and demands begin to billow upward before this opposition to unfathomable heights . . . . For the most part such a "knighthood" will consist of young people, who feel it incumbent upon them to hew their way through a world which makes for its own realization rather than that of their ideals, and who hold it a misfortune that there should be family ties, civic society, state laws, professions, and all the rest of such things at all, because conditions of such solidity and so inevitably restricted are so cruelly opposed to their ideal dreams and the infinite claims of their souls.

We have there, obviously, the chivalric knighthood of the young "Marcusites" in all the advanced countries of the Western world today — a spirit rooted not in the grand Hegel, as is sometimes pretended, but only in his prophecy about the romantic children of the prosaic bourgeoisie. Observing that this modern-style Epopoeia can have every sort of denouement, tragic or comic, as well as prosaic, Hegel concludes his discussion with a general word of praise: "In this history we may see the same old type of the adventurous spirit with this distinction, that here the spirit discovers its real significance, and all that is wholly fantastic in it receives its necessary correction."[70]

The *manner* of the lyric poet is far removed from all of this. When he utters himself in the second, subjective voice, the poet is wrapped up in his interior life, unable or unwilling to realize his will in action. There may be a very powerful national consciousness enveloping his existence, but he does not absorb or let himself be absorbed by it. Leaving its objectivity behind, he descends into his own private domain, to peer into the subjective center of his existence — that same center out of which comes the spontaneity of tears and laughter.

Poetic speech is no doubt a means of relief for the heart's excessive joys and sorrows, hopes and fears, and, generally, for the "blind tumult of passion" that crowds the soul. But genuine lyric utterance does not merely provide an emotional outlet; rather, "it creates therefrom an object which is purified from all mere contingency of the passing mood; an object in which the soul-life of this deliverance returns once more to itself freely and with self-conscious satisfaction, and remains there at home." If the poet has acquired a sufficient mastery of his language, the original spontaneous overflow of emotion is transmuted, through tranquil recollection, into a "poetic song of universal validity."[71]

Precisely because of its subjectivity, lyric poetry can take for its content an infinite variety of experiences, so that when the entire wealth of lyric poetry of any nation is taken together more is expressed of the national character than can be summed up in its epic poems. Stressing this point, Hegel says further:

> While we regarded as necessary for the full bloom of the true Epos a phase of the nation's growth which was, speaking generally, undeveloped, at least in the sense that it had not ripened in the prosaic acceptance of its actual life, the times which favor most of all lyrical composition are those which already are in possession of more or less fixed social conditions. [Lyric Poetry] ... requires an artistic culture already secured, so that it may assert itself as the flower and independent product of the individual's natural endowment thus trained to a perfect result. For these reasons the Lyric is not limited to particular epochs of the spiritual development of a people, but is capable, rather, of blossoming in any era. To an exceptional degree is it favored in most recent times, in which everybody is entitled to have and express his own views and emotions.[72]

Hegel reminds us that many of the minor narrative-type forms such as the epigram, ballad, romance, and poems *d'occasion* lend themselves also to lyrical expression. This is particularly true, he notes, of the "witty epigrams of the Greek anthology which have lost the epic manner," as also of the old English ballads, charged with an "emotional emphasis calculated to make both heart and voice thrill and falter with anguish."[73] Among the modern Germans he praises particularly the ballads of Burger for their "somber tone of naiveté," of Goethe for "the impeccable clarity of their emotional, no less than imaginative vision," and of Schiller for their "superb emotional emphasis on the fundamental thought" awakened by the tales they relate.[74]

But the lyric voice is not perfectly heard in such narrative-type poems. For its perfection it needs to be divested finally "of all *dependence* on external occasion or purpose."[75] Epic poetry is the poetry of consciousness absorbed in its object; lyric poetry is that of self-consciousness absorbed in itself. Anticipating Whitman's famous line, Hegel says of the lyric poet that "his supreme subject is himself"; and he illustrates his point by citing the practice of Pindar and Sappho, Catullus and Horace, as well as the moderns. Comparing Pindar's manner with that of Homer, be remarks: "Homer, as an individual person, is in his Epos so entirely sacrificed that people nowadays are loth to admit that he ever existed at all. His heroes live on forever. Pindar's heroes are for us little better than empty names. He himself, however, the self-celebrated and self-honored, remains before us immortal as the poet. The heroes of whom he is the lyric singer are famous only as his subjects."[76]

As forms of the free lyric, Hegel discusses first of all the class of hymns, dithyrambs, paeans, and psalms, of which the Old Testament "outcries of the soul to the One" are the consummate perfection;[77] then he takes up the class of odes, in the modern meaning of the term, which celebrate some matter of great importance — whether heroes, love, beauty, art, or friendship, and the like — in terms of the author's completely subjective emotional involvement; and finally he considers what he calls the *genuine song*, which is neither an outcry to God nor the celebration of any given matter but merely the voice of the poet talking, as Eliot expressed it, to himself or to nobody. It is the latter kind of lyric poetry that is truly universal. No people of any cultural development, Hegel writes, is ever so barren as to be totally lacking at any time in singers of such songs; for it is just such poetry which, "in contrast to the Epopoeia, does not so much die as it is forever awakened anew. This field of blossom starts up afresh every spring."[78]

Within the range of this most universal kind of song, Hegel distinguishes two main tendencies: "On the one hand the poet may express his emotional inner life quite openly and without reserve, so that he communicates to us all that he has experienced. On the other hand, and in extreme contrast to this, he may suffer us to surmise through his very speechlessness, what is brought to focus in the unopened chamber of his heart." The first type is the song of the East, and more particularly of the Mohammedan Persians, with its "careless hilarity and contented expansiveness . . . which loves to dilate itself hither and thither in all the breadth of sensuous perception and witty conceit."[79] Such poetry makes joys of its sorrows. In Hafiz, for instance, "we hear often enough," Hegel writes, "of the poet's woes and laments . . . but our poet persists through grief, no less than through happiness, as free of care as ever."[80] There is more of the sublime than of the romantic in this, according to Hegel; and in a brief but very provocative essay on the subject, Hegel contrasts the Persian and Arabic song generally with the ancient Hindu song, and also with Goethe's *Divan* which be says comes closer to expressing the Mohammedan spirit than any other writing of the West.

The second type of genuine song, on the contrary — Hegel writes — "applies with more force to our Northern self-concentration and subjective intimacy which, in its compressed tranquillity, is often enough able to seize hold of objects that are wholly external and to put suggestions in *them*, while the essentially suppressed spirit is on the other hand unable to express itself or find a bent, so that, like the child with whom that father in the Erl King rides through the night and the wind, it must finally stifle . . . its own gasping breath and die."[81]

Hegel's treatment of lyric poetry is full of gems of criticism of individual poems, with the emphasis as often on the technique of verse as on the emotional and intellectual content. Anacreon, Sappho, Pindar, Catullus, Horace, Ovid, David the Psalmist, Hafiz, Saadi, Dante, and Petrarch, are all characterized and distinguished through an analysis of typical poems or lines; though, of course, when it is a question of versification or diction, examples are more often than not drawn from the modern German lyricists. Hegel praises Klopstock, for instance, for having "wrested our poetry from the stupendous insignificance of the Gottsched period, which with its blockish superficiality had completely destroyed the life of all that is noble and of worth in the genius of our race,"[82] and Schiller, for having universalized the song of Germany in its new mode. But his highest praise is reserved for the lyric poetry of Goethe, "in which we Germans unquestionably possess the most consummate, profound, and influential compositions of modern times. If they are wholly the expression of the poet, they are equally the treasure of his people; and, in fact, as the genuine growth of his native soil, are completely in accord with the profoundest tones of our national life and genius."[83] Goethe towers over lyric poetry in the modern era, according to Hegel, as Homer and Dante tower over the epic poetry of the ancient and medieval worlds.

With the third voice of poetry, the dramatic voice, we find, as Hegel expresses it, "the objective character of the Epos essentially united to the subjective principle of the Lyric."[84] As in the epic so in dramatic poetry, we have "directly before our vision an essentially independent action as a definite fact." Yet, instead of its being presented to us as "an event of the past resuscitated by the narrative alone," the action of drama "is made to appear as actually realized in the particular volition, morality or immorality of the specific characters depicted, which thereby become central in the principle of *lyric* poetry."[85]

Historically, dramatic poetry has divided itself into three kinds: tragedy, comedy, and the so-called drama of real life, which is a sort of mean between the two or, more precisely, the theatrical counterpart of the modern novel. In that real-life drama, as also in comedy, dramatic poetry tends to dissolve rapidly into the prose of ordinary existence; but it finally does so, Hegel asserts, only after the "garland of all the arts" has been completely woven — which is to say, only after having attained, in tragedy, the highest phase of development to which art in general can aspire.

According to Hegel, this three-fold dramatic synthesis of the epic and lyric voices is the distinctively Western form of poetic utterance. The other two voices have had a considerable development among oriental peoples, he acknowledges; but the dramatic voice — that of *personae* recognizing and address- ing one another as *personae* – has never been heard in Arabic and Mohammedan poetry and has but faintly uttered itself among the Chinese and Hindus. And the reason, from Hegel's point of view, is that genuinely dramatic action presupposes a plurality of free agents, each possessed of a "will to find in the self the free cause and source of the personal act and its consequence." Where a sense of personal responsibility is lacking, there can be no tragedy; and, "to a still more emphatic degree," Hegel adds, "is this free claim of the personal life . . . a necessary condition for the appearance of comedy."[86]

The term Islam itself, Hegel observes, implies a repudiation of the principle of dramatic responsibility, particularly since the pledge of submission is addressed to Allah, the One predominant Power, in whom there is no distinction of per- sons, as among the Olympian gods or in the Christian trinity of Father, Incarnate Son, and Holy Ghost. Something resembling the responsible actions of individuals is discernible in the theatrical art of the Chinese and Hindu; but, as Hegel explains, "here, too . . . these do not so much amount to the execution of any free and individual action: they merely reflect the animated life of events and emotions in definite situations, which are displayed in their course as they actually hap- pened."[87]

For the beginnings of genuine drama in all its forms we must therefore turn to the Greeks. In the Orient, only one is free, whether as God ruling directly over his subjects or as God's first minister; and where only one is free there can be no dramatic confrontations or collisions. Among the Greeks *many*, but not yet all, were deemed to be free; so that dramatic confrontations were a reality, yet only among free citizens who knew themselves to be responsible not only for their own personal deeds but also for the deeds of slaves and dependent aliens, as well as women and children. In the modern world,

finally, *all* human beings are held to be essentially free —
potentially as children, and actually as adults — so that each
person, if he is to be recognizable as a person, must sooner or
later hold himself responsible for all that he does or suffers to
be done to him. And this must be true, according to Hegel, even
and particularly in the instance of the slave who has permitted
himself to be enslaved or to continue in slavery when, in the
profoundest depth of his soul, he knows that he has always been
as free as his master to prefer and risk and suffer death rather
than endure enslavement.

From this Hegelian point of view, the development of
drama is tragic when free men are few and exceptional, and it
becomes more and more comic, in the noblest sense of the
word, as equality in freedom is universalized. In tragedy, as
Hegel expresses it, heroic types "are thrown into confusion in
virtue of the abstract nature of their sterling volition and
character, or they are forced to accept that with resignation, to
which they have been themselves essentially opposed."[88] In
comedy, on the contrary, there is no heroic confrontation, but
a triumph of personality "in its character of infinite
self-assuredness." It is a triumph in which all free men, not just
heroes, can share equally. What is inseparable from the personal experience of comedy, Hegel writes, "is an infinite
geniality and confidence, capable of rising superior to its own
contradiction, and experiencing therein no taint of bitterness
or sense of misfortune whatever. It is the happy frame of mind,
a hale condition of soul, which, fully aware of itself, can endure
the dissolution of its aims and achievements."[89]

Of the intermediary form, which is neither tragedy nor
comedy, Hegel says very little, even though in his time as in ours
theatrical pieces of its class had come to predominate on the
English and European stage. The principle aim of such real-life
dramas, he observes, is essentially theatrical; they seek less "to
affect us as genuine poetical productions than to reach our
emotions generally as men and women." Or, more precisely:
"They aim on the one hand simply at recreation, and on the
other at moral education of the public taste. But while doing so
they are almost equally concerned to provide ample opportunity to the actor for the display of his trained art and virtuosity

in the most brilliant manner."[90]

As we have already noted, Hegel's theory of tragedy is the one part of his poetics that has received serious and intelligent study in the English-speaking world, due, for the most part, to the labors of A. C. Bradley. Only in one significant respect does Bradley fail to do justice to the comprehensiveness of the Hegelian theory, and that has to do with Hegel's alleged preference of ancient over modern tragedy. Bradley insists that, "rightly or wrongly," one gets the impression from the *Aesthetics* that, in Hegel's view, the principle of tragedy "is more adequately realized in the best classical tragedies than in modern works." That impression is supported, Bradley argues, by certain implications of Hegel's distinction between classical and romantic art. Hegel appears to have taught, as Bradley reads him, that the classical art of Greece, in which "beauty held a position such as it never held before and will not bold again," is art par excellence; from which it follows that modern or romantic art, with its "boundless subjectivity," is essentially defective in comparison. Unlike its classical predecessor, ro- mantic art admits "common and un-beautiful reality into the realm of Beauty;" and one can readily see, Bradley concludes, "how all this is connected with those characteristics of modern tragedy which Hegel regards as necessary and yet as, in part, drawbacks."[91]

Bernard Bosanquet, on the contrary, has argued that the opposite of Bradley's view is correct. "It has been said," Bosanquet observes, "that Hegel's classification is a descending series. This is not so; the romantic arts are the culmination of art as such, though it is mere truth to say that they are not the culmination of beauty in the narrow sense."[92] Needless to say, we support this view.

In his long discussion of the differences between ancient and modern drama, Hegel has summed up his entire theory of tragedy in terms of those differences. He there notes, first of all, that the Greeks developed two distinct types of tragic situation: one dealing with the opposition "between ethical life in its social universality and the family as the natural ground of moral relations;"[93] the other exploring the dilemma of moral respon- sibility incurred for deeds committed in fact but not with

conscious intent. The first type is best represented, Hegel
asserts, in the *Antigone* of Sophocles. Defining with precision
his high estimate of that play (which is similarly singled out for
praise by Aristotle), he writes: "Of all that is noble in the ancient
and modern world — I know pretty nearly all of it, and it is right
and possible to know it — the *Antigone* appears to me, from this
point of view, the most excellent, the most satisfying work of
art."[94] What is satisfying, artistically is the fact that each of the
plays protagonists, Creon as well as Antigone, is in a tragic
situation of the first type: both acknowledge a double obliga-
tion — on the one hand, to respect their family ties, and on the
other, to respect their political obligations as rulers and off-
spring of rulers. That is to say, the tragic conflict in the *Antigone*
is not the opposition between protagonists, as many critics of
recent times have imagined; on the contrary, "imminent in the
life of both" is the value each combats, and "they are seized and
broken by that very bond which is rooted in the compass of
their own social existence."[95]

Turning to the second type of tragic situation — the dilemma of responsibility for deeds done under external constraint — Hegel observes that we find in some Greek examples
of it "a real approach to our modern point of view." Identifying
the masterpiece of this type, which he sets beside the *Antigone*,
Hegel says unequivocally: "The most perfect example of this in
ancient drama is to be found in the ever admirable *Oedipus at
Colonus*." The hero of that play, we are told, "resembles Adam,
losing his happiness when he obtains the knowledge of good
and evil." Oedipus, who had sought to avoid doing what was
fated, finally assumes full moral responsibility for all that he has
done and chooses to live among the Erinyes, or Furies, until all
the disruption in him is extinguished and his soul is purified.
What makes the play almost modern in its point of view, Hegel
explains, is the emphasis on psychological reconciliation worked
out by Oedipus "in and for himself," through his own "essential
character."[96]

Yet there remains an essential difference between ancient
and modern tragedy; and in spelling it out, Hegel unequivocally declares his ultimate preference, which is not what Bradley would have us believe. Hegel notes, first of all, that from the

"point of view of our profounder modern consciousness of right and wrong," the crimes of Oedipus and of other ancient tragic heroes do not appear as "deeds for which the true personality of the perpetrator was responsible." It is not easy for us to feel at home with heroes who, without revealing their psychological motivation, make it "a point of honor . . . that they are guilty." The modern world insists on the distinction between the subjective attitude of self-conscious individuality and the "objective significance of the fact accomplished."[97]

There are in Greek literature, especially in Euripides, instances of characters who examine their consciences and weigh their motives, thereby vacillating in their resolve. But in the "supreme results of ancient tragedy," Hegel reminds us, the truly heroic personalities invariably identify their individuality "with an ethical pathos which is substantive." This is never the case in the best examples of modern tragedy. The great romantic heroes make their tragic decisions in the complex depths of personality, where the sanctions of moral law or social responsibility have no compelling power. Whether morally justified, or wrong and criminal in their deeds, the modern heroes invariably act as they do, not out of interest in the "ethical vindication of the truly substantive claims of right, but for the simple reason that they are the kind of men they are."[98] According to Hegel, the highest mastery in the representation of fully developed characters of this sort was attained by the English dramatists of the Renaissance; and among these modern masters, "soaring above the rest at an almost unapproachable height, stands Shakespeare."[99]

Shakespeare, Hegel asserts, has revealed in his great heroes and heroines the innermost essence of tragic experience. Exploring the extreme limits of evil and folly as well as moral nobility, he has endowed his characters with a degree of intelligence and imagination that "makes them free artists" in themselves, capable of contemplating their own lives as works of art. Because of the incomparable universality of his characterizations and the variety of situations included in the "infinite embrace of his world-stage," Shakespeare's works have gained entrance everywhere except in those rare quarters where national conventions of art are too narrow and specific. On this point of universality, Hegel makes a telling comparison: "A similar position of advantage, such as that we allow to Shakespeare, would be attributable to the tragedies of the ancients, if we did not, apart from our changed habits in respect to scenic representation and certain aspects of the national consciousness, make the further demand of a profounder psychological penetration and a greater breadth of particular characterization."[100]

But the tragedies of Shakespeare do not all equally satisfy the profounder requirements of the modern point of view. In *Macbeth*, for instance, the disposition of the tragic hero who listens to the "equivocal sisters of fate," allowing himself to be driven to crime by their "double-tongued" promises and false admonitions, hardly differs from that of the ancient Oedipus or Orestes, both sent to destruction by oracular and evidently divine utterances.[101] Despite the depths of personality and motivation that Shakespeare explores in *Macbeth*, there is nevertheless through it all a *fixedness* in the characterization that links it with the perspective of the ancients. Macbeth, Hegel writes:

> is forced by his character into the fetters of his ambitious passion. At first he hesitates, then he stretches his hand to seize the crown; he commits a murder in order to secure it, and in order to maintain it storms on through the tale of horror. This regardless tenacity, this identity of the man with himself, and the object which his own personality brings to birth is the source of our abiding interest in him. Nothing makes him budge, neither the respect for the sacredness of kingship, nor the madness of his wife, nor the rout of his vassals, nor destruction as it rushes upon him, neither divine nor human claims — he withdraws from them all into himself and persists . . . . The action of Macbeth [is] a descent of the soul into savagery, accompanied by a result which, when all irresolution is thrown to the winds, and the dice are cast, leaves nothing further able to restrain it.

This *fixedness* of Macbeth differs from the ancient characterizations in the single important respect that comparable stability of purpose in ancient heroes is invariably "penetrated with a pathos which may be vindicated on ethical grounds."[102]

There is, indeed, in Hegel's judgment, only one Shakespearean play in which the modern, romantic point of view is consistently maintained throughout. Its hero, Hegel says, has a type of consciousness that is much purer than Macbeth's "which believes in witches," and much more sober, thorough, and solid than that of the ancient heroes, who put their trust in the frenzy of priestesses, or in the voices of trees and birds, or in dreams. This purer type of consciousness cannot allow itself to be lifted out of its moral dilemma by external determinations, for good or evil. Its tragic mistrust, therefore, finds no relief. In attempting to represent such self-consciousness, "with all the intimate traits of its evolution," in "self-destructive conflict with circumstances,"[103] Shakespeare produced the work of art that is for Hegel the supreme masterpiece of all human art, ancient or modern: that insoluble psychological enigma, that "Mona Lisa" of literature, as T. S. Eliot calls it[104] — the tragedy of *Hamlet*.

Hegel's theory of comedy has also had some impact on modern literary criticism; and again, the medium has been A. C. Bradley, whose brilliant essay "The Rejection of Falstaff" is an application of the Hegelian insights.[105] In widely scattered pages of the *Aesthetics*, Hegel says much that is interesting about ancient comedy, both Greek and Roman; but it is significant that the entire course of lectures on the fine arts culminates in what he has to say finally about the comic genius of Shakespeare as compared with Aristophanes and Molière. The major point of difference, according to Hegel, between Aristophanic and almost all subsequent comedy is revealed by exploring the question as to whether "the comic characters are an object of laughter only to the audience, or also to the characters themselves." Aristophanes, the creator of genuine comedy, confined himself to the latter alternative; but since then it is the former that has prevailed. It has been the standpoint not only of Plautus and Terence and the Renaissance comic dramatists, Hegel writes, but also "of Molière — and particularly in his best plays, which are by no means farces."[106]

Molière's characters, unlike those of Aristophanes, are in bitter earnest about the objects aimed at, and are therefore —

in Hegel's judgment — "quite unable to join with satisfaction in the laughter, when they are finally deceived . . . . They are in short merely the disillusioned objects of a laughter foreign to themselves." Molière's Tartuffe, and Orgon, and the Miser, are typical, and the theme is generally the same: that socially titillating transvaluation of values which shows us, in an amusing way, how "the real masters are the servants."[107]

On the other hand, beside this prosaic form, the modern era has also "elaborated a world of comedy which is both comic and truly poetical in nature" — the comedy of exploited self-assurance. It is a dramatic achievement that fully matches that of Aristophanes, even to the point of paralleling its development. And as the master who . . . outshines all others in this field" Hegel once again cites for us the name of Shakespeare.[108]

Shakespeare's comic rogues, no less than his tragic heroes and villains, are all self-conscious poets, endowed with an imaginative power that enables them to be "independent spectators of themselves." This is, obviously, true of the great tragic figures; but "in like manner," Hegel writes, "Shakespeare's more vulgar characters, such as Stephano, Trinculo, Pistol, and that hero among them all, Falstaff, though saturated with their own debasement, assert themselves as fellows of intelligence, whose genial quality, possessed of a large and open atmosphere of its own, enables them to take in anything, and makes them, in short, all that great men are."[109]

It is in the "spirit of negation" of such comedy — a negation that negates its own negativity — that art in general attains its consummation, opening the way, as Hegel expresses it, to "a dissolution of all that human art implies." In tragedy, the loftiest significance of man's spiritual dilemma is revealed to him: he sees himself as a responsible being who is yet not responsible for his being at all. It is a simultaneous view of the glory and the vanity of man's condition. In high comedy, the glory of the tragic vision is shattered — but so also is the vanity; and all that remains in the midst of such dissolution, Hegel concludes, "is the free activity of subjective life [*Subjectivität als solche*] which is displayed, in and along with the dissolution, as aware of itself and self-assured."[110] In Aristotelian terms, we should have to say, therefore, that it is not tragedy but comedy, of the order of Shakespeare's Falstaff, that offers the ultimate aesthetic catharsis.

NOTES

1. W. D. Ross, *Aristotle* (London, 1930), p. 290.

2. A. C. Bradley, "Hegel's Theory of Tragedy," *Oxford Lectures on Poetry* (London, 1950), p. 69.

3. *Poetics*, 4 (1448[b] 1f.), Ingram Bywater, tr., in *The Basic Works of Aristotle*, R. McKeon, ed. (New York, 1941), pp. 1457-8. All translations from Aristotle have been adapted slightly in accordance with the Bekker text.

4. *Rhetoric*, I, 11 (1371[a] 33-4), H. Rhys Roberts, tr., in McKeon, p. 1365.

5. *Metaphysics*, I, 2 (982[b] 11f), W. D. Ross, tr., in McKeon, p. 692.

6. *Poetics*, 4 (1448[b] 13f), McKeon, pp. 1458-9.

7. *Ibid.*, 9 (1451[b] 1f), pp. 1463-4.

8. *Metaphysics*, XIII, 4 (1078[b] 14f), McKeon, p. 894.

9. *Ibid.*, I, 6 (987[b] 10f), p. 701.

10. *Ibid.*, I, 9 (991[a] 29f), p. 708.

11. *Hegel's Lectures on the History of Philosophy*, E. S. Haldane, Francis H. Simson, trs. (New York, 1953), II, 1-373 *passim*.

12. *Metaphysics*, XII, 10 (1075[a] 12f), McKeon, pp. 885-6.

13. *Ibid.*, VII, 9 (1034[a] 36f), p. 796.

14. *Peotics*, 26 (1462[a] 7ff), McKeon, p. 1487.

15. *Ibid.*

16. Bradley, *Oxford Lectures on Poetry*, p. 69.

17. G. W. F. Hegel, *Lectures on the Philosophy of Religion*, E. B. Speiers, J. B. Sanderson, trs. (New York, 1962), II, 249.

18. G. W. F. Hegel, *The Philosophy of Fine Art*, F. P. B. Osmaston, tr. (London, 1920), II, 182-3; *Sämtliche Werke*, Herman Glockner, ed. (Stuttgart, 1964), XIII, 17. *The Philosophy of Fine Art* will hereafter be referred to as *PFA*; quotations therefrom have been adapted in accordance with the German text of *Sämtliche Werke*, hereafter referred to as *SW*.

19. *The Introduction to Hegel's Philosophy of Fine Art*, Bernard Bosanquet,

tr. (London, 1905), pp. 185-6.

20. *Nichomachean Ethics*, X, 7 (1177ᵇ 26f), W. D. Ross, tr. McKeon, p. 1105.

21. *PFA*, III, 185-6; *SW*, XIII, 432-3).

22. *PFA*, II, 17-8, 138 and III, 41; *SW*, XII, 418, 518 and XIII, 278-9. See also John Edwin Sandys, *A History of Classical Scholarship* (Cambridge, 1908), III, 65f.

23. *Poetics*, 1 (1447ᵃ 16f), McKeon, p. 1455.

24. *Ibid.*

25. *Ibid.*, 2 (1448ᵃ 1ff), p. 1456.

26. *Ibid.*, 3 (1448ᵃ 19f), pp. 1456-7.

27. *PFA*, IV, 5; *SW* XIII, 222.

28. *PFA*, IV, 102; *SW* XIII, 321-2.

29. *PFA*, II, 23; *SW* XII, 422.

30. *PFA*, II, 25-6; *SW*, XII, 424-5.

31. *Introduction*, Bosanquet, tr., p. 184.

32. *Ibid.*, p. 197.

33. *Ibid.*, pp. 198-9.

34. *Ibid.*, p. 187.

35. *Ibid.*

36. *Ibid.*, p. 190.

37. *Ibid.*, pp. 204-5.

38. *PFA*, III, 257-8; *SW*, XIV, 45.

39. *PFA,* III, 339; *SW*, XIV, 125-6.

40. *Introduction*, Bosanquet, tr., p. 206.

41. *PFA*, III, 347; *SW*, XIV, 133.

42. *PFA*, III, 383; *SW*, XIV, 170.

43. *PFA*, IV, 10; *SW*, XIV, 227.

44. *PFA*, IV, 5; *SW*, XIV, 222.

45. *PFA*, IV, 19; *SW*, XIV, 236.

46. *Introduction*, Bosanquet, tr., p. 171.

47. *Ibid.*, p. 172.

48. *PFA*, IV, 16; *SW*, XIV, 233.

49. *PFA*, IV, 21; *SW*, XIV, 238.

50. René Wellek, *A History of Modern Criticism: 1750-1950*, Vol. II, *The Romantic Age* (New Haven, 1955), p. 323.

51. T. S. Eliot, "Three Voices of Poetry," *On Poetry and Poets*, (New York, 1961), p. 96.

52. *Ibid.*, p. 112.

53. T. S. Eliot, *The Criterion*, XIV (April, 1935), 433.

54. *PFA*, IV, 23; *SW*, XIV, 240.

55. *PFA*, IV, 111; *SW*, XIV, 331.

56. *PFA*, IV, 112; *SW*, XIV, 332-3.

57. *PFA*, IV, 175; *SW*, XIV, 399.

58. *PFA*, IV, 176; *SW*, XIV, 400-1.

59. *PFA*, IV, 177; *SW*, XIV, 402.

60. *PFA*, IV, 164; *SW*, XIV, 388.

61. *PFA*, IV, 117-8; *SW*, XIV, 338-9.

62. *PFA*, IV, 147-8; *SW*, XIV, 369-70.

63. *PFA*, IV, 150; *SW*, XIV, 372.

64. Erich Auerbach, *Mimesis*, (Princeton, 1956), p. 191.

65. *Ibid.*, p. 194.

66. *PFA*, II, 373; *SW*, XIII, 213.

67. *PFA*, II, 373-4; *SW*, XIII, 213-4.

68. *PFA*, IV, 190; *SW*, XIV, 416.

69. *PFA*, IV, 171; *SW*, XIV, 395.

70. *PFA*, II, 375-6; *SW*, XIII, 215-6.

71. *PFA*, IV, 194; *SW*, XIV, 420.

72. *PFA*, IV, 206-7; *SW*, XIV, 434.

73. *PFA*, IV, 200; *SW*, XIV, 426-7.

74. *PFA*, IV, 201; *SW*, XIV, 428.

75. *PFA*, IV, 214; *SW*, XIV, 443.

76. *PFA*, IV, 215; *SW*, XIV, 443-4.

77. *PFA*, IV, 226; *SW*, XIV, 456.

78. *PFA*, IV, 231; *SW*, XIV, 461.

79. *PFA*, IV, 231-2; *SW*, XIV, 462.

80. *PFA*, II, 94; *SW*, XII, 491.

81. *PFA*, IV, 232; *SW*, XIV, 462.

82. *PFA*, IV, 244; *SW*, XIV, 475.

83. *PFA*, IV, 247; *SW*, XIV, 478.

84. *PFA*, IV, 248; *SW*, XIV, 479.

85. *PFA*, IV, 104; *SW*, XIV, 324.

86. *PFA*, IV, 308; *SW*, XIV, 540-1.

87. *PFA*, IV, 309; *SW*, XIV, 541.

88. *PFA*, IV, 301; *SW*, XIV, 533.

89. *PFA*, IV, 302; *SW*, XIV, 534.

90. *PFA*, IV, 307-8; *SW*, XIV, 540.

91. Bradley, *Oxford Lectures on Poetry*, pp. 76, 94.

92. Bernard Bosanuqet, *A History of Aesthetic* (London, 1949), p. 352.

93. *PFA*, IV, 318; *SW*, XIV, 551.

94. *PFA*, IV, 324; *SW*, XIV, 556.

95. *Ibid.*

96. *PFA*, IV, 325-6; *SW*, XIV, 557-8.

97. *PFA*, IV, 319-21; *SW*, XIV, 551-3.

98. *PFA*, IV, 335; *SW*, XIV, 567.

99. *PFA*, IV, 337; *SW*, XIV, 568.

100. *PFA*, IV, 273; *SW*, XIV, 503-4.

101. G. W. Hegel, *The Philosophy of Mind*, I. B. Baillie, tr. (London, 1910), p. 740.

102. *PFA*, II, 356.9; *SW*, XIII, 196-9.

103. *PFA*, IV, 340; *SW*, XIV, 571-2.

104. T. S. Eliot, *Selected Essays 1917-1932* (New York, 1932), p. 24.

105. Bradley, *Oxford Lectures on Poetry*, pp. 245-75. See also E. F. Carritt, *The Theory of Beauty* (London, 1923), p. 316: "[Hegel's] theory is profoundly suggestive. Its elaboration would be justified if only because it has surely stimulated Mr. A. C. Bradley's inimitable essay on Falstaff."

106. *PFA*, IV, 345; *SW*, XIV, 576-7.
107. *PFA*, IV, 346-7; *SW*, XIV, 578.
108. *PFA*, IV, 348; *SW*, XIV, 579.
109. *PFA*, II, 366; *SW*, XIII, 207.
110. *PFA*, IV, 349; *SW*, XIV, 579.

HEGEL AND THE IDEA OF ARTISTIC BEAUTY, OR THE IDEAL

I. Introduction and Bibliographical Note on Translation

Georg Wilhelm Friedrich Hegel was born in Stuttgart, capital of the Duchy of Württemberg, on August 27, 1770. Württemberg, one needs to recall, did not become a part of the German Empire until 1871, after it had been defeated as an ally of Austria in the Austro-Prussian war. In that duchy's South German, distinctly Swabian atmosphere, Hegel received his cultural formation until the age of eighteen, when he went off to Tübingen to study theology. The years at Tübingen (1788-93) proved to be a time of great cultural and social ferment, the excitement of which he shared with his newfound university friends, the young poet Friedrich Hölderlin and the precociously mature philosopher Friedrich Schelling, both of whom would become famous long before Hegel.

In the German universities of that time, Immanuel Kant was the dominant intellectual force. His great *critiques* of pure and practical reason, and of judgment or aesthetics published between 1781 and 1790, were demonstrating, on a theoretical level, the power of thought to uproot the present from the past. In France, that same power had already exercised itself on a practical level to uproot and sweep away social, religious, and political institutions as old as France itself. For Hegel and his friends, the French revolutionary deeds that seemed to mirror Kant's revolutionary thought had an irresistible fascination. As England's romantic poet William Wordsworth would later say of the moment:

> Bliss was it in that dawn to be alive,
> But to be young was very heaven.

[From *Hegel on the Arts*, abridged and translated by Henry Paolucci, Frederick Ungar Publishing Co., New York, 1979, pp. i-xxx; 1-10.]

After completing his studies at Tübingen, Hegel took a post in Berne, Switzerland, as a tutor in a private home. He returned to Germany in 1797, living first in Frankfurt am Main (still as a tutor) and then in Jena, where his friend Schelling had already established himself. Jena had become a flourishing cultural center, numbering Schiller, Fichte, the Schlegel brothers, Tieck, and Novalis among its residents.

To qualify as a university instructor at Jena, Hegel wrote a dissertation in Latin on the "orbits of the planets." In it, as in later writings on the mathematical sciences, he argued that Kepler's empirical laws were of more permanent scientific value than Newton's gravitational theory in which the curvilinear simplicity of Kepler's ellipses is analyzed into vectors of rectilinear force. This was followed by an essay on "The Differences in the Systems of Fichte and Schelling" (1801) in which Hegel interprets the absolute idealism of Fichte (with its "ascendancy of the Ego over Nature") and the naturalistic idealism of Schelling (with its attempt to "reconcile Nature and Ego") as complementary responses to the Kantian critical philosophy. The essay acquires importance in retrospect, however, because of its suggestion that Hegel might himself attempt a synthesis that would reinterpret the thought of Kant, Fichte, and Schelling the way the critical dialectic of Socrates and the idealism of Plato are reinterpreted in the developmental, naturalistic system of Aristotle.

The first significant result of Hegel's effort to make himself a modern Aristotle was his *Phenomenology of Mind* (*Phänomenologie des Geistes*, 1807), which he himself characterized as a journey of discovery and relentless self-criticism on a "highway of despair." In the midst of it, he suddenly felt himself thrust up spiritually into the highest reaches of aesthetic, religious, and philosophic excitement. It was as if the "scattered pages" of his education to that point had suddenly been drawn into a single volume, bound by the kind of *love* that the Greeks called *philosophia* – love of wisdom.

The final pages of the *Phenomenology* were being prepared for print while the Emperor Napoleon — the French Revolution on horseback — was leading his army to victory in the Battle of Jena. That army was supposed to be bringing liberty, equality, and fraternity to all mankind everywhere, and its symbolic significance looms large in the pages of Hegel's first major book. But its immediate practical effect was to put him out of a job. With teaching closed to him, he took a post as editor of a newspaper in Bamberg and then (in 1808) as rector of a classical gymnasium in Nuremberg. There he married and, while revising the school curriculum and teaching its upper classes, he wrote his extensive *Science of Logic (Wissenschaft der Logik*, 1812-16).

In the fall of 1816, Hegel was called to occupy a chair in philosophy at the University of Heidelberg. He there completed his third major work, the *Encyclopedia of the Philosophical Sciences (Encyclopädie der philosophischen Wissenschaften*, 1817), designed to serve as an integrative handbook for students attending his university lectures. That work, with its three subdivisions on the *Science of Logic,* the *Philosophy of Nature,* and the *Philosophy of Mind, is* perhaps the boldest, and certainly the most successful attempt of any thinker since Plotinus to systematize the thought of an entire civilization. As Hegel several times indicated, he intended it to be the sort of comprehensive work Aristotle himself might have attempted had he lived to complete the systematic exposition of his thought on the design broadly sketched in several notable passages of his *De Anima, Ethics, Politics,* and *Metaphysics.* In the last paragraph of the *Encyclopedia,* Hegel in fact humbly eclipses himself, giving the final word to Aristotle. Cited in Greek is the famous passage of the *Metaphysics* in which Aristotle defines the being of God as *living thought* or, more precisely, as a pure act of thinking that nourishes itself by actually thinking through all that is potentially thinkable. The effect of the passage at the close of the *Encyclopedia* is to suggest that the entire system elaborated to that point provides a post-Kantian confirmation of Aristotle's view that man experiences the divine actuality of rational life in its transcendent fullness when his thinking — I (the *cogito* of Descartes' *cogito ergo* sum — I think therefore I am) is fully absorbed in thinking of itself as thinking — I *(nóesis noéseos nóesis).*

From Heidelberg, Hegel was soon called to the university of Berlin, where he delivered his first lecture on October 22,

1818. His fourth major work, *The Philosophy of Right (Grundlinien der Philosophie des Rechts)*, appeared in 1821. He continued to write while at Berlin, publishing an enlarged second edition of his *Encyclopedia* and several monograph-length articles in learned journals. But the great intellectual labor of this final period went into the year-long series of university lectures he delivered on the philosophy of history, fine art, and religion, and on the history of philosophy, all destined to be published posthumously. He was preparing a third edition of his *Encyclopedia* when he died on November 14, 1831.

The posthumously published Berlin lectures fill at least a dozen volumes in Hegel's collected works. Those on fine art or aesthetics *(Vorlesungen über die Ästhetik)* were compiled and edited by Heinrich Gustav Hotho, using Hegel's own very extensive handwritten notes as a basis, but enriching them with student transcriptions of the very lectures themselves as delivered in the years 1823, 1826, and 1828-29. The first edition consisted of three volumes issued in 1835, 1837, and 1838, and a revised second edition followed in 1842-43. Scholars who have gone over the manuscript materials since then agree that, especially in the second edition (which is the basis for this Milestones of Thought abridgment), Hotho "did his work brilliantly."

In his review of the T. M. Knox translation of the entire *Aesthetics (Times Literary Supplement,* January 2, 1976), Professor John Casey aptly observed that "Hegel's lectures on fine art form in many ways the most attractive introduction to his thought." That Hegel approached the study of art with a staggeringly rich cultural preparation is now widely recognized. His years as teacher and rector in a classical gymnasium at Nuremberg gave him a thorough mastery of the works of the ancients in their original languages. Those works, he said on September 29, 1809, in a commencement address, "contain the most noble food in the most noble form: golden apples in silver bowls . . . incomparably richer than all the works of any other nation and of any other time."

But Hegel's cultural preparation was by no means limited to bookish acquaintance with Greco-Roman classical literature and art. His letters of later years reveal that he frequently attended concert halls and opera houses and that he repeatedly visited the great German art galleries. As Professor Carl Friedrich of Harvard notes, "during his Berlin professorship, he made three long trips, to the Low Countries and Brussels, 1822, to Vienna, 1824, and to Paris, 1827," the main purpose of which appears to have been "to see the great works of art and architecture" which he so vividly describes in his lectures. In Vienna, Professor Friedrich further notes, Hegel was "enchanted with Italian opera, and his letters to his wife were expressing not only general joy, but detailed appreciation. When Mendelssohn produced, for the first time after generations, Bach's Passion according to St. Matthew in Berlin, Hegel was greatly impressed. His taste in music, contrary to Schopenhauer's, was altogether of a high order."

Confirming Friedrich's judgment, Professor Casey too speaks of the "quite prodigious range" of personal experience and knowledge of the arts that Hegel brings to bear in elaborating his lectures on fine art. The "exalted importance" Hegel gives to art in his philosophical system, "although explicable in purely philosophic terms," Casey adds, "also answers to the experience of his own life. In this he is to be contrasted with Kant whose writings on aesthetics, greatly though they influenced Hegel, are strangely detached from any obvious love of the arts." How far beyond Kant and Schopenhauer we may have to go for an approach to the arts based on love and refinement of taste at all comparable to Hegel's has been pointedly suggested by A. C. Bradley, the leading Shakespearean critic of modern times, where he writes: "Since Aristotle dealt with tragedy and, as usual, drew the main features of his subject with those sure and simple strokes which no later hand has rivaled, the only philosopher who has treated it in a manner both original and searching is Hegel."

Aristotle's theory of tragedy has of course come down to us as an isolated fragment. Hegel's, on the contrary, is part of a complete poetics, which deals fully with epic and lyric poetry and comic drama as well as tragedy; and which is in turn part of a complete aesthetics, where the treatment of architecture, sculpture, painting, music, and the narrative, lyric, and comic genres of poetry is not less searching and original than the treatment of tragedy.

The systematic exposition of Hegel's aesthetics links the five major arts in a "progression" that borders on the technology of utilitarian construction at one extreme and on the prosaic sounds or signs of expository discourse at the other. The most "solid" of them, architecture, *encloses* three-dimensional space. Suggesting rather than directly expressing its meaning, it is, in Hegel's scheme, the symbolic art par excellence. What it symbolizes, what it prepares an environment for, is directly expressed in the classical perfection of sculpture, the solidity of which does not enclose but rather fills space. Next in order come the *romantic* arts — the less-than-three-dimensional arts — of painting, music, and poetry.

The perspective in the romantic arts is internal. In painting, for instance, it is as if we had penetrated the solidity of a Greek statue in order to look out of its otherwise coldly-vacant eyes with the warmth of life. From such an internal perspective, by means of pigments and lines on a two-dimensional surface, painting gives us love-suffused, vivid representations of all that could conceivably "seem to be" in the architecturally enclosed space of sculpture's "fitting temple," or in the boundless reaches of imaginable space beyond. Music, penetrating more deeply, takes art beyond spatial dimensionality altogether. In its pulsing point of time, at the very center of artistic vitality, the whole gamut of subjective feelings and passions receives infinitely variable rhythmic, melodic, and harmonic expression.

Architecture is the most outward, music the most inward of the arts. Where then does poetry fit in this progression? Hegel reminds us that poetry's medium is neither spatial nor temporal in a physical sense. Its words, which need not be sounded aloud or written, are signs addressed directly to our imaginative intelligence, where they are able, as Hegel expressed it, to produce the *effects* of all the other arts without the material means. First there is epic or narrative poetry. It creates for our mind's eye worlds and figures as objective as works of architecture and sculpture and as warmly pigmented as the finest paintings. At the opposite extreme, lyric poetry sings its unheard melodies directly into our souls. But it is poetry's "third voice" — drama — that literally brings the effects of all the other arts together, not only by combining the characteristics of epic and lyric, but by actually getting itself performed, three dimensionally, on stage. There, enclosed in a set built by architectural stagecraft, figures modeled in flesh and blood rather than marble or bronze are rehearsed to play their parts in carefully "blocked" colorful scenes, all the while uttering in cadenced speech the profoundest thoughts and sentiments, whether of pure tragedy, or comedy, or a mixture of both, that serve imaginatively to shape their identities as *dramatis personae* – or characters of the play.

Fascinatingly suggestive as this Hegelian account of the progression of the arts may be in itself, its genuine importance and novelty for the history of aesthetics lies in its underlying philosophic concept. There is here a decisive break with the fundamental attitudes of the neo-classical or "Enlightenment" aesthetics which had dominated the preceding two centuries. According to that aesthetics, art's perfection consisted in a rationally-disciplined "imitation of nature," so that the result would be, in Alexander Pope's phrase, "nature still – but nature methodized." Rejecting that reigning neoclassical conception, Hegel gives us an elaborately integrated analysis and richly illustrated interpretation of the five major arts as progressively dematerialized media for the expression of a content which they share not with any more or less scientific or rationalist "study of nature" but with religion and philosophy.

The neo-classical aesthetics of "Enlightenment" was willing enough to share its content with philosophy, provided philosophy remained rationalistically critical toward the claims of any form of religion that went beyond naturalistic deism. In art, as in human ethical and political behavior, whatever was not rational in a naturalistic sense was deemed to be a defect. Even the masterworks of classical Greco-Roman art, which had served the Renaissance masters as models of unsurpassable perfection, came to be sharply downgraded under strictly rationalistic scrutiny. Too much was still discernible in them, it was alleged, of the ethnic and religious attitudes inherited by the Greeks from their Asiatic cultural ancestry. The Enlightenment's self-appointed task was, in fact, to free not only art, but all human activity from the "burden of history."

The expectation was that, with the weight of centuries of ethnocentric prejudice and monkish ignorance lifted from their shoulders, the enlightened populations of the present might indeed before long inaugurate for all mankind a global "reign of reason" that might yet prove perpetual.

Such an essentially anti-historical rationalist attitude had made any serious appreciation of the art of the Ancient Near and Far East, to say nothing of medieval Christendom's art, virtually impossible. And not until Enlightenment's vaunted reason had given way to terror and dictatorship in France was there a reaction that reaffirmed not only the value but the necessity of historical-rootedness for civilized existence.

According to Hegel, the break with rationalistic abstraction came first in poetry itself. In that sudden outburst of romantic lyricism that gave us Goethe and Schiller in Germany, Coleridge, Wordsworth, Byron, Keats, and Shelley in England, and their peers and successors throughout Europe, the stifling rules and restraints of the neo-classical approach to art were "cast aside" everywhere, permitting the "rights of genius, its works and its effects," to prevail at last against the "presumption of such legalisms and such watery wastes of theory."

Owing principally to the appearance of "genuinely living poetry," Hegel proceeds to explain, "there has sprung up a receptivity for and freedom to enjoy and recognize great works which have long been available, whether those of the modern world or the Middle Ages or even of wholly foreign peoples in the past, e.g., the Indian. These works, because of their age or foreign nationality, have of course something strange about them for us, but they have a content which outsoars their foreignness and is common to all mankind, and only by the prejudice of theory could they be stamped as products of bad taste."

Here it is that Hegel impresses upon us the importance and significance of the great categories of symbolic, classical, and romantic art, in terms of which he elaborates not only his "progression" of the five major art forms but his entire aesthetics. When brought face to face with masterworks of art that "lie outside the circle and forms" prescribed by neo-classical aesthetic theories, serious thinkers must of necessity, Hegel says, consider the concept of artistic beauty in a "deeper way than was possible for such theories." This has led in the first place to "recognition of a special kind of art — "Romantic Art"; but it has led also, Hegel adds, to a heightened appreciation of the heretofore inadequately defined concept of "Symbolic Art." In Hegel's view, each of these "other" kinds of art has plainly produced masterpieces worthy of comparison with those of our familiar classical and neo-classical art —however much an anti-historical, rationalistic bias may have tended to blind us to that fact.

Hegel has, of course, been tracing the origin of the so-called Romantic Movement, of which he himself is indisputably the greatest philosophical thinker. All his works, but especially his lectures on history, art, religion, and philosophy, are permeated with its powerfully excited sense of history's vital continuity and developmental force, apart from which even rationalistic "enlightenments" are impossible as well as inexplicable. In every field that he approached historically — anthropology, phenomenology, psychology, law, ethics, economics, sociology, and politics, as well as art, religion, and philosophy — Hegel's influence has been that of a trailblazer. "We may be critically inclined toward this Hegelian heritage," Professor Friedrich has said by way of introducing a survey of its impact on the contemporary world, "but we cannot gainsay its universal significance." The Hegelian "insistence on the unity of culture," he reminds us, "is now so widely accepted that it is difficult to believe that it was once a revolutionary principle." Its impact on social activists and creative artists as well as philosophers of every variety, from Marxist materialists and Italian idealists to American pragmatists and contemporary European existentialists, has been "so all-engulfing" that to survey it, Friedrich concludes, "would fall little short of an intellectual history" of the century and a half since his death.

What sort of trailblazer Hegel has proven to be in opening up for comparative study the cultural legacy of the peoples of the Near and Far East, we can better judge, perhaps, by noting the impact he has had on specialists in that vast sphere of study. The most eminent cultural archeologist of our time, W. F. Albright, for instance, reviews the state of interpretative research in his field as part of the introduction to his classic book, *From the Stone Age to Christianity: Monotheism and the Historical Process,* and then concludes: "For all the arbitrary and romantic elements in Hegel's philosophy of history, both philosophers and historians must remain forever in his debt. For the first time he brought together the data of history in a rational synthesis, exhibiting the progress of humanity from its Asiatic cradle to modern Western Europe and clearly recognizing the fact of cultural evolution." Albright organizes his own approach to the artistic-religious legacies of the peoples of the ancient Near East on Hegelian lines, including his interpretations of the verses of the Old and New Testaments. From a Jewish cultural perspective, in a specialized study on Hegel and Judaism, Professor Emil L. Fackenheim asks at one point whether Hegel's philosophical approach was capable of doing justice to the Jewish cultural experience. "Surprisingly, our answer," he concludes, "must be emphatically affirmative: Hegel not only *might* have developed an adequate *Grundidee* as his thought emphatically exposed itself to the Jewish religious self-understanding; his philosophy is, perhaps, of all philosophies the *only one* capable of doing so."

Moving further to the East, we cite the judgment of Kurt F. Leidecker, a specialist in the art and philosophy of India and Chinese Buddhism. He notes that modern scholarship has indeed made available mountains of materials that were unknown to European scholars in Hegel's day. Yet the Hegelian philosophical system is as a whole "so essentially oriental in itself," he adds with emphasis, that nothing could be more valuable as a pattern for organizing oriental studies today. "The dialectic," Professor Leidecker concludes, "is the greatest and permanent achievement of Hegel and within its context he can be and was the trailblazer for the synthesis between Orient and Occident."

But perhaps from a more purely aesthetic standpoint, the excitement that Hegel's trailblazing interpretations of non-classical art are apt to arouse in a culturally receptive reader has been best epitomized by the French critic Edmund Scherer, who is so highly and deservedly praised by Irving Babbitt in his *Masters of Modern French Criticism.* Hegel has taught us in his aesthetics, Scherer wrote back in 1861, "the respect and intelligence of the facts . . . . What a marvelous understanding of the past we have in consequence! How it lives again before our eyes! The affiliations of people, the advance of civilizations, the character of different times, the genius of languages, the sense of mythologies, the inspiration of national poetries, the essence of religions, are so many revelations due to [the impact of Hegelian thought on] our aesthetic. It prefers to contemplate and study rather than judge . . . . It has given up the barren method which consists in opposing one form of beauty to another, in preferring, in excluding. It bears with everything. It is vast as the world, tolerant as nature."

Hegel's aesthetics is indeed tolerant, in the sense that it "makes room" for appreciative study of every conceivable kind of artistic experience and expression. But it is in no sense a naturalistic aesthetics. Hegel in fact excludes any consideration of natural beauty from his theory of art, beyond what needs to be said to show that it can have no conceptual significance in an aesthetics competent to interpret varieties of art that are essentially religious in content. In his *Theory of Beauty*, E. F. Carritt of Oxford University had noted that Hegel's approach to art offers a "necessary propaedeutic to the appreciation of art produced by ancient and alien people" precisely because it rejects, as we have already noted, the naturalistic predilections of neo-classical criticism. In neo-classical criticism neither nature nor art, Hegel argued, could be accorded its due, because "methodized" nature is no more natural than it is artistic. While liberating itself from "imitation of nature," romantic aesthetics had in effect also liberated nature for the kind of appreciative study that John Ruskin was later to accord it. Contrasting Ruskin's attitude with Hegel's, Professor Carritt offers this striking comparative assessment: "Hegel's aesthetic prepossessions were as markedly humanist and dramatic as Ruskin's were naturalistic; and by its profound analysis of the Oriental, Classical, and Medieval minds as these expressed themselves in architecture, sculpture and poetry, the *Aesthétik* must stand, for the appreciation of this kind of beauty, in the place which is filled for the love of nature by Ruskin's studies in cloud and mountain form or in the morphology of plant and glacier."

Pressing the contrast between artistic and natural beauty, Hegel notes that, when animated by love, what our senses report to us of this "mighty world of eye and ear" is, as Wordsworth acknowledged, "both what they half create, and what perceive." The "nature lover," so far from being a passive observer, is already in part an artist. And art's perfection, thereafter, consists in freeing itself altogether from "natural bondage," so that it shows itself finally to have been *ideal* from beginning to end, in content as well as form.

The great critic Johann Joachim Winckelmann had stressed that very point in his studies of the ideal beauty of Greek art. According to Winckelmann, the content expressed in the masterworks of Greek art is never a merely natural "thing," but is always rather the *ideal itself* (in a Platonic sense) of the thing. Thus, in Greek art, a reciprocal or ideal adequacy of content and form becomes attainable; and that, Hegel agrees, is in fact the characteristic excellence of Greek artistic beauty, especially as we find it expressed in the perfection of Greek sculpture.

Hegel cannot, however, stop there. His concern is to determine how the masterpieces of symbolic and romantic art compare with Greek art in this respect. According to Bernard Bosanquet in his *History of Aesthetic,* Hegel was the first philosopher or critic to attempt such a comparison on the basis of Winckelmann's insight. Writing with great precision, Bosanquet therefore lays down this emphatic judgment:

> Hegel's treatment of the Ideal is the greatest single step that has ever been made in aesthetic. Winckelmann had portrayed the Ideal as in its perfection one and abstract. Kant, while recognizing it as an embodiment of life, had on this very ground excluded it from aesthetic, because relative to the will. It was Hegel who, while maintaining its aesthetic nobility in the sense of Winckelmann and crediting it with the full aesthetic purity, demanded but denied it by Kant, at the same time accepted the extension and differentiations of it so as to constitute the principle and matter of art in all its phases and limits.

With that "greatest single step that was ever made in aesthetic," Hegel raised the concept of art beyond anything that could have been claimed for it by the neo-classicists or the ancient Greeks themselves. Once it is clear that the true content of all genuine art must of necessity be ideal, not naturalistic, it becomes possible to draw comparisons, at least in terms of content, between the masterworks of Greek art and those of peoples who never so much as pretended to draw artistic inspiration from nature but who sought, rather, to represent in art an ideal "presence" of spirit in the universe, experienced as supernatural and divine. Focusing on content, Hegel can therefore insist that art is "a way of bringing to our minds and expressing the Divine," which is to say, "the deepest interest of mankind and the most comprehensive truths of spirit." Art, Hegel says further, "shares this vocation with religion and philosophy, but in a special way, namely by displaying even our highest spiritual experience objectively, thereby bringing it nearer to the senses, to feeling, and to nature's mode of appearance."

Hegel reminds us that the Greeks, who had inherited their sense of divinity from the Near East, very early identified their art and religion. That meant, in effect, that their gods had early been accorded idealized human form. Homer and Hesiod, Herodotus had said, have "fashioned" our gods for us; and Hegel notes further that, by the time of Phidias, the Greek religious experience had been so thoroughly absorbed in artistic expression that, beyond art's limits, nothing at all distinctive was left to which religious worship could lay exclusive claim. When philosophy came on the scene, it too insisted on a total assimilation of the divine and human, if not on a physical level, then certainly in thought, and in the aesthetic catharsis of high tragedy.

In the Near and Far East and among the peoples of Western Christendom the experience of divinity has been very different, and the art expressing that diversity of experience has differed accordingly. When God is experienced as unfathomable mystery or annihilating necessity or outpouring love, artistic expression must either fall short of or transcend the reciprocal adequacy of content and form that characterizes the classical ideal. Falling short of such adequacy, artistic expression is symbolic; transcending such adequacy, it is romantic.

These are not, for Hegel, relationships of inferiority or superiority. The symbolic, classical, and romantic kinds of art are three distinctive ways of expressing artistically what is expressible also in distinctive, historically-rooted forms of religious worship and philosophic speculation.

In any event, as Hegel insists, it has been in works of art — symbolic, classical, or romantic — "that nations have deposited their profoundest intuitions and ideas; art is thus often the key, and in many nations the sole key, to their philosophy and religion." Art, religion, and philosophy are in the end, for Hegel, "moments" of absolute spirit, by which he means that in their highest reaches, they are activities of *convergent* significance. They are related, one may say, like meridians of a terrestrial globe. Far apart at the equator, they draw closer and closer as we trace them upward, till they meet at the pole in a shared point, which is as much the culmination of religious and philosophic experience as it is of artistic experience. Where they are furthest apart, these meridians are clearly recognizable as man's commonest activities of *making, behaving,* and *explaining.* All peoples make, behave, and explain; and even the most primitive of them sooner or later develop manual skills, customary norms, and imaginatively suggestive myths that serve as explanations. In one corner or another of the world, some few people subject the three activities to the discipline of reason; and the result, then, is, in the first case, technology or productive science; in the second, rationalized ethical behavior, or practical science; and in the third, disciplined empirical study, or theoretic science.

But in all three of these spheres, it is possible to rise above the discipline of reason. There, as if under a higher than human control, technology becomes fine or inspired art, rational behavior becomes obedience to the categorical imperatives of religious revelation, and empirical science becomes God-centered speculative philosophy or theology. As moments of absolute spirit, the three activities are then within sight of the point of final convergence. According to Hegel, art's ultimate object must be, in other words, to perfect the activity of *making,* even as religion perfects *behaving* and philosophy perfects *explaining.*

An image of such convergence of art, religion, and philosophy upon a common point is provided by Dante in the opening and closing cantos of his *Paradiso,* and Hegel takes note of its significance for aesthetic theory. Dante tells us in the second canto that he is there about to "cross waters" that had been navigated before only by holy men and philosophers, saints and sages. Saints have crossed those waters in pursuit of religion's highest good; sages in pursuit of philosophy's highest truth. Dante means to cross them in pursuit of art's highest beauty. In the end, the lines pursued by saint, sage, and poet meet in a triadic unity or trinity that is at once good, true, and beautiful.

According to Hegel, it is romantic art — the art of the gothic cathedrals, medieval painting, and Bach, as well as Dante and Shakespeare — that seeks to absorb itself, or rather to let itself be absorbed, in the absolute unity of truth, goodness, and beauty. Classical art holds back. It seeks to cling to the moment of beauty's perfection before it confounds itself with the high objects of religion and philosophy. Symbolic art characteristically overshoots the point of convergence. In the process, it more often than not leaves beauty behind, even as it succeeds in expressing a disquiet, a tremor of mystery and majesty, and indeed a sublimity that is awe-inspiring in a way that Classical beauty, always ideally balanced, can never be.

Hegel at one point says that "symbolic art *seeks* the perfect unity of inner meaning and external shape which classical art *finds,* . . . and which romantic art *transcends.*" In transcending the balance achieved by classical art, romantic art of course "reverts, even if in a higher way, to that difference and opposition of the two sides which in symbolic art remained unconquered" — but, Hegel hastens to add, "with this essential difference, that, in romantic art, the Idea, the deficiency of which in the symbol brought with it deficiency of shape, now has to appear, *perfected* in itself as spirit and heart."

In other words, when Dante in the *Paradiso* says that words fail him in his attempt to represent his "vision of God," we must not imagine that he has not adequately comprehended what he has seen. Words fail him, on the contrary, because, as Hegel explains, the perfection of what he has fully comprehended "is not susceptible of an adequate union with the external, since its true reality and manifestation it can seek and achieve only in itself." Dante may have attempted too much in his *Paradiso*, even as it has been said of Shakespeare (most recently by T. S. Eliot) that he attempted too much in *Hamlet*. But can one presume on that account to insist that, having attempted too much, Dante and Shakespeare had of necessity to fail — even though in the one case the result was the greatest epic of the modern world and in the other, as Hegel thought, the greatest tragedy of all times? Obviously to speak of failure in terms of the ideal of classical beauty is to speak of success in terms of romantic art. Precisely by seeming to fail in the classical sense, Dante and Shakespeare manage in the end to represent for us exactly what they had in mind, thereby expressing more, and somehow expressing it better than the medium of expression they employed would seem to allow. "In this way," Hegel concludes, "romantic art is the self-transcendence of art but within its own sphere and in the form of art itself."

Bosanquet's brilliant chapter on Dante and Shakespeare in his *History of Aesthetic* provides a thoroughly Hegelian assessment of the achievement of these two greatest poets of the Western world; and it is significant that in his recent book, *Trope and Allegory: Themes Common to Dante and Shakespeare,* Francis Fergusson has broken with the "fashionable view that Shakespeare was an uncommitted skeptic," in order to join Bosanquet (and Hegel) in affirming, on the contrary, that Shakespeare and Dante were "writing out of the same context of a classical-Christian heritage," and that they are indeed the twin towering geniuses of the romantic art of the modern world.

But the reader must feel the *comprehensive* power of Hegel's analyses and interpretations for himself. The perfect beauty of the classical art of Greece gets its due in the pages of his *Aesthetics*, yet never at the expense of the restless symbolic aspiration of Eastern art or the self-consuming romantic transcendence of the art of medieval Christendom and the entire modern world.

My abridgment and translation of Hegel's lectures on the philosophy of fine art, or aesthetics, is based on the second, revised edition of the *Vorlesungen über die Ästhetik* prepared by H. G. Hotho in 1842-3. Originally issued in three volumes, that second edition has recently been re-issued in two-volume versions (Berlin, 1955; Frankfurt/Main, 1965, 1966), edited by F. Bassenge.

In preparing this Milestones of Thought volume, my method has been to abridge the German text first — eliminating sections, paragraphs, phrases, and words that could be eliminated without sacrificing or distorting the meaning of what remained —and then to translate from the German and edit my version to make it as idiomatic and clear as possible. My primary concern has been to insure continuity of meaning for the reader where large sections have been omitted. In all the transitions, I have tried to retain the bones and sinews of Hegel's organic articulation of his subject, the general frame of which is, I think, clearly traceable in my abridgement, which reduces the work to approximately one-sixth its original length. Every care has been taken, of course, to leave the major statements of aesthetic theory and the analyses and interpretative evaluations of particular works of art intact, in language that is at once idiomatic English and faithful to Hegel's philosophic and critical expression.

The full course of Hegel's lectures on aesthetics has twice been translated into English in its entirety; and there have been several additional translations of major parts, especially of Hegel's general Introduction *(Einleitung)*. Most of these translations have been based on the first or second Hotho editions, but in some instances the translators have acknowledged dependence on an early French translation: G. W. F. *Hegel: Cours d'esthetique analysé et traduit par Charles Bénard* (5 vols., Paris, 1840-52). The first complete translation into English was *G. W. F. Hegel: The Philosophy of Fine Art*, translated, with notes, by Francis Plumptre Bereford Osmaston (4 vols., London, 1920), based on the 1835 Hotho text; the second is Hegel's *Aesthetics: Lectures on Fine Art*, translated by T. M. Knox, with a Translator's Preface and notes (2 vols, Oxford, 1975), based, like my abridged version, on Hotho's second edition. In his Preface, Professor Knox gives an objective evaluation of the Osmaston translation. Both he and Osmaston acknowledge that the English version of Hegel's Introduction by Bernard Bosanquet — *The Introduction to Hegel's Philosophy of Fine Art*, translated from the German, with Notes and a Prefatory Essay, by Bernard Bosanquet (London, 1886) — is a model translation that has become a philosophical classic in its own right. For an evaluation of the T. M. Knox translation, stressing its interpretative significance as compared with Bosanquet's treatment of the Introduction, see the review by Anne and Henry Paolucci in *The Owl of Minerva: Quarterly Journal of the Hegel Society of America*, Vol. 8, No. 3 (March, 1977), pp. 4-7.

SUPPLEMENTARY READINGS IN ENGLISH

Bosanquet, Bernard (1892, 1894). *A History of Aesthetic.* London: Allen & Unwin.

Bradley, A. C. (1909, 1961). "Hegel's Theory of Tragedy." In *Oxford Lectures on Poetry.* London: Macmillan.

Clark, Richard C. (1970). "Hegel: Bibliographical Spectrum." In *Hegel in Comparative Literature, Review of National Literatures*, I, 2, 273-292, New York: St. John's University.

Hofstadter, Albert (1974). "On Artistic Knowledge: A Study of Hegel's Philosophy of Art." In *Beyond Epistemology: New Studies in the Philosophy of Hegel*, edited by F. G. Weiss. The Hague: Martinus Nijhoff.

Kaminsky, Jack (1962, 1970). *Hegel on Art: An Interpretation of Hegel's Aesthetics.* Albany: State University of New York (SUNY).

Kedney, John Steinfort (1885, 1897). *Hegel's Aesthetics: A Critical Exposition.* Chicago: Scott, Foresman & Co.

Knox, Israel (1936). *The Aesthetic Theories of Kant, Hegel, and Schopenhauer.* New York: Columbia University.

Paolucci, Anne (1978). "Hegel's Theory of Comedy." In *Comedy: New Perspectives, New York Literary Forum*, I, 89-108. New York: New York Literary Forum.

Paolucci, Anne and Henry Paolucci (1962, 1975, 1978). "Introduction." In *Hegel on Tragedy.* New York: Doubleday; Harper & Row; Greenwood.

Paolucci, Henry (1970). "The Poetics of Aristotle and Hegel." In *Hegel in Comparative Literature, Review of National Literatures*, I, 2, 165-213. New York: St. John's University.

II. The Idea of Artistic Beauty or the Ideal

These lectures deal with *Aesthetics*. Their subject is the wide *realm of the beautiful – which is* to say, the realm of *art*, and more precisely, of *fine art*.

Artistic rather than natural beauty is the subject matter of aesthetics, which may thus be called, more properly, the philosophy of fine art

The word *Aesthetics* in its literal sense is perhaps not quite appropriate here, for it means, strictly speaking, the science of sensation or feeling. Yet it is now commonly used in our more specialized sense, and may therefore be permitted to stand. We should bear in mind, however, that a more accurate expression for our science is the "Philosophy of Art," and better still, the "Philosophy of Fine Art."

With that expression we at once exclude from consideration the *beauty of nature*. In ordinary usage we speak of beautiful color, a beautiful sky, a beautiful river, and, even more, of beautiful flowers, animals, and, above all, beautiful human beings. Whether there is a natural beauty to be recognized as existing beside artistic beauty is not our concern here. We wish merely to assert that *artistic* beauty stands higher than the beauty of nature. But "higher" is of course an altogether indefinite expression. We mean that the beauty of art belongs to mind and that mind only is capable of truth. Thus to be truly beautiful, a thing must have an element of mind in it and indeed be a product of mind. In this respect the beauty of nature exists for us as but a reflection of the beauty of mind, as a thing incomplete and imperfect in itself, the real substance of which is contained in mind.

As a matter of historical fact, for all that is said about the beauties of nature, no one has as yet taken it into his head to give us a scientific, systematic account of such beauty. The aspect of utility has been emphasized; we have had, for example, scientific catalogues of medically useful natural things, offering detailed descriptions of minerals, chemical compounds, plants, and animals. But we have not had any comparable analysis and classification of natural things to emphasize their beauty.

Insofar as works of art are produced by mind, they are in themselves essentially spiritual. They have sensuous being for us, of course, but it is a sensuousness pervaded by mind. In the merely external things of unintelligent nature, mind finds itself at a distance; but in works of art, it has to do with its very own. Indeed, artistic productivity belongs as much to mind as thought itself; and thus, when mind subjects art to scientific consideration, it is in fact only satisfying its own inmost need.

To begin with, we meet generally with two opposite ways of treating our subject scientifically. On the one hand, we find a purely external approach. It busies itself with actual works of art, arranging them to show historical patterns and initiating discussion of their particular characteristics; or it may sketch out theories to guide us both in criticizing and in producing works of art. On the other hand, we find science leaving particular works of art behind to generalize about the beautiful as such, thereby creating a merely abstract philosophy of the beautiful.

An empirical approach to art is indispensable, of course; yet, on this side, it is only the *scholarship* of the history of art that has had a permanent scientific value, and one that it cannot but continue to have. Its task is to enrich our aesthetic appreciation of particular works of art by supplying us with what we need to know of the historical circumstances that conditioned their production. Theorizing in the strict sense is not a part of such scholarship, though there may be an occasional straying in that direction. Yet if a reader doesn't let this distract him, he will find that such scholarship provides the philosophy of art with a wealth of historical material, into the details of which philosophy cannot enter.

The opposite approach to art leaves particular works aside and seeks to understand in a purely theoretical way what beauty is in itself. It was Plato who first required of philosophic study that it deal with things not in their particularity but in their universality. He held that truth was not in the singleness of individual good actions, true opinions, beautiful human beings or works of art, but in *goodness, beauty, truth* themselves. Still, in the sphere of art, even for the mere idea of beauty, the Platonic abstraction must fail to satisfy the deeper philosophical wants of the mind today. An idea of the beautiful must indeed be our starting point for a philosophy of art; but our conception must from the beginning reconcile the two approaches we have mentioned, combining metaphysical universality with what is genuinely particular.

Coming closer to a scientific treatment of our subject, we take for granted, as an introductory conception, that a work of art is no natural product but a thing brought into being by human activity, created by mind. But the question at once occurs: What is man's need to produce works of art? On the one hand, it may appear that such works are products of idle fancy or chance. On the other, they seem sometimes to originate in the highest of human impulses, supplying what seems to be an absolute need of man and being wedded in this respect to the most universal religious interests and world-perspectives of entire epochs and peoples. It is art in this latter sense, conceived as an absolute rather than a merely contingent need of man, that concerns us here.

Man's need for art, no less than his need for religion and philosophy, is rooted in his capacity to mirror himself in thought

On its formal side, man's need for art is rooted in the fact that he is a *thinking* consciousness. Man is not only *immediate* and *single*, like all other natural things; as mind, he also *reduplicates* himself, existing for himself because he thinks himself. He does this, in the first place, *theoretically*, by bringing himself into his own consciousness, so as to form an idea of himself. But he also realizes himself for himself through *practical* activity. This he does by reshaping external things, by setting the seal of his inner being upon them, thereby endowing them with his own characteristics. Man's spiritual freedom consists in this reduplicating process of human consciousness, whereby all that exists is made explicit *within* him and all that is in him is realized *without*. Here not only artistic making but all human behaving and explaining — whether in the forms of political and moral action, religious imaginative awareness, or scientific knowledge — has its ground and necessary origin.

What distinguishes art from other things made by man is, first of all, that it is made for man's *sensuous* apprehension in such a way as to address itself ultimately to his *mind,* which is to find a spiritual satisfaction in it. The sensuous shapes and sounds of art present themselves to us not to arouse or satisfy desire but to excite a response and echo in all the depths of consciousness of the mind. The sensuous can be thus *spiritualized* in us because in art, it is the *spiritual* that appears in sensuous shape. A man-made sensuous thing is a true work of art, in other words, only in the measure that it has been brought into being through mind, by genuinely spiritual productive activity. In such activity, the spiritual and sensuous aspects must be fused as an undivided unity. This is what constitutes genuinely artistic productive imagination, or *phantasy.* When such phantasy is truly artistic, it is the imaginaion of a great mind and heart that seizes and creates both ideas and shapes so as to exhibit the profoundest and most universal human interests in completely formed sensory representations.

With that we put aside any notion that art's purpose is the *imitation* of *nature. To* take what already exists, just as it is, simply to make it over a second time as an exact copy — that we may at once dismiss as a superfluous labor. The result, at best, must fall far short of nature. Imitations are, after all, *one-sided* deceptions, *i.e.,* appearances of reality addressed to one sense only, and therefore hardly more than parodies of what is genuinely living. Pleasure is no doubt to be found in the skill and industry required to produce strikingly realistic copies of nature, but it is pleasure that is soon enough chilled into boredom and repugnance. When it becomes a question only of whether a natural thing has been *correctly* copied, what disappears in the process is the very idea of *objective beauty.* It is of course essential to art to have natural shapes as part of its foundation. But what the natural world supplies, cannot be art's *rule,* and much less can mere imitation of external appearance *as* external be its *end.*

To conclude our introductory remarks, we must ask finally: What then is the true content of art, and with what aim is it to be presented? A common view is that it ought to offer us, through our senses, *all* that finds a place in human experience, all that can arouse and animate the heart and mind of a human being, whether he be cultured or uncultured. To draw the human heart through the whole significance of life by means of external representations of its innermost movements is what, from this perspective, constitutes the peculiar and pre-eminent power of art. Linked with this is the notion that art has also a power to mitigate and even purge the fierceness of our impulses, passions, and desires — which is to say that, while it is itself sensuous, art is somehow nevertheless able to deliver man from the power of sensuousness,

Related to this, in turn, is the notion that art ought ultimately to *teach*. That art has taught, that it has been in fact the first *instructress* of peoples, is certainly true. But to suggest that *didactic* utility in the moral or spiritual sphere is its end and that its sensuous basis is a mere means, amounts to denying it a vocation and purpose of its own. The sensuous and the spiritual are both essential to art. The contrast or struggle of the two in the mind of man makes him, it has been said, an amphibious animal forced to live in two contradictory worlds at once. His consciousness wanders between them, shuttle-cocked back and forth, unable to satisfy itself wholly in either. The common understanding demands that this contradiction be resolved, yet it remains fixed in the antithesis. The solution demanded remains for it a mere *ought*. When the cultural experience of an entire age sinks into this contradiction, it becomes philosophy's task to show that neither side possesses truth in itself, that each is one-sided and self-dissolving, that the truth lies in the conciliation and mediation of the two, and that such mediation or *reconciliation* is in reality already accomplished and is always self-accomplishing.

The sensuous and the spiritual which struggle as opposites in the common understanding are revealed as reconciled in the truth expressed by art

That points us toward what we must vindicate as a higher standpoint for art. Against the view that art is a means of instruction and moral improvement, aspiring to something that remains an *ought to be,* we must maintain rather that its purpose is to reveal *the truth* in an arresting sensuous form, representing for mind the reconciliation of opposites just described. There we have the idea of art in its inner necessity, traced to what has been, historically speaking, its point of origin. In the modern world, brought to focus on the antithesis we have described, philosophy in general has had a re-awakening; and it was that re-awakening that gave us the beginnings of a truly scientific aesthetics as well as a higher sense of the importance of art.

To have recognized that artistic beauty is and has been a means of resolving the contradiction between abstract mind and actual nature must stand as one of the great achievements of modern times. It was indeed Kant who brought philosophical thinking to focus on the "reconciled contradiction," though he did not elaborate its essence scientifically or present it as the only true reality. In his *Critique* of the power of judgment, which he defines as "the power of thinking the particular as contained under the universal," he gives us a treatment of the beautiful in art that cancels any severance of universal and particular, end and means, conception and object. In artistic beauty, perception and feeling are exalted into spiritual universality, and the sensuous and conceptual find justification and satisfaction all in one. Yet Kant in the end requires that we accept this apparent reconciliation not as the truth and reality of art in itself, but as something merely subjective, experienced as such in both the production and appreciation of works of art.

Thus we may say that while Kant's criticism is the startingpoint for a true conception of artistic beauty, that conception could not assert itself as a higher grasp of the true unity of necessity and freedom, of particular and universal, of sensuous and rational, till it had overcome the basic deficiencies of Kantian thought. It is Schiller who presses beyond the subjectivity and abstractness of Kant's thinking. Accepting the principles of unity and reconciliation as the truth of art, as actualized in art, Schiller touched the profoundest depths of the true concept of artistic beauty.

After Schiller, the unity of opposites which he first grasped scientifically as the principle and essence of art was taken up, by an advance in philosophy, as the *Idea itself* — principle of all existence and knowledge — to be recognized in that capacity as the sole truth and reality. This insight, as developed in Schelling's philosophy, brings science to its absolute standpoint. As we have seen, art had already begun to assert its true nature and dignity in relation to the highest human interests, but it was only now that the actual *concept* of art and its place in scientific theory were discovered. Though at times not without a significant measure of distortion, art was now accepted in its high and genuine vocation.

Scientifically treated, art stands on the same ground as religion and philosophy

Indicating briefly the place of aesthetics as it relates to the other philosophical sciences, we may say to begin with that, where it rises highest, art's sphere is shared with religion and philosophy. Each of the three — art, religion, and philosophy — is a moment of absolute mind, and they differ from one another only in the *forms* in which they bring their content, the absolute, to human consciousness. The differences in form, moreover, are implicit in the shared content. Mind in its truth is absolute, which means that it is not an abstraction lying outside the objective world, but is rather present in objectivity as our finite minds experience what is objective, whether as finite in the natural sphere or as absolute on the levels of artistic, religious, or philosophic awareness. Distinguishing the three forms of the finite mind's awareness and apprehension of the absolute, we may say that the *first* is an immediate and for that reason *sensuous* knowing, a knowing in the configuration of the sensuous and objective itself, in which the absolute is brought to our contemplation and feeling; that the *second* form is imaginative or *pictorial* thinking; and that the *third* and last is the *free* thinking of absolute mind.

Art is thus the most immediate self-gratification of absolute mind. Its truth is the absolute as an object in sensuous form, which is for art the only adequate form. Religion adds worship to pictorial thinking, and thereby, in a subjective sense, transcends art's way of apprehending the absolute. In worship, the subject so identifies himself with the absolute content that its *inner* presence for him, in ideas and depth of feeling, becomes for the absolute itself the essential element of existence. Philosophy, in turn, unites the forms of apprehension of art and religion. The *objectivity* of art here loses its characteristically external sensuous form, but only so that it may be exchanged for what is the highest form of the objective, the form of *thought;* and the *subjectivity* of religion is purified, similarly, into the subjectivity of *thinking.* For thinking is, on the one hand, the most intimate, truest subjectivity, while true thought, the Idea, is at the same time the most effectual and most objective universality which can apprehend itself in its true form only in thinking.

Having linked art with religion and philosophy as proceeding from the absolute Idea, and having defined art's end as the sensuous representation of the absolute itself, we must next try to indicate, briefly, how the basic divisions of aesthetics as a science may be deduced from this very concept of artistic beauty. Granted that the content of art is the Idea, and that its form lies in the plastic use of images accessible to sense, we must first examine how art succeeds in reconciling these two sides — its content and its form — into a full and united totality. What is first required is that the content which is to be given artistic representation be inherently worthy of such representation. The result is, otherwise, only a bad combination: a content that will not lend itself to plastic, external representation is forced into it, a prosaic matter is expected to manifest itself in a form antagonistic to its very nature.

Related to this is the requirement that the content of art must not be anything inherently abstract. This does not mean that only something sensuously concrete, as opposed to all that is spiritual and intellectual, will do. For, in fact, everything that is genuinely true, in mind as in nature, is inherently concrete, having both subjectivity and particularity in itself, as well as universality. If, for example, we take God simply in his *Oneness,* merely as the *Supreme Being,* we have only a lifeless abstraction. As such, God is not apprehended in his concrete truth and cannot therefore provide material for art, least of all for plastic art. That explains why the Jews and Turks have not used art to represent their God —who is by no means an abstraction of the understanding for them — in the positive way that Christians have used it. For in Christianity, God is conceived in his truth as thoroughly concrete in himself, which is to say, as person and subject and, more closely determined, as spirit or mind. What he is as spirit manifests itself to religious consciousness as the Trinity of Persons which is for itself nevertheless One. Here we have essentiality, universality, and particularity in reconciled unity; and such unity alone constitutes the concrete. To be true in itself, any content must have such unity; and art can therefore require nothing less of whatever it is to represent in sensuous form.

But the form, too, must be no less individual and wholly concrete in itself. Indeed, it is only insofar as both have a measure of concreteness that the two elements of art, the content and the form, can coincide. The natural shape of the human body, for instance, is sensuously concrete in a way that enables it to represent spirit, which is in itself also concrete. We must reject the view that the human body, as an actual phenomenon, is only accidentally chosen to supply art with a true form. A content that is inherently concrete involves in itself the element of manifestation. And the sensuously concrete manifestation, in turn, addresses itself to the inward being, for which it in fact exists as perceptible and imaginable. This alone is the reason that shape and content must be made to conform in art. Unlike the *merely* sensuous concrete things of external nature, a work of art is not naively self-centered; it is instead essentially a question, an address to the responding human soul, an appeal to affections and to mind.

In Ideal artistic beauty, perfection of form derives ultimately from perfection of content

It follows from this that the Idea embodied in actual works of art — the *Idea* as the *beautiful in art* — cannot be the *Idea* as *such* in the way that a metaphysical logic conceives it. If the Idea and its sensuous shape in art are to be reciprocally adequate, the Idea as such must already have been specially determined in itself to be fit for true expression. So determined, or molded, the Idea becomes the *Ideal.* The reciprocal adequacy required is not something merely formal, as if this or that idea might do equally well, so long as the actual shape given it, of whatever kind, represents only that specific idea. The truth required of the Ideal is in that case confounded with mere *correctness,* which consists in nothing more than giving appropriate expression to any meaning in such a way that the meaning is immediately recognizable in the objective expression. The Ideal is nothing of the sort. Any content whatever can be given a representation which, judged by the standard of its own nature, is wholly adequate; yet it would not therefore gain the right to claim for itself the artistic beauty of the Ideal. Contrasted with ideal beauty, such a representation might appear quite defective. Defectiveness in art, as we shall later show, is not to be ascribed only and always to lack of skill. On the contrary: *defectiveness of form* arises from *defectiveness of content*. Greater or lesser skill in apprehending or imitating nature's forms is not the chief thing here. Art that may be quite perfect technically, and in other respects, may nevertheless be defective in terms of the Ideal of art. Only on art's highest levels can the Idea and its expression be reciprocally adequate in the Ideal sense. The outward shape the Idea then receives is the essentially true shape because the content of the Idea which that shape expresses is the essentially true content. This correspondence of the true Idea with the true shape it generates for itself is the Ideal.

But that correspondence can actualize itself in art only through the unfolding and reconciliation of the divergent aspects of the Idea, and it is in the process of such unfolding and reconciliation that artistic beauty comes to exhibit itself as a *totality of particular stages and forms.*

Art's progression through diverse forms — forms that are in fact nothing but the different possible relations of content and shape — may be regarded as an advance either of the Idea in itself or of the shape in which it gains existence. Since each is immediately bound up in the other, perfection of the Idea as content is reflected in perfection of shape; and correspondingly what are defects in the artistic shape prove to be defects also in the informing Idea. But, as we shall see, there are three basic relations that may obtain between the Idea and its outward artistic representation. As each serves to define and characterize a distinctive art form, we have three such forms to consider: first the Symbolic, then the Classical, and finally the Romantic.

PART TWO

◇◀◀◀◀▷▶▶▶◇

SCIENCE AND ASTRONOMY

GALILEO: *THE ASSAYER*

In which Galileo ridicules those who prefer the books of men to the great open book of Nature itself.

It seems to me that I detect in Sarsi [an Aristotelian disciple] the fixed persuasion that in philosophizing one has to rely on the opinions of some famous author, as if this mind of ours would remain sterile and barren unless it were wedded to another persons thoughts. Perhaps he thinks philosophy is a book of fiction or some other kind of imaginative work like the *Iliad* or *Orlando Furioso*, in which it is of least importance that what is written be true.

My dear Sarsi, that's not how the matter stands. Philosophy is written in this grandest of all books which forever lies open before our eyes (I mean the universe), but which cannot be understood if one does not first learn to understand the language and interpret the characters in which it is written. It is written in mathematical language, and the characters are triangles, circles, and other geometrical figures, without which it is humanly impossible to understand a single word; without these, there is only aimless wandering in a dark labyrinth . . . .

I cannot omit to . . . indicate, further, how ill-founded is Sarsis conclusion that scientific knowledge must be deficient if the number of disciples is few. Perhaps Sarsi thinks that good philosophers are to be found like squadrons of soldiers in every camp. My belief, dear Sarsi, is that they fly like eagles, and not like starlings. Indeed, the truth is that eagles, because they are rare, are rarely seen and even less often heard; whereas the starlings that fly in throngs, wherever they alight, "filling the

[From *The Achievement of Galileo*, Twayne Publishers Inc., New York, 1962. Original translation.]

sky with shrieks and noises," stir up the whole world. But, if only true philosophers were indeed like eagles, and not rather likethe phoenix! My dear Sarsi, "infinite is the throng of fools," that is to say, those who know nothing, myriads there are who know next to nothing of philosophy; some few know a trivial bit of it; fewest of all know a part or two; God alone is He who knows all.

So that, to state exactly the point I want to make regarding the scientific knowledge men can attain by demonstrations and human speculation, I am convinced that as it attains greater perfection, it will propose to draw ever fewer conclusions; fewer still will it pretend to prove, and, as a consequence, so much less will it please, and less, proportionately, will the number of its adherents be. On the other hand, high-sounding titles, coupled with grandiose and numerous promises, attracting the natural curiosity of men, keeping them perpetually tangled up in fallacies and chimeras, never enabling them to taste the sharpness of a single proof, from which the reawakened taste would learn how insipid indeed has been its usual fare — such is the sort of thing that will keep an infinitude of persons busily interested. And it will be the happiest of accidents for anyone, guided by extraordinary natural insight, to be able to free himself from the benighted and confused labyrinths in which he, with everyone else, would otherwise forever wander, ever entangling himself the more.

To judge anyones views in matters of science, therefore, from the number of followers, I hold to be quite unsound. But, while I believe that the best philosophy will have very few adherents, I do not, as a consequence, maintain conversely that those views and doctrines are necessarily perfect which have the fewest adherents. For I can well conceive of someone entertaining views so erroneous that he would of necessity be forsaken by everyone else.

GALILEO: TWENTIETH CENTURY QUESTIONS

> *It is a curious fact that, just when the man in the street has begun to believe thoroughly in science, the man in the laboratory has begun to lose his faith.*
> Bertrand Russell
> (from *The Scientific Outlook*)

I

Natural science has come a long way since that dawn of self-confidence in the opening decades of the seventeenth century when Galileo, by joining mathematics with experimentation, and by defending their union with convincing eloquence, opened up to a "vast and most excellent science," as he himself called it, "ways and means by which other minds more acute than mine will explore its remote corners." In the intervening centuries, remote corners of that science have, in fact, been explored by acute minds, many of them far better trained in mathematics and far better equipped for systematic experimentation than Galileo was; so that, quantitatively considered, the scientific knowledge he possessed amounts to but a fragment of what is available to any good physicist today. And yet, as Albert Einstein has remarked, the ways and means of advance have indeed been those conceived and perfected by Galileo. He it was who first saw and then was able to convince men of science that all knowledge of the real world of space and time must start with and end in experience, that ideas arrived adequately trained in mathematics can so much asat by pure thinking, without observation, are completely empty as regards

[From *The Achievement of Galileo*, Twayne Publishers, Inc., New York, 1962.]

reality; he it was who first insisted that the source of experience, the "great book of Nature," is a book written in mathematical characters, and that, therefore, only minds begin to read intelligently. "Because Galileo saw this," Einstein has written, and particularly because he drummed it into the scientific world, he is the father of modern physics —indeed, of modern science altogether."

But, while continuing to adhere strictly to his ways and means, modern mathematical physicists, for the most part, are far less confident about results than Galileo was. His earliest writings reveal that, even before he became a Copernican, Galileo had been convinced, as Descartes was later to be, that ultimate material reality is essentially mathematical, and that what is true of mathematical objects, therefore, is equally true of material objects. Thus, for instance, he could say: "if you had a perfect sphere and plane, though they were material, you need not doubt that they would touch at one sole point . . . . Nay, pursuing the question with more subtle contemplations, you would find that it is much harder to procure two bodies that touch with part of their surfaces than with one point only." The argument of these words is typical of Galileo's lifelong polemic against the Aristotelian scientists of his day who believed that, by applying mathematical techniques and reasoning to the study of natural phenomena, one could acquire, at best, only abstract, relative knowledge, convenient, like mnemonic devices, for summarizing facts and "saving appearances," but inadequate for comprehending the essential reality of material things. Galileo believed, on the contrary, that precisely such mathematical study alone enables the human intellect to break through appearances and gain true knowledge of the underlying reality of the empirical world. God, he did not hesitate to say, may know infinitely more than we can ever know, but what we know mathematically we know as well as He does.

This confidence of Galileo in the certitude of knowledge acquired by mathematical and experimental study served, in his own day and for centuries thereafter, to attract many studious minds away from other books, over which there was much disputing, to the book of nature. But today, in the era of post-Planckian and post-Einsteinian physics, few competently trained persons can pretend to enjoy such confidence. "Mathematics and experiment," Professor Tobias Dantzig has recently written, "reign more firmly than ever over the new physics, but an all-pervading skepticism has affected their validity." And Bertrand Russell, to the same effect, has asserted: "Science, which began as the pursuit of truth, is becoming incompatible with veracity, since complete veracity tends more and more to complete scientific skepticism."

Many thoughtful persons of our time have welcomed the change in attitude that has made modern physicists "humble and stammering" where their predecessors, heirs to the confidence of Galileo and Newton, were "proud and dictatorial." But the best scientists, the Plancks and Einsteins, have not welcomed the change. While admitting that an "unbridgeable chasm" seems, for the present, to separate natural reality, with its infinite and perhaps ultimately indeterminate complexity, and the abstract representations of scientific formulas, they refuse to resign themselves to the present state of things. "Some physicists," Einstein wrote, "among them myself, cannot believe that we must abandon, actually and forever, the idea of direct representation of physical reality in space and time; or that we must accept the view that events in nature are analogous to a game of chance." But there is, clearly, a ring of nostalgia rather than of prophecy in this Einsteinian protest. And it could hardly have been otherwise with the man whose own cultural importance as a scientist consists largely in his having shaken the confidence of dogmatists by reducing to the humble status of convenient hypotheses the great Galilean and Newtonian principles of terrestrial and celestial mechanics which, for more than two hundred years, had been held to be true in an absolute sense.

Rare is the educated man today who would insist, against Einstein, that Newton's principle of inertia, which posits an unobservable state of affairs, is anything more than an assumption, valid, scientifically, only to the extent that it introduces simplicity and economy in mathematical representations of the complicated phenomena of motion; but there are still many who, in spite of Einstein, persist in believing that the Copernican system defended by Galileo has been established as "true" in an absolute sense. Giorgio de Santillana, for instance, in his popular book *The Crime of Galileo*, says that, if Galileo himself was unable to provide "conclusive physical proof" of the new system, it was simply because he "could not yet produce Foucault's pendulum." Santillana is, of course, thoroughly aware of the revolution effected by Einstein and has frequently expressed his full accord with its results, so that it is difficult to understand why he is unable to grasp its implications with regard to the Foucault and other experiments designed to "prove" that the earth is indeed in motion. Morris R. Cohen, on the contrary, in an essay illustrating the significance of the Einsteinian revolution, has stated its implications with regard to all such proofs in these emphatic terms:

> The reader who knows something of the history of science will recognize that our example shows Einstein's later theory of relativity as reopening the issue between Galileo and those who condemned him for saying that the earth *is* in motion . . . . It would be vain to repeat against Einstein the old arguments for the absolute rotation of the earth, based on Foucault's pendulum or the bulging of the earth at the equator. He shows that it is possible to define a space with regard to which the fixed stars are rotating. In such a space the earth may be considered at rest, and the phenomena which in Newtonian mechanics are called gravitational and centrifugal would change places. Since both are proportional to the mass of the earth there would be no experimental difference.

Professor Cohen has here merely paraphrased words of Einstein himself, which have become commonplaces in popular expositions of his thought but which are nevertheless precise.

Philipp Frank, equally emphatic in his exposition, is perhaps more explicit when he writes:

> From Einstein's principles one could derive the description of the motions of celestial bodies relative to any system of reference. One could demonstrate that the description of the motion of planets becomes particularly simple if one uses the system of fixed stars as a system of reference, but there was still no objection to using the earth as system of reference. In this case, one obtains a

description in which the earth is at rest and the fixed stars are in a rotational motion. What appears to be in the Copernican heliocentric system the centrifugal force of the rotating earth becomes in the geocentric system a gravitational effect of the rotating fixed stars upon the earth.

The Copernican system became for the first time in its history not only mathematically but also philosophically true. But at the same moment the geocentric system became philosophically true, also. The system of reference had lost all philosophic meaning. For each astronomical problem, one had to pick the system of reference that rendered the simplest description of the motions of the celestial bodies involved.

Thus one must conclude that while twentieth-century science fully acknowledges its debt to Galileo for its mathematical-experimental method, it has unequivocally decided against him in his defense of the Copernican system. The dogmatism of the apocryphal *eppur si muove*, with which his case was originally appealed to posterity, has been repudiated by the best modern scientists; and with the popularization of *relativity*, their repudiation of it is rapidly filtering down into non-scientific circles.

Yet, when we turn from writings about Galileo to read for ourselves the text of his defense of the Copernican system, we are bound — if we have not been forewarned — to be startled by what we find in its opening pages. For nothing could be more "modern," nothing could be more consistent with the post-Einsteinian attitude of modesty toward scientific knowledge, than the preface which Galileo himself provided for his *Dialogue on the Great World Systems*. Galileo thus summarizes what he means to accomplish in his dialogues:

> Three main topics are to be treated. First, I will endeavor to show that all experiments that can be made upon the Earth are insufficient means to conclude for its mobility but are indifferently applicable to the Earth, movable or immovable; and I hope that on this occasion many observations will come to light that were unknown to the ancients. Secondly, we will examine the celestial phenom-

> ena that make for the Copernican hypothesis, as if it were
> to prove absolutely victorious, adding by the way certain
> new observations which yet serve only for astronomical
> facility, not for natural necessity. In the third place, I will
> propose an ingenious fancy . . . that the unknown prob-
> lem of the tides might receive some light, admitting the
> Earth's motion.

Galileo is here saying in popular language precisely what Cohen and Frank have said in their expositions of the implications of Einstein's later theory of relativity: that it cannot be demonstrated experimentally whether the earth is in motion or not; that preference of one system over another is a matter of "astronomical facility," not "natural necessity;" that in the case of a particular problem, like explaining the tides, one assumption may prove to be more "convenient" than another. And, if we turn from the opening to the closing pages of the *Dialogue*, we find an even more explicit avowal of a scientific relativism: the famous interlocutors, Simplicio, Sagredo, and Salviati agree there that identical observable phenomena may be brought about, or accounted for, in diverse ways, many of them beyond the capacity of the human intellect to comprehend.

The trouble with the "relativism" which we find in the opening and concluding pages is that, as the scholars assure us, Galileo did not mean it. He was persuaded that, with his many experiments, and particularly with his excitingly new telescopic observations of the moon, sun, planets and stars, he had added to the mathematical exactitude of the Copernican system sufficient empirical support to establish it as absolutely true. The relativistic modesty of his preface and conclusion, all scholars agree, was forced upon him by ecclesiastical critics who would not otherwise have permitted the work to be published.

A number of interesting questions force themselves upon our attention at this point. How did it happen that the opponents of Galileo were able to anticipate and favor, in the seventeenth century, an attitude which the disciples of Galileo science were not to assume until the time of Ernst Mach, Hertz, Poincaré and Einstein? When they forced him to recant what he had always believed, when they forced him to profess solemnly on his knees the view he had pretended to uphold in the preface and conclusion of his *Dialogue*, were the ecclesiastical opponents of Galileo, paradoxically, forcing him to be scientifically right in spite of himself? Such questions surely are implied in Professor Cohen's assertion that Einstein, with his later theory of relativity, has reopened the issue "between Galileo and those who condemned him for saying that the earth *is* in motion."

But as we read more deeply into the great dialogues of Galileo, other, even more important questions are apt to occur to us. Was Galileo really a precursor of Newton in formulating the law of inertia? He has been called by some the "creator" of that law, though, as Santillana remarks, "he could not help recoiling from the full formulation of his own inertial principle." Yet when we turn to the text, we find him, in fact, upholding the very antithesis of the Newtonian formulation. Like the modern adherents of the field-theory, Galileo held it to be impossible "that any movable body can have a natural principle of moving in a straight line." Contrary to Newton's view that all curved motions are compounded of rectilinear motions, and quite in accord with the twentieth-century view, he believed that all apparently rectilinear motions are either actually curved or compounded of curved motions. Indeed it was primarily because the Copernican system "ennobled" the earth by attributing to it the "effortless motions" of a heavenly body that Galileo was drawn — so he tells us — to its defense.

II

Many philosophers since Giordano Bruno have reproached Andreas Osiander harshly for the preface which he added to the book of Copernicus. The recommendations made to Galileo by Bellarmine and Urban VIII have been treated with hardly less severity since the day when they were first published. Physicists of our own time have weighed more minutely than their predecessors the exact value of the hypotheses employed in astronomy and physics; they have witnessed the dispelling of many illusions, which not long since still passed for certitudes; it is their duty, today, to acknowledge and to declare that logic was on the side of Osiander, Bellarmine and Urban VIII, and not on the side of Kepler and Galileo; that the former grasped the precise import of the experimental method and that the latter were mistaken in its regard.

The history of science, however, honors Kepler and Galileo, whom it ranks among the great reformers of the experimental method, whereas it does not so much as mention the names of Osiander, Bellarine or Urban VIII. Is this the height of injustice on its part? May it not be true, on the contrary, that those who attributed to the experimental method a false import and an exaggerated value worked more effectively and contributed much more toward the perfecting of this method than those who, from the outset, had a more precise and just appreciation of it?

The Copernicans plunged headlong into an illogical realism, when everything seemed to be pressing them to avoid such error, when by attributing to astronomical hypotheses the correct value determined by so many men of authority it would have been easy for them to avoid both the quarrels of the philosophers and the censures of the theologians. Such strange behavior calls for an explanation! But can it be explained otherwise than by the attraction of some great truth, a truth perceived too vaguely by the Copernicans for them to formulate it in its purity, to extricate it from the erroneous affirmations beneath which it concealed itself; but a truth so keenly felt that neither logical precepts not practical counsels could weaken its invisible attraction. What was this truth? That is what we must now attempt to define.

Through antiquity and the Middle Ages, Physics appears to us made up of two parts, one so completely distinct from the other that they are, so to speak, opposed to one another; on one side we find the Physics of celestial and imperishable things, on the other the Physics of sublunary things subject to degeneration and decay.

Those things which the first of the two Physics deals with are reputed to be of an infinitely higher nature than those which the second deals with. From this one concludes that the first is incomparably more difficult than the second; Proclus teaches that sublunary Physics is accessible to man, whereas celestial Physics transcends him and is reserved for divine Intelligence;

Maimonides shares this opinion of Proclus; according to him, celestial Physics is full of mysteries, knowledge of which God has reserved for Himself alone, whereas terrestrial Physics is to be found, fully worked out, in the work of Aristotle.

Contrary to what the men of antiquity and of the Middle Ages thought, the celestial Physics which they had constructed was singularly more advanced than their terrestrial Physics.

From the age of Plato and Aristotle, the science of the stars was organized according to the plan which we today still impose on the study of nature. On one hand there was Astronomy; geometers like Eudoxus and Callipus formed mathematical theories by means of which they could describe and predict celestial movements, while observers noted the degree of correspondence between the mathematical predictions and natural phenomena. On the other hand there was Physics proper, or to use the modern terminology, celestial Cosmology; thinkers like Plato and Aristotle speculated on the nature of the stars and on the cause of their movements. How were these two parts related to one another? What precise line of division was there between them? What affinity united the hypotheses of the one with the conclusions of the other? These are questions which astronomers and physicists discuss throughout antiquity and the Middle Ages, which they resolve in different ways, because their minds are guided by diverse tendencies very similar to those which appeal to modern men of science.

Much was required before the Physics of sublunary things would attain in its own good time the same degree of differentiation and organization. It, too, in modern times will divide itself in two parts very similar to those into which celestial physics from antiquity was divided. In its theoretic part it will combine mathematical systems which will reveal by their formulas the precise laws of the phenomena. In its cosmological part it will seek to grasp the nature of corporeal things, of their attributes, of the forces to which they respond or which they exert, of the combinations they can form among themselves.

During antiquity, during the Middle Ages and the Renaissance, it was difficult to make this division; sublunary Physics was hardly aware of mathematical theory. Two subdivisions of this physics, Optics or *Perspective* and statics or *Scientia de ponderibus*, had alone assumed this form, and physicists were greatly embarrassed when they wanted to assign to *Perspective* and to the *Scientia de ponderibus* their rightful places in the hierarchy of sciences. Except for these two subdivisions, the analysis of the laws which regulate phenomena continued to be purely qualitative, lacking precision; it had not yet freed itself from cosmology.

In Dynamics, for example, the laws of free-falling bodies, dimly perceived since the fourteenth century, the laws of the movement of projectiles, vaguely surmised in the sixteenth century, remained entangled in the metaphysical discussions on local movement, on natural movement and forced movement, on the coexistence of mover and movable. Only in Galilleo's day, at the very time that its mathematical character was becoming more precise, do we see the theoretic part free itself from the cosmological part. Until then, the two parts had remained intimately united, or rather, entangled in an inextricable manner. Their aggregate constituted the Physics of local movement.

On the other hand, the old distinction between the Physics of celestial bodies and the Physics of sublunary things underwent a gradual effacement. Following Nicholas of Cusa, following Leonardo da Vinci, Copernicus had dared to regard the Earth as one of the planets. By his study of the star that had appeared then disappeared in 1572, Tycho Brahe had shown that the stars too could come into being and pass away. In discovering the sunspots and the mountains of the moon, Galileo brought to completion the union of the two Physics into a single science.

Consequently, when a Copernicus or a Kepler or a Galileo declared that astronomy should take as its hypotheses propositions the truth of which has been established by Physics, that assertion, seemingly one, included in reality two quite distinct propositions.

Such an assertion, in fact, could mean that the hypotheses of astronomy were judgments on the nature of celestial things, and on their actual movements; it could mean that in regulating the correctness of these hypotheses, the experimental method enriched our cosmological knowledge with new truths. This first meaning is found, so to speak, on the very surface of the assertion; it is immediately apparent; it is this meaning which the great astronomers of the sixteenth and seventeenth centuries saw clearly, it is this same one which compelled their allegiance. Now, taken with this meaning, their assertion was false and harmful; Osiander, Bellarmine and Urban VIII regarded it, justifiably, as opposed to logic; but this assertion was to breed countless errors before the decision to reject it was finally reached.

Underlying this first sense, illogical but obvious and seductive, the assertion of the Renaissance astronomers contained another; in demanding that astronomical hypotheses accord with the teachings of physics, they were in effect demanding that the theory of celestial movements rest on foundations that could also support the theory of the movements we observe here below; they were demanding that the course of the stars, the ebb and flow of the sea, the movement of projectiles and falling bodies be saved with one and the same set of postulates formulated in the language of mathematics. Now this sense remained deeply hidden; neither Copernicus or Kepler nor Galileo saw it clearly; it remained, however, disguised yet fruitful underneath the obvious but erroneous and dangerous sense which alone these astronomers seized. And while the false illogical meaning which they attributed to their principle brought forth polemics and quarrels, it was the true but hidden meaning of this same principle which gave birth to the scientific endeavors of these pioneers; while they were striving to maintain the correctness of the first sense, they were moving unconsciously toward establishing the accuracy of the second sense: while Kepler was multiplying his attempts to account for the movements of the stars with the aid of the properties of the currents of water or of magnets, while Galileo was endeavoring to accord the paths of projectiles with the movement of the earth or to derive from this last movement an explanation of the tides, both of them thought they were proving that the Copernican hypotheses were founded in the very nature of things; but the truth which they were introducing little by little into the sphere of science is that one and the same Dynamics should, by means of a single set of mathematical formulas, represent the movements of the stars, the oscillations of the ocean and the fall of heavy bodies; they thought they were correcting Aristotle; they were preparing for Newton.

In spite of Kepler and Galileo, we today hold with Osiander and Bellarmine that the hypotheses of physics are but mathematical artifices designed to *save the phenomena*; but thanks to Kepler and Galileo, we now call upon them to *save, as a single whole, all the phenomena of the inanimate universe.*

III

Galileo's writings hold many surprises and illustrate his extraordinary capacity to convey through written words the excitement of a "watcher of the skies when a new planet swims into his ken," as well as his flair for literary controversy and the stylistic artistry of his dialogues — artistry that has earned him, in the judgment of the best Italian critics, a leading place among the master prose writers of the Italian language. In particular, the dialogue form — which he used in his major works — when well used is a marvelous vehicle for surprise: if it is not to lapse into a monologue, divergent positions on the matters discussed must be given eloquent and consistent expression. Thus, for dramatic effect the author may unwittingly give utterance to arguments which he himself has rejected as false, but which may appear startlingly fresh and true to readers of subsequent generations. For readers like ourselves, in the post-Einsteinian era, this is especially true.

PIERRE DUHEM: *TO SAVE THE PHENOMENA*

[Pierre Duhem was primarily a theoretical physicist. Yet, as Louis De Broglie, Nobel Prize-winning physicist, has written: "Apart from his strictly scientific works which were brilliant indeed, notably in the domain of thermo-dynamics, he acquired an extremely extensive knowledge of the history of the physico-mathematical sciences and, after having given much thought to the meaning and scope of physical theories, he shaped a very arresting opinion concerning them, expounding it in various forms in numerous writings." The philosopher Ernst Cassirer has credited Duhem with having carried to rigorous fulfillment the philosophic efforts of Mach, Hertz, Poincaré, and others, to establish an autonomous basis for physical theory, purging it of the last residues of burdensome metaphysics. Philipp Frank, has hailed him as "the greatest and most accurate student of the history of physics."

The chief monument of historical research left to us by Pierre Duhem is his massive Le Système du Monde, Histoire des Doctrines Cosmologiques de Platon à Copernic, *in ten volumes, five published posthumously, the last in 1959. This thoroughly documented work reviews the history of astronomy and cosmology from the ancient Greek, through the Roman, early Christian, Arabic, and medieval periods, to the time of Copernicus, tracing the development through all its evolutions, revolutions, and involutions, showing how the science of each epoch is nourished by the systems of past centuries, indicating how often the scientific certainties of one proud age are laughed at as absurdities in the next, while as often today's absurdities are seen forcing themselves forward into acceptance as the high truths of tomorrow. A master of Latin and Greek philology and a competent paleographer, Duhem resorted in his researches as often as possible to*

[From *The Achievement of Galileo*, Twayne Publishers, Inc., New York, 1962. Original translation, New York, 1961.]

*original materials, and was able thereby to correct many of the
traditional errors perpetuated from generation to generation by
historians of science who work only from published documents and
other secondary sources.*

The mass of erudition supporting Le Système du Monde *is so
enormous as to appear overwhelming on first acquaintance. Duhem,
however, drew out its central thread of meaning in advance, for
separate publication in a series of short essays under the Greek title*
Sozein ta Phainomena *(To Save the Phenomena):* Essai sur la
Notion de Théorie Physique de Platon à Galilée, *the final portion
of which is presented here.*

*One of the main purposes of all Duhem's historical writings and
the chief object of his* Sozein ta Phainomena *was to provide a
safeguard in the future against the two most serious derangements –
"the mad ambition of dogmatism as well as the despair of Pyrrhonian
skepticism" – to which the minds of physicists, in the past, have been
especially prone. His work is, therefore, particularly important today
when many of the leading contemporary physicists are pressing the
essential skepticism of the relativist and indeterminist positions to its
most extreme consequences, driving the last defenders of Galilean and
Newtonian dogmatism from the field. The special relevance of Duhem's
work in this area was indicated; the reader will recall, by Professor
Morris R. Cohen, in his discussion of the philosophical implications
of Einstein's later theory of relativity, which, as he says, "brings fresh
support to the views of the great . . . physicist and historian of science,
Pierre Duhem."]*

————————

Astronomical hypotheses are mere artifices designed to
"save" phenomena; provided they fulfill this end, they need not
be true or even probable.

This view seems to have been generally accepted, by
astronomers and theologians from the time of the publication
of Copernicus' book and Osiander's preface, to that of the
Gregorian reform of the calendar. On the contrary, in the
course of the half-century that extends from the reform of the
calendar to the condemnation of Galileo, we find it relegated
to obscurity, indeed, even violently opposed in the name of a

widespread realism that seeks to find in astronomical hypotheses affirmations regarding the nature of things, and which requires henceforth that these hypotheses accord with the doctrines of Physics and with the texts of Scripture . . . .

J. Kepler is, beyond any doubt, the most convinced and the most illustrious representative of this new realism.

In the preface itself of his first work, the *Mysterium cosmographicum*, printed in 1596, Kepler informs us that six years earlier, at Tubingen, as assistant to Michel Maestlin, he had already been captivated by the system of Copernicus: "From that moment, I was intent upon attributing to the Earth not only the movement of the outermost movable sphere but also the solar movement; and while Copernicus attributed these motions to the earth for mathematical reasons, I would attribute them for physical, or, if you prefer, metaphysical reasons."

Kepler is Protestant, but profoundly religious; he would not regard the Copernican hypotheses as conformable to reality if they were contradicted by Holy Scripture; before entering upon the terrain of Metaphysics or Physics, therefore, he must traverse that of Theology. "From the outset of this discussion on nature," so he writes at the beginning of Chapter I of his *Mysterium cosmographicum,* "we must take care to say nothing contrary to Holy Scripture."

Thus Kepler indicates for the Copernicans the way they will thereafter be obliged to follow: as realists, they require that their hypotheses conform to the nature of things; as Christians, they acknowledge the authority of the sacred Text; hence they are led to reconcile their astronomical doctrines with Scripture, and are constrained to assume the role of theologians.

They might have avoided such constraint had they thought of astronomical hypotheses what Osiander thought of them; but those who pursued faithfully the indications of Copernicus and Rhaeticus could not endure the doctrine expressed in the famous preface. "Some persons," said Kepler, "make much of the example of an exceptional demonstration in which, from false premises, by means of a rigorous syllogistic deduction, one is able to draw a true conclusion; on the strength of this example they try to prove that the hypotheses entertained by

Copernicus might be false and that, nevertheless, true phenomena could derive from them as from their proper principles; I have never been able to accept such a view .... All that Copernicus discovered *a posteriori,* all that he demonstrated by observation, can, I do not hesitate to assert, be demonstrated *a priori,* by means of geometric axioms, in a manner that would overcome all hesitation and that would even win the approval of Aristotle himself, were he still alive. . . ."

Kepler is not content to criticize the doctrine upheld by Osiander . . . ; he means, further, to put into practice that realism the principles of which he had set down; evidence of this realism is supplied us by that greatest of the works which his genius produced, the *Epitome Astronomiae Copernicanae.*

Its realism is manifest from the opening of the first book of the work: "Astronomy," says Kepler, "is a part of Physics," and the importance of this aphorism is at once revealed in what the author tells us *De causis hypothesium:* "The third part of the astronomer's 'baggage' is Physics; generally it is not considered necessary for the astronomer; and yet the Science of the astronomer has a great bearing on the object to be attained by this part of Philosophy which, without the astronomer, would remain incomplete. Indeed, astronomers should not be allowed absolute license to assume anything at all, without sufficient reason. You should be able to offer likely reasons for the hypotheses which you assume to be the true causes of phenomena; you should, therefore, search for the foundations of your astronomy in a higher science, that is to say, in Physics or in Metaphysics; furthermore, with the geometric, physical or metaphysical arguments supplied by your particular science to support you, you are not prevented, in turn, from moving beyond the limits of this science to discover objects pertaining to these higher doctrines."

In the course of his *Epitome,* Kepler takes every possible occasion to support his hypotheses with arguments supplied to him by Physics and Metaphysics. What a Physics and what a Metaphysics! But this is hardly the place to describe what strange dreams, what childish fancies, Kepler designated by these two names. We do not have to examine how Kepler constructed his astronomy; we have to know, simply, how he wanted it to be constructed. And, we now know, he wanted the science of celestial motions to rest on foundations guaranteed by Physics and by Metaphysics; he insisted that astronomical hypotheses be in no way contradicted by Scripture.

We find, moreover, a new ambition manifesting itself in Kepler's writings: Founded on true hypotheses, Astronomy can, by means of its conclusions, contribute to the progress of the Physics and Metaphysics which have supplied it with its principles . . . .

When Galileo accepted the Copernican system, he did so in the same spirit . . . ; he wanted the hypotheses of the new system to be, not artifices designed for the calculation of tables, but propositions conforming to the nature of things; he wanted them to be established on the grounds of Physics. One might, indeed, say that physical confirmation of the Copernican hypotheses is the center toward which all, even the most diverse, of Galileo's researches tend; his observations as an astronomer, his theories as a pioneer in mechanics converge toward this same end. Further, because he insisted that the foundations of Copernican astronomy be truths, and because be did not believe that a truth could contradict Scripture, which he acknowledged to be of divine inspiration, he was bound to attempt to reconcile his assertions with biblical texts; when the time arrived for him, he turned theologian; his celebrated letter to Marie-Christine of Lorraine bears us out.

In claiming that the hypotheses expressed physical truths, in declaring that they did not seem to him to contradict the Holy Scriptures, Galileo was, like Kepler, wholly in the tradition of Copernicus and Rhaeticus. He set himself against those who represented the tradition of Tycho Brahe, the Protestant, and the Jesuit Rodolphe Clavius. What these had said around the year 1580 the theologians of the Holy Office solemnly proclaimed in 1616.

They seized on these two fundamental hypotheses of the Copernican system:

Sol est centrum mundi et omnino immobilis motu locali;

Terra non est centrum mundi nec immobilis, sed secundum se totam movetur, etiam motu diurno.

They asked themselves whether or not these two propositions had the two characteristics which, by common accord, Copernicans and Ptolemains alike required of all admissible astronomical hypotheses: Were these propositions compatible with sound Physics? Were they reconcilable with divinely inspired Scripture?

Now, for the Inquisitors, sound Physics was the Physics of Aristotle and Averroes; it laid down for them, unequivocally, the answer that they were to give to the first question: the two hypotheses challenged were *stultae et absurdae in Philosophia.*

As for Scripture, the consultants of the Holy Office refused to accept any interpretation of them which was not supported by the authority of the Fathers; the answer to the second question consequently forced itself upon them: The first proposition was *formaliter haeretica,* the second was *ad minus in fide erronea.*

The two propositions censored had neither one nor the other of the two characteristics which were supposed to distinguish all admissible astronomical hypotheses; they were to be wholly rejected, therefore, not to be used even for the sole purpose of *saving the phenomena;* thus the Holy Office prohibited Galileo from teaching the Copernican doctrine *in any fashion.*

The condemnation carried through by the Holy Office was the result of a clash between two "realist" positions; this violent opposition might have been avoided, the debate between the Ptolemaics and the Copernicans might have been limited to the field of Astronomy, if the wise precepts concerning the nature of scientific theories and the hypotheses on which they rest had been heeded; these precepts, formulated by Posidonius, Ptolemy, Proclus, Simplicio, had come down directly, through an uninterrupted tradition, to Osiander, to Reinhold, to Melanchthon; but they now seemed to be wholly forgotten.

And yet there were at hand voices of authority to call attention to them once again.

One of these voices was that of Cardinal Bellarmine, the same who in 1616 was to examine the Copernican writings of Galileo and Foscarini; as early as April 12, 1615 Bellarmine had written Foscarini a letter full of good sense and prudence from which some passages are here given:

It seems to me that Your Reverence and Galileo will act prudently by contenting yourselves to speak *ex suppositione* and not in absolute fashion, as I have always believed Copernicus to have spoken. It is well to say that in assuming the Earth to move and the sun to remain stationary one can "save" all the appearances better than can be done with eccentrics and epicycles; there is no danger in that and it suffices for the mathematician. But to want to affirm that the sun really remains stationary at the center of the universe, that it turns only upon itself without moving from east to west, that the Earth occupies the third sky and that it turns with great speed around the Sun, is very perilous; it is likely not only to irritate all the philosophers and all the scholastic theologians, but also to harm the faith and to render false Holy Scripture . . . .

If it could be demonstrated with certainty that the Sun stands at the center of the Universe, that the Earth is in the third sky, that it is not the Sun that turns around the Earth but the Earth that turns around the Sun, then we should have to proceed with great circumspection in the explication of the Scriptures . . . . But I shall not believe that such a demonstration is possible until it can be shown to me. It is one thing to prove that one can "save" appearances by supposing that the Sun is at the center of the Universe and that the Earth is in the heavens, but quite another thing to demonstrate that the Sun is really at the center of the Universe and the Earth really in the heavens. Regarding the first demonstration, I believe it can be given; but regarding the second, I strongly doubt it; and in a case of simple doubt, you must not abandon Scriptures as the Holy Fathers have expounded them . . . .

Galileo knew of the letter addressed by Bellarmine to Father Foscarini; several writings edited between the time when he learned of this letter and his first condemnation contain answers to the Cardinal's arguments; examination of these writings, from which excerpts were first published by M. Berti, enables us to grasp the vital thought of Galileo regarding astronomical hypotheses.

One piece written toward the end of the year 1615 and addressed to the consultants of the Holy Office warns them against two errors: the first is to claim that the mobility of the Earth is, in some way, *a great paradox* and *a manifest piece of folly*, which has not been proved as yet and which can never be proved. The second is to believe that Copernicus and the other astronomers who have assumed this mobility "did not believe that it was true in fact and in nature" that they have only admitted it as a supposition in order to account for the appearance of the celestial movements more easily, in order to make astronomical calculations more convenient.

In affirming that Copernicus believed in the reality of the hypotheses formulated in *De Revolutionibus;* in proving by an analysis of this work that Copernicus did not admit the mobility of the Earth and the immobility of the Sun only *ex-suppositione,* as Osiander and Bellarmine would have it, Galileo was upholding historical truth. But what interests us more than his judgment as an historian is his opinion as a physicist. Now this is easily inferred in the piece we are analyzing. Galileo thought that the reality of the movement of the Earth is not only demonstrable but already demonstrated.

This thought emerges even more clearly in another text; there, not only do we see that Galileo thought the Copernican hypotheses could be demonstrated, but we learn further how he understood the demonstration to have been carried out:

> To refuse to believe that the movement of the Earth is susceptible of demonstration so long as such demonstration has not actually been provided is to act very prudently; we do not, therefore, expect anyone to believe such a thing without demonstration; we would expect only that for the good of the Holy Church one examine with extreme severity all that those who maintain such a doctrine have produced or might produce; that none of their assumptions be admitted unless the arguments that sustain it greatly exceed the arguments of the other side; that their judgment be rejected unless supported by 90 percent of the arguments. But in turn, when it shall have been proved that the opinion advanced by the philosophers and astronomers of the opposite side is unquestionably false, that it is of absolutely no weight then one ought not to scorn the opinion of the first side, one ought not to consider it so paradoxical as to be forever beyond the

possibility of clear demonstration. We may reasonably propose such broad conditions for this dispute; in fact, it is clear that those holding to the side of error cannot support themselves with any argument or any experience that is valid: on the contrary, on the side of truth everything must harmonize and agree.

It is certainly not the same thing to show that by assuming the Sun as stationary and the Earth as moving, appearances are saved, and to demonstrate that such hypotheses are really true in Nature; but what is otherwise and much more true is that with the commonly accepted system these appearances cannot be accounted for, so that this system is unquestionably false; similarly it is clear that the system which accords very closely with appearances can be true, and, in a given situation, one neither can or ought to seek another or greater truth than that which answers for all the particular appearances.

If one were to press this last proposition just a bit further, one could easily draw from it the doctrine that Osiander upheld, that Bellarmine upholds; that is to say, precisely the doctrine which Galileo attacks. Logic thus constrains the great Pisan geometer to formulate a conclusion directly contrary to that which he thought to establish. But in the lines that precede, his thought is clearly apparent.

The pending dispute appears to his mind's eye as a sort of duel. We are confronted with two doctrines, each of which claims to be in possession of the truth; but one speaks the truth, the other lies; who will decide? Experience. That doctrine of the two with which experience will refuse to accord will be judged erroneous and, by the same token, the other doctrine will be declared to accord with reality. The refutation of one of these two conflicting systems guarantees the certainty of the opposing system, just as, in geometry, the absurdity of one proposition carries with it the certitude of the contradictory proposition.

If anyone doubts that Galileo really held the opinion which we attribute to him on the subject of the proof of an astronomical system, he will be convinced of it, we believe, by reading the following lines:

The most expedient and surest way to show that the

position of Copernicus is not contrary to Scripture would be, as I see it, to show by a thousand proofs that this proposition is true and that the contrary position cannot in any way stand; consequently, since two truths cannot contradict one another, it must follow that the position admitted to be true accords with Holy Scriptures.

On the value of the experimental method and the art of using it, Galileo has pretty much the same opinion as that which Francis Bacon will formulate; he conceives the proof of a hypothesis in imitation of the demonstration by absurdity used in geometry; by condemning one system as erroneous, the experiment confers certitude upon the opposing system; positivistic science advances by a series of dilemmas, each of which is resolved with the help of an *experimentum crucis*.

This manner of conceiving the experimental method was destined to enjoy great vogue, for it is very simple; but it is entirely false, for it is too simple. Admit that the phenomena cease to be saved by the Ptolemaic system; that system would certainly have to be considered false. It will not in the least follow that the Copernican system is true, for the Copernican system is not purely and simply the contrary of the Ptolemaic system. Admit that the Copernican hypotheses succeeded in saving all known appearances; one will conclude from this that these hypotheses may be true; one will not conclude that they are certainly true; to justify that conclusion it would first have to be proved that no other combination of hypotheses were conceivable that could save appearances just as well; and this last demonstration has never been given. In Galileo's own time, was it not possible to save all the observations that could be mustered in favor of the Copernican system just as well by the system of Tycho Brache?

These remarks were made often enough in Galileo's time. Their truth had flashed upon the eyes of the Greeks the day when Hipparchus succeeded in saving the solar movement as well by means of an eccentric as by means of an epicycle; St. Thomas Aquinas had formulated them with the greatest clarity; Nifo, Osiander, Alexander Piccolomini, Giuntini, had repeated them after him. Once again an authoritative voice was to remind the illustrious Pisan of them.

Cardinal Maffeo Barberini, who was soon to be elevated to the papacy under the name Urban VIII, had a meeting with Galileo, after the 1616 condemnation, to discuss the Copernican doctrine; Cardinal Oregio, present at this meeting, has left us an account of it; in this meeting the future pope, by means of arguments similar to those which we have just recalled, laid bare the hidden error of this Galilean argument: since all the celestial phenomena accord with the Copernican hypotheses while they are not saved by the Ptolemaic system, the Copernican hypotheses are certainly true; hence they are of necessity in accord with Holy Scripture.

According to Oregio's account, the future Urban VIII advised Galileo "to note carefully whether or not there is agreement between the Holy Scriptures and what be had conceived regarding the movement of the Earth, for the purpose of saving the phenomena that are manifest in the sky and all that philosophers commonly regard as settled, by means of observation and a minute examination in what has to do with the movements of the sky and the planets. Granting, in effect, everything this great scientist had conceived, he asked him if it were beyond the power and wisdom of God to arrange and move the orbs and planets in another way, and do this, however, in such a way that all the phenomena manifest in the skies, all that is taught concerning the movements of the stars, their order, their position, their distance, their arrangement, still could be saved.

"If you mean to say that God cannot or knows not how to do this, you must prove," added the holy prelate, "that all this could not, without involving contradiction, be obtained by a system other than the one you have conceived; God, indeed, is capable of all that does not lead into contradiction; moreover, since God's science is not inferior to his power, if we say that God could do it, we must also say that be could know it.

"If God knew how and was able to arrange all things in a way other than what you have imagined, and this in such a way that all the results enumerated were still saved, we are not in the least obliged to reduce divine power and wisdom to this system which you have conceived.

"Having heard these words, the great scientist remained

silent."

The man who was to become Urban VIII bad reminded him clearly of this truth: the confirmations of experience, howsoever numerous and precise they might be, could never transform a hypothesis into a certitude, for it would be necessary, in addition, to demonstrate this proposition: that the same facts of experience would, necessarily, contradict all other hypotheses that might be conceived.

Were these very logical and reasonable admonitions of Bellarmine and Urban VIII sufficient to convince Galileo, to sway him from his exaggerated confidence in the scope of the experimental method, in the worth of astronomical theories? We may well doubt it. In his celebrated *Dialogue* of 1632 on the two great systems of the World, he asserts from time to time that be treats the Copernican doctrine as a pure astronomical hypothesis, without claiming it to be true in nature; these protests, which contradict the proofs accumulated by Salviati, one of the speakers, to sustain the reality of the Copernican positions, are undoubtedly nothing more than pretexts to break the interdiction laid down in 1616. At the very moment when the dialogue is about to end, Simplicio, the peripatetic butt and target, to whom is assigned the thankless task of defending the Ptolemaic system, concludes with these words:

> I confess that your thought seems to me much more ingenious than many of those I have had occasion to hear; even so, I do not hold it true, or conclusive; in fact, I keep always before my mind's eye a very solid doctrine which I received from a very learned and eminent person and before which we must pause. Indeed, I would like to ask you both this question: Can God with his infinite power and his infinite science give to the element of water the oscillating movement that we observe, in any other way than by making the containing vessel move? . . . . If the answer is yes, I conclude at once that it would be foolhardy to want to limit and constrain divine wisdom and power to one particular conjecture alone.

"An admirable and truly angelic doctrine," Salviati answers. "One can answer, in a way that agrees just as well, by means of another doctrine which is divine: although he allows us to argue about the constitution of the World, God adds . . . that we are in no condition to discover the work which his hands have fashioned."

Perhaps through the mouth of Simplicio and of Salviati, Galileo wished to address a delicate piece of flattery to the Pope; perhaps he also wished to answer the old argument of Cardinal Maffeo Barberini with a touch of ridicule. Urban VIII took it in this guise: against the impenitent realism of Galileo be gave full license to the intransigent realism of the peripatetics of the Holy Office; the condemnation of 1633 confirmed the sentence of 1616.

HEGEL AND THE CELESTIAL MECHANICS OF NEWTON AND EINSTEIN

My object here is, first, to review Hegel's criticism of Newton's "system of the world" and then to examine critically the many aspects of it that seem to anticipate the approach to mathematical physics, which is today associated with the name of Einstein.

One must emphasize that Hegel's criticism was well informed. Certainly he knew the *Philosophiae naturalis principia mathematica* and *Opticks* first hand and had the requisite training in mathematics to comprehend what he read. Through hundreds of well-documented pages of his *Science of Logic* (large and small) and *Philosophy of Nature*, Hegel explores the meaning of Newton's fluxional calculus, his concepts of space, time, mass, inertia, centripetal and centrifugal forces, his laws of motion, his gravitational world-system, and, finally, his theory of light and colors. Particularly under the headings "Quantity" and "Measure" in the *Logic* and "Mechanics" in the *Philosophy of Nature*, Newton's doctrine provides much of the empirical datum upon which the Hegelian philosophical dialectic operates. And that represents no small tribute to the achievement of Newton, especially when we bear in mind that, according to Hegel, "without the working out of the empirical sciences on their own account, philosophy could not have reached further than with the ancients" (*HP* 3, p. 176)[1]

I

Unfortunately for Hegel's reputation, some of his pages on Newton have a vein of rather heavy-handed humor running

[From *Hegel and the Sciences*, BSPS Vol. 64. Edited by Robert S. Cohen and and Marx W. Warsofsky. D. Reidel Publishing Co., 1984.]

through them that can easily be mistaken for *lése-majesté* or, worse, an ethnic slur against the British people. Such passages are few, but ethnic pride and sensitivity have sought them out and, at least among sanguine admirers of the greatness of Newton — *qui genus hunwnum ingenus superavit*[2] — their effect has been to draw upon Hegel an imputation of gross scientific ignorance and presumption.

Even at its worst, however, Hegel's criticism nowhere matches the sustained sarcasm of the anti-Peripatetics of the century before Newton — the Galileos and Bacons, for instance — who pilloried Aristotle for his "bad" science, regardless of the fact that he had been revered for centuries as, in Dante's phrase (*Inf.* IV, 131), the "teacher of those who know" — *maestro di color che sanno*. Still, there is no denying that the Newtonian *sacramenta* are subject to much abuse in the pages of the German philosopher; and, despite the reigning relativism of our age, it is a bold scholar who will presume, as J. N. Findlay has, to qualify it as "much *fine* abuse."[3]

Admittedly hard to take, on a first reading, is Hegel's comparison of Newton with Molière's *bourgeois gentilhomme* — all to the advantage of the latter! Molière's M. Jourdain was "surprised to learn that he had talked prose all his life, not having had any idea that he was so accomplished"; but he, at least, learned — Hegel observes — whereas Newton seems never to have realized "that he thought in and had to deal with notions of the understanding, while he imagined he was dealing with physical facts" (*HP* 3, pp. 323-324). On the same level is Hegel's discussion of what the English generally understand by the term Philosophy and why it is that among them "Newton continues to be celebrated as the greatest of philosophers." In England, he explains, not only the empirical sciences but also the mechanical arts are confounded with philosophy; "and the name goes down as far as the price-lists of instrument-makers." With grudging admiration, as well as irony, Hegel in the same passage commends the heirs of the tradition of Bacon and Newton for at least taking the name of philosophy seriously enough to apply it to the study of matters of the greatest importance to them — like political economy, free trade, and the imperial administration, as well as chemistry, mineralogy,

natural history, agriculture, and the arts — whereas in most
other lands "the name of philosophy is now generally used only
as a nickname and insult, or as something odious" (*L* [W, 1975],
§ 7, pp. 11 -12).[4]

More abusive, from a Newtonian standpoint, is Hegel's
rejection of the *Principia*'s "proofs" of Kepler's laws — proofs
which he characterizes as "demonstrational jugglery and coun-
terfeiting" (*SL* [J/S] 2, p. 290); and most offensive of all,
perhaps, is his assessment of the *Opticks*, where he speaks not
only of *ineptitude, incorrectness,* and *thoughtless inconsistency,* but
also of *stupidity, blind prejudice,* and *dishonesty* (*PN*, § 320,
Remark, p. 199).[5]

It is no wonder, therefore, that, for longer than a century
in Newton's English-speaking world, most scholars have responded by refusing to take Hegel's *Naturphilosophie* seriously,
or even to read it at all — as, it is said, the seventeenth century
Aristotelians of Padua refused to take Galileo seriously, or even
to look through his optical tube. The fact is that, whereas the
French and Italians, less sensitive to criticism of Newton, have
had translations of the complete Encyclopedia of Hegel, including the *Naturphilosophie*, since the 1860s, the English-
speaking academic community, on the contrary, has delayed
until this bicentennial anniversary of Hegel's birth the labors of
filling the gap between the excellent versions of the *Logic* and
the *Philosophy of Mind*, which Professor Wallace provided three
generations ago.

But this year is destined evidently to mark a turning point
in the fortunes of Hegel's *Philosophy of Nature*. Thanks largely
to the sustained interest of Professor Findlay, we now have an
excellent translation — that of A. V. Miller — presented to us by
Findlay with a challenge that the Anglo-American academic
community will sooner or later have to accept. Back in 1958,
Professor Findlay had written of the *Naturphilosophie*:

> This part of the system is one that many Hegelians have
> thought fit to ignore entirely, mainly on account of the
> outmoded character of the science on which it reposes.
> Nothing can, however, be more unfit than this ignoring,
> and, in view of Hegel's undoubted greatness, more imper-
> tinent. *The Philosophy of Nature* is an integral part of

Hegel's system, and one can no more understand that system without taking account of it, than one can understand Aristotelianism while ignoring the *Physics* or the *History of Animals*, or Cartesianism while ignoring the physical portions of the *Principles of Philosophy*. In Hegel's theory of Nature, as in the parallel theories of Aristotle and Descartes, one sees the philosopher's principles at work, casting their slant upon our talk and thought about the world around us. The complete misunderstanding of Hegel's idealism by British philosophers, and its reduction to a refined form of subjectivism, are probably due to their ignoring of the *Naturphilosophie*.

... Hegel's grasp of contemporary science was, moreover, informed and accurate: the reading of the *Naturphilosophie* is made easy by its wealth of experimental illustration, and by its long citations from contemporary treatises. Hegel gives one the sciences of his own day, together with the interpretations he puts on them. [His views remain] as worthy of study, and of detailed scholarly comment, as are the views of Aristotle, or (in recent times) of Whitehead.[6]

In his foreword to the Miller translation, Professor Findlay says that his object in publishing it has been primarily utilitarian, to make its thought accessible "to students and teachers, particularly in regions where prejudiced simplifications might otherwise be their only route of access to it." The work itself is proof, he asserts, "that Hegel, like Aristotle and Descartes and Whitehead, is one of the great philosophical interpreters of nature, as steeped in its detail as he is audacious in his treatment of it." Praising its "thoroughgoing realism," Findlay concludes that what is to be admired most in it is Hegel's manifest "willingness, unusual in philosophers, to read, digest, and take full account of so much detailed scientific material, a willingness which puts him on a pinnacle of scientific information and understanding shared only by Aristotle" (*PN*, pp. viii-ix, xxv).

Thus, under unprecedentedly favorable auspices, we now have the *Philosophy of Nature* before us in a thoroughly English context. There can no longer be, therefore, any excuse among us for the "impertinence" of ignoring its doctrine — including the details of its criticism of Newton. Still, it remains to be seen how that criticism will fare under the closer scrutiny it is now certain to receive. Studied popularly in its fullness, it may appear to be all the more presumptuous and ill-informed and lead to a general discrediting of the rest of the Hegelian System — the *Philosophy of Mind* as well as the *Logic* — precisely on the grounds that the System is an integrated whole. "Nature, and the world or history of spirit, are the two realities" — says Hegel in the closing pages of his *History of Philosophy*; and the "ultimate aim and business of philosophy is to reconcile the thought of the Notion with reality" (*HP* 3, p. 545). If the Newtonian perspective, which is also the Darwinian, is true, and the Hegelian perspective false, what is the use, apart from antiquarianism, of a renaissance of interest in the *Naturphilosophie*? If Hegel's notion of the reality of nature is inadequate, then there can be no truth, no *adequatio intellectus et res*, in his general synthesis. And, except for truth's sake, why should the Anglo-American academic community take Hegel seriously when it can get as much of German dialectical philosophizing as it apparently needs in the doctrine of Karl Marx, which leaves the greatness of Newton and of Darwin intact?

II

Before focusing on Hegel's systematic elaboration of his criticism of Newton's science which is developed in the larger *Science of Logic* and culminates in the *Philosophy of Nature*, we would do well to consider briefly the condensed expressions of it in scattered pages of his *Phenomenology of Mind*, *History of Philosophy*, and smaller *Logic*. Newton is not named in the *Phenomenology*, but his chief contribution to the development of scientific thought — the concept of force — is taken up as part of the phenomenology of consciousness under the heading "Force and Understanding, Appearance and the Supersensory World (*Kraft und Verstand, Erscheinung und übersinnliche Welt*)." In attempting to understand the perpetual flux of the world of appearances (*phenomena*), consciousness labors to look through the phenomena to see what, in reality, sustains them. In the process of "thinking through" appearances, the understanding, Hegel says, discovers or fashions for itself a supersensory model which stands for it in place of the complexities of the restless sensory world. As Hegel expresses it, continued reflection develops that supersensory model into a "kingdom of laws," which is "no doubt beyond the world of perception — for this exhibits the law only through incessant change — but likewise present in it, and its direct immovable copy or image" (*Phen* [B], p. 195).[7]

In the first stages of this reduction of phenomenal complexity to the simplicity of reflection, laws of the understanding are discovered or formulated singly, to account for a relatively narrow range of phenomena. But the understanding longs for unified comprehension; and its tendency is, as Hegel says,

> to let the many laws coalesce into a single law, just as, e.g., the law by which a stone falls, and that by which the heavenly bodies move have been conceived as one law. When the laws thus coincide, however, they lose their specific character. The law becomes more and more abstract and superficial, and in consequence we find as a fact, not the unity of these various determinate laws, but a law which leaves out their specific character; just as the one law, which combines in itself the laws of falling terrestrial bodies, and of the movements of celestial bodies, does not, in point of fact, express both kinds of laws. The unification of all laws in universal attraction expresses no further content than just the bare concept of law itself, a concept which is therein set down as existing. Universal attraction says merely that all things retain their difference with respect to one another. The understanding presumes that in this it has found a universal law that expresses universal reality as such; but in fact it has merely found the notion of law in itself, though in such a way as to permit it to assert that all reality, in itself, is subject to law (*Phen* [B1, pp. 196-197).

The important point to stress here is that Hegel exhibits this activity of the understanding as an essential moment in the phenomenological process. What Newton did *had* to be done by human consciousness. The idea of universal gravitation "is therefore of the greatest importance," Hegel concludes, "because it is directed against the unthinking way of representing reality that makes everything appear to have happened by accident, and for which qualitative distinctiveness has the form of merely sensory differentiation" (*Phen* [B] , p. 197).

Newton thus comes off rather well in the *Phenomenology* — in marked contrast with the caustic treatment we get of him in the lectures on the *History of Philosophy*. There Hegel calls the author of the *Principia* an intellectual "barbarian" for having treated the basic concepts of his natural science as if they were physical facts — sensuous things, to be dealt with "as men deal with wood and stone." Especially barbaric, according to Hegel, was the Newtonian attitude summed up in the maxim, "Physics, beware of metaphysics," which amounts to saying, "Science, beware of thought." The worst of it is, Hegel continues, that physical scientists since Newton's time have for the most part

> faithfully observed this precept, inasmuch as they have not entered upon an investigation of their conceptions, or thought about thoughts . . . . And this is even now the case. In the beginnings of physical science we read of the power of inertia, for instance, of the force of acceleration, of molecules, or centripetal and centrifugal forces, as of facts which definitely exist; what are really the final results of reflection are represented as their first grounds (*HP* 3, p. 323).

Yet here again, Hegel acknowledges the value of Newton's scientific work in "introducing to physics the determinations respecting forces, which pertain to reflection." By setting "the laws of forces in the place of the laws of phenomena," Newton "raised science to the standpoint of reflection," and for that he deserves high praise. He is to be blamed, according to Hegel, only for imagining that he is still functioning on the level of sensory perception, free of metaphysics, when, by undertaking to "compose" the empirically derived laws of phenomena out of the interrelations of "component" forces, he has obviously slipped back into metaphysics without knowing it — which is to say, ignorantly. The harshest part of Hegel's judgment here is his prophecy that physical science will make no significant advance in the theoretical sense until it gives up the naive Newtonian dogmatism that confounds abstract concepts of the understanding with the reality of nature (*HP* 3, pp. 322-324).

That surely was a "hard saying" in the first decades of the nineteenth century. Today, however, it has become the prevailing view of the most expert practitioners in the field. In his

Physics and Microphysics, for instance, the Nobel Prize-winning physicist Louis de Broglie writes:

> For scientists, and in particular for the theorists, there is a certain danger in trying to ignore the efforts of philosophers and especially their work as critics . . . . Thus many scientists of the present day, victims of an ingenuous realism, almost without perceiving it, have adopted a certain metaphysics of a very materialistic and mechanistic character and have regarded it as the very expression of scientific truth. One of the great services that the recent evolution of physics has rendered contemporary thought, is that it has destroyed this simplified metaphysics, and with the same stroke has caused certain traditional philosophic problems to be considered in an entirely new light . . . . For the development of science to continue, we must embark on, or at any rate touch upon, questions of philosophic import and sometimes consider their new and very original solutions.[8]

Discussing the reluctance of the Newtonians to abandon their long-cherished concepts of space, time, motion, and force, the same author observes that too many physicists even today would no doubt "prefer merely to perfect and amend the existing theories rather than be obliged constantly to reconstruct them." But a willingness to abandon long-cherished concepts is, he concludes, "the condition and ransom of scientific progress."[9]

In the smaller *Logic*, Hegel does not explicitly discuss the Newtonian celestial mechanics. He does, however, discuss the logical presuppositions upon which any analysis of laws of phenomena (such as Kepler framed) into laws of forces (such as Newton framed) ought to be based, if it is to make philosophical sense. And this he does at considerable length under the subheadings "Repulsion and Attraction," "Quantity," "Magnitude," "Quantum," "Number," "Degree," "Quantitative Ratio," "Measure," "Thing," "Properties," "Matter," "Form," "Phenomena," "Forces," and "Expression of Forces" — all of them terms we now familiarly encounter in contemporary treatises on post-Planckian physical theory.

Under the heading "Repulsion and Attraction," Hegel

draws a parallel between Newtonian physics and the ancient atomism of Leucippus and Democritus. In both systems, particles of matter and an enveloping void are posited as the ultimate constituents of nature, with the void serving as a separating or repulsive principle. The Newtonian advance over the old doctrine consists in having posited "an attractive by the side of a repulsive force," which — Hegel acknowledges — "certainly gives completeness to the contrast" between the Democritean Full and Empty (*L* [W, 1975], § 98, p. 143). Still, what Aristotle criticized in ancient atomism remains to be criticized, according to Hegel, in the Newtonian doctrine.

The old atomists traced fixed patterns (equivalents of the Newtonian laws of forces) through all the manifold flux and multiplicity of the phenomenal world. But when required to say what, in the first place, caused the atoms to start bumping together, acting and reacting as they do in their great web of necessity, the reply of the Democriteans was simply: a primordial, fortuitous swerving, a whirl of indeterminate origin — which is another way of saying that, in the final analysis, like our modern Heisenbergians, Democritus ascribed all things to chance. ("*Democrito*," Dante wrote in the fourth canto of the *Inferno*, "*che 'l mondo a caso pone*" [who ascribes the world to chance].)[10] And it can easily be demonstrated that, despite the popular view which holds that Necessity is the atomists' God, Dante's phrase is drawn straight out of the very precise Aristotelian analysis of the Democritean doctrine in Book IV of the *Physics* — an analysis upon which Hegel dwells in his Lectures on the *History of Philosophy*.) The Newtonians, when all is done, do precisely the same — Hegel argues; for, despite all their talk of matter and void, inertia and gravity, it is a *chance thrust* dating from some indeterminate moment of the remotest past that is assumed to have originally set the planets in course to be pushed and tugged as they are by centrifugal as well as centripetal forces.

Hegel's concern in all of this is to indicate that the Newtonian mechanics, despite pietistic and deistic protests to the contrary, is essentially a materialist doctrine. He is, of course, aware that, as a man of God, Newton strenuously resisted the assimilation of his doctrine to that of the avowed materialists. "I feign no hypotheses" about final causes, Newton had pleaded in the celebrated General Scholium of the *Principia*, where, indeed, he explicitly rejects as untenable the Cartesian theory of vortices on the grounds that no merely mechanical causes could give birth to so much orderly motion as we can trace in the heavens. By asserting that such orderliness presupposes an intelligent creation, Newton had hoped, as Hegel remarks, to leave unimpaired the "honor of God as the Creator and Governor of the World" while at the same time excluding him from consideration in the actual search for underlying forces (*L* [W, 1975], § 136, p. 195).

Under the sub-headings "Force" and "Expression of Force" in the smaller *Logic*, Hegel discusses at length why it is that Newtonian science would sooner or later have to give up its veneer of theistic piety. "Contrasted with its deinfinitized world of independent forces and matters," he writes, "the only terms in which it is possible to describe God will present him in the abstract infinity of an unknowable supreme Being in some other world far away." And that, Hegel continues, is "precisely the position of materialism," from as far back as Democritus and Epicurus down to the "free-thinking" deism and agnostic atheism of the Enlightenment. The medieval Church, confronted with the renaissance of ancient doctrines, was in that respect right, therefore, Hegel says, in resisting the "search for underlying causes" as impious, as tending to deny to God the things that are God's, which are assigned instead to indeterminate causes. From the vantage point of religious faith, no less than from that of philosophy, it must be acknowledged, Hegel says, that "the finite forms of the understanding certainly fail to fulfill the conditions for knowledge either of Nature or of the formations of the world of Mind as they truly are" (*L* [W, 1975], § 136, p. 195).

Yet while religion has a right to be dissatisfied with the results, it has no right to frustrate the labors of the understanding, whose "finite forms" are — for Hegel — indispensable moments in the development of consciousness to the level of truly scientific comprehension. In words that anticipate the scientific posture of Pierre Duhem in the concluding sections of his masterful *Aim and Structure of Physical Theory*, Hegel writes against the false claims of religious piety:

> On the other hand, it is impossible to overlook the formal right which, in the first place, entitles the empirical sciences to vindicate the right of thought to know the existent world in all the speciality of its content, and to seek something further than the mere abstract faith that God creates and governs the world. When our religious consciousness, resting upon the authority of the Church, teaches us that God created the world by his almighty will, that he guides the stars in their courses, and vouchsafes to all his creatures their existence and their well-being, the question Why? is still left to answer. Now it is the answer to this question which forms the common task of empirical science and of philosophy (L [W, 1975], § 136, p. 195).

Defending the practice against the piety of the Newtonians, Hegel asserts that when religion appeals to the "unsearchableness" of the decrees of God, it is, in effect, aping the agnosticism of the enlightenment rationalists. "Such an appeal," he concludes, "is no better than an arbitrary dogmatism which contravenes the express command of Christianity, to know God in spirit and truth, and is prompted by a humility which is not Christian, but born of ostentatious bigotry" (L [W, 1975], § 136, p. 196).

III

The larger *Science of Logic*, which provides what amounts to a running commentary on the terse paragraphs of the *Logic* of the *Encyclopedia*, takes us to the philosophic core of Hegel's criticism of the Newtonian celestial mechanics. No one pretending to assess the adequacy of that criticism can afford to ignore, or skim over, what Hegel has to say about Quantity, Quantum, and Quantitative Ratio in his book-length discussion of "Magnitude," or about Specific Quantity, Real Measure, and the Measureless (as transition to Essence) under the heading "Measure," or about Mechanism, Chemism, and Teleology under the heading "Objectivity." As in the smaller Logic, Hegel is here examining the preconceptions and methods of study of all sciences that take not abstractions but the concrete realities of nature and mind as their qualitatively determined objects.

Under "Magnitude" and "Measure," Hegel examines, among other things, the basic notion of the Newtonian- Leibnizian calculus and traces the history of the mathematical infinite and infinitesimals upon which that calculus is built; he considers at length the difficulties of assimilating analytical calculus to analytical geometry and of applying both to the analysis of accelerated rectilinear and non-uniform curvilinear motion; and, anticipating things to come in our own time, he speculates on the possibility of developing a mathematics of qualitative quanta which would be a science of measures, competent to deal with the qualities as well as the quantities of existent things (as, for instance, Einsteinian and Planckian physics now deals with qualitatively determined quanta, or measures, of space, time, light, and a host of electro-magnetic phenomena).

The first explicit reference to Newton comes under the sub-heading "Quantum" and it consists of singularly high praise. Considering the "chief determinations which have been offered in mathematics about the infinite," Hegel asserts un-equivocally that "no correcter determination of the thought can be made than that offered by Newton." The problem of the mathematical infinite is ancient. It was first clearly defined by the Eleatics (notably Zeno) in their efforts to demonstrate the irrationality of the Heraclitean "flux"; and Zeno's paradoxes have remained vital paradoxes for mathematical physicists to this day — Hegel insists — despite all the walking to and fro of old Diogenes and cynics of more recent times. That Hegel was competent to deal with the problem in its abstractest geometrical and algebraic as well as logical aspects, he has amply demonstrated not only in the *Science of Logic* itself, but also in the *History of Philosophy*, where he takes it up as often as it surfaces in his sources.

Newton tells us that he "invented the methods of series and fluxions in the year 1665," and his first published treatise on the subject, *Methods of Fluxions and Infinite Sequences*, appeared in 1674. But Hegel is concerned, as he says, with Newton's maturest thought on the subject, which is that of the *Principia*. Hinting at what he will later criticize, Hegel writes:

I here set apart the determinations belonging to the idea

of motion and velocity (from which latter chiefly he took the name of *fluxions*), for there the thought appears not in its due abstraction, but concrete and mixed with unessential forms.

In praise of the duly abstract thought, Hegel says:

Newton explains these fluxions (*Princ. Mathem. Phil. Nat. L. i. Lemma XI, Schol.*) by saying that he takes them not as *indivisibilia* (a form used by earlier mathematicians, Cavalieri and others; it contains the concept of a Quantum determinate in itself), but as vanishing *divisibilia*; and, further, not as the sums and ratios of determinate parts, but as the limits (*limites*) of the sums and ratios. It will be objected, he says, that vanishing magnitudes have no final ratio, because the ratio before they vanish is not the last, and, after they have vanished, no longer exists. But by the ratio between vanishing magnitudes must not be understood the ratio that exists either before or after, but that *with which* they vanish (*quacum evanescunt*). And, similarly, the first ratio of becoming magnitudes is that with which they arise (*SL* [J/S] 1, pp. 271-272).

After noting that the "magnitudes at the point of vanishing" are understood by Newton to be "quanta no longer," Hegel makes clear that, in his judgment, Newton has here adequately expressed the notion of transition from quantity to quality which is so essential an element in the Hegelian dialectic. As much Newtonian as Hegelian is the statement that: "The limit of the magnitudinal ratio is that point where it is and it is not — or, more precisely, where the Quantum has vanished, and the ratio, therefore, is preserved only as qualitative quantity-ratio" (*SL* [J/S] 1, p. 272).

But while Newton grasped the concept of the qualitative quantity-ratio and expressed it clearly, in practice — says Hegel — the author of the *Principia* let it slip through his fingers. And the same must be said of the other great mathematicians of the period, including Newton's master Barrow, as well as Fermat, Leibniz, Lagrange, Landen, Euler, and their successors. It seems, Hegel writes, that "when mathematicians turn to practice, the finite determinateness of quantity returns, and the operation can no longer do without the idea of a Quantum which is merely relatively small" (*SL* [J/S] 1, p. 277). Indeed, the idea of the relatively small, of increment, of addition, "of growth of *x* by *dx* or *i*, and so on," Hegel concludes, "must be considered the fundamental evil inherent in these methods — as an enduring obstacle which makes it impossible to disengage the determination of the qualitative moment of quantity from the idea of ordinary Quantum" (*SL* [J/S] 1, p. 274). In other words, the evil is that those "ghosts of departed quantities" (as Bishop Berkeley called them) are too easily mistaken for never-perishing *indivisibilia*, and the transition from quantity to quality is lost to thought.

If mathematicians could take another approach so as to develop a mathematics of qualitative quantity-ratios, Hegel observes, the result would be a magnificent instrument for the advancement of a truly physical as distinct from an abstractly mechanical science. Such a mathematics, he writes, would have to be in essence —

> a science of measures — a science for which much has been done empirically, but little in a truly scientific, that is philosophic, manner. Mathematical principles of Natural Philosophy — as Newton called his work — if they were to fulfill this determination in a philosophic and scientific meaning deeper than that which was reached by Newton and the whole Baconian generation, must contain quite other things in order to bring light into these regions, dark as yet, but most worthy of contemplation (*SL* [J/S] 1, p .361).

Later, in the *Philosophy of Nature*, Hegel will add on this theme:

> The truly philosophical science of mathematics as *theory of magnitude*, would be the science of *measures*; but this already presupposes the real particularity of things, which is found only in concrete *Nature*. On account of the external nature of magnitude, this would certainly also be the most difficult of all sciences.

Newtonian science, Hegel stresses, is not a science of measures. In fact, all that most needs to be measured in nature — the actualities of space, time, and the light by means of which spatial measurements are possible — is taken for granted by the Newtonians, exactly as defined in the abstract presuppositions of their calculus. That calculus was developed, it is true, to deal with motions of qualitatively determined phenomena; but, in the process, the traditional mathematical spirit of abstraction took over. Forgetting the qualitative forms of the phenomena of falling bodies and orbiting planets, the mathematicians focused on the terms of the ratios in the formulas — with the result that products of analysis (of the decomposition of the magnitude of a phenomenon, such as motion) there received, in Hegel's words —

> an objective meaning, such as velocity, accelerated force, and so on; according to this newly acquired objective meaning they were to produce correct propositions and physical laws; their objective connections and relations, too, were to be determined by analytic means; for instance, it was said that in a uniformly accelerated motion, there existed a special velocity proportional to the periods of time, while besides, an accretion was added uniformly from the force of gravity. In the modem analytical form of mechanics such propositions are regularly cited as results of the calculus (*SL* [J/S] 1, p. 289).

Hegel was well aware that Newton had not arrived at the conclusions demonstrated in Book Three of the *Principia* (where the universal law of gravitation is expounded as the System of the World) by means of the analytical calculus and geometry he uses there. Newton himself says, at the beginning of that book, that the method of exposition there was an afterthought, and that he introduced it rather to prevent than to facilitate general understanding. He had at first, he says, written the entire book in a more direct, popular way; but afterwards, "considering that such as had not sufficiently entered into the principles could not easily discern the strength of the consequences, nor lay aside the prejudices to which they had been many years accustomed," Newton decided to avoid any direct confrontation with ignorance and prejudice by choosing "to reduce the substance of this Book into the form of Propositions (in the mathematical way), which would be read by those only who had first made themselves masters of the principles established in the preceding books."[11]

What might have become of the great law of universal gravitation of that Third Book, had Newton not *reduced* his exposition to the form of Propositions, in a mathematical way, one can hardly guess. But perhaps the Ernst Machs and Einsteins would have got at its absolute space and time, the essentially non-empirical character of its laws of motion, and its oddly convenient equivalence of inertial and gravitational mass, much sooner. In the light of what has since become the fate of Newton's mathematical "proofs," it was eminently fair and extraordinarily perceptive for Hegel to have said over 150 years ago:

> It will be impossible to deny that in this sphere much has been accepted as proof — chiefly veiled under the kindly mist of the infinitesimally small — on no other ground than that the result was already known beforehand, and the proof, which was arranged in such a manner as to produce the result, at least effected the illusion of a framework of proof — which illusion was preferred to mere belief or empirical knowledge. But I do not hesitate to regard this method as no better than demonstrational jugglery and counterfeiting; and I include even some of Newton's demonstrations, and especially such as belong to those just mentioned, for which Newton has been extolled to the skies and above Kepler, because what Kepler had discovered empirically *he* demonstrated mathematically (*SL* [J/S] 1, p. 290).

Hegel then proceeds to explain that, by its very nature, the mathematics of Newton and his peers is unable to "prove the magnitudinal determinations of physics in so far as they are laws based upon the qualitative nature of the moments." The qualitative element is lost in the processes of the calculus; and it is rather a moral than a scientific question why, to many mathematicians, it has seemed against the honor of their discipline — so Hegel phrases it — to "acknowledge simply experience as source and sole proof of empirical propositions" (*SL* [J/S] 1, p. 290).

Needless to say, Hegel has long since won his point on this score. Modern mathematicians and the best mathematical physicists of recent years are all of a mind in acknowledging — and indeed often boasting — that they no longer hold, with

Galileo, Descartes, and Newton, that mathematics of itself, or mathematically conducted experiments, can lead to true knowledge of the realities of Nature. As Professor Tobias Dantzig expressed it in his *Number: The Language of Science*:

> The mathematician may be compared to a designer of garments, who is utterly oblivious to the creatures whom his garments may fit. To be sure, his art originated in the necessity for clothing such creatures, but this was long ago; to this day a shape will occasionally appear which will fit into the garment as if that garment had been made for it. Then there is no end of surprise and delight! There have been quite a few such delightful surprises. The conic sections, invented in an attempt to solve the problem of doubling the altar of an oracle, ended by becoming the orbits followed by the planets in their courses about the sun . . . . The absolute differential calculus, which originated as a fantasy of Riemann, became the mathematical vehicle for the theory of Relativity . . . . Mathematics and experiment reign more firmly than ever over the new physics, but an all-pervading skepticism has affected their validity. Man's confident belief in the absolute validity of the two methods has been found to be of an anthropomorphic origin, both have been found to rest on articles of faith.[12]

Bertrand Russell, who (with Alfred North Whitehead) gave us an updated *Principia Mathematica* in 1914, has said to the same effect: "It is a curious fact that, just when the man in the street has begun to believe thoroughly in science, the man in the laboratory has begun to lose his faith"; and, again: "Science, which began as the pursuit of truth, is becoming incompatible with veracity, since complete veracity tends more and more to complete scientific scepticism."[13]

But the truly great scientists of our time, the Einsteins and Plancks, have not been content that mathematical science, which once boasted of its certainty, should now boast of its uncertainty. Einstein admits that, in its pursuit of the open questions of the Galilean and Newtonian mechanics, mathematical science has been led inevitably — as Hegel predicted — to Democritean, or Heisenbergian, indeterminism. But, according to Einstein, that is hardly an outcome to gladden the scientific heart. "Some physicists," he wrote in 1941, "among them myself, can not believe that we must abandon, actually and forever, the idea of direct representation of physical reality in space and time."[14] Hegel, too, refused to abandon that idea. Like Aristotle long before him, he sought, by means of a dialectical criticism of the limits of mechanistic science and its mathematical methods, to prepare the way for a truly philosophic science of nature — a science that can not only represent but also comprehend in its truth the qualitative reality of nature, from the merest externality and duration of space and time, up through the great chain of inorganic and organic being, to the animal existence — birth, life, health, reproduction, disease, and death — of thinking man.

IV

With one notable exception, all references to Newton in the *Philosophy of Nature* are confined to the first part — Mechanics —where the object of study is matter in the abstract, as contrasted with the qualified matter of Physics and the living matter of Organics. Under Mechanics, the sub-divisions are: "Space and Time" (including the abstract concepts of Place and Matter); "Matter and Motion, Finite Mechanics" (including the concepts of Inert Matter, Thrust, and Falling); and "Absolute Mechanics" (with Universal Gravitation, Kepler's Laws, and Transition to Physics as sub-headings). The subdivisions and subheadings obviously represent a graded order, ranging upward from the simplest and most abstract object of study in mechanics (space) to what in Hegel's judgment is the most complex and least abstract (the solar system as described in Kepler's laws). The fact that Universal Gravitation is placed beneath Kepler's Laws in the graded order reveals at a glance that here, as elsewhere, Hegel will represent Newton's "System of the World" to us as a "reductionist" analysis of a higher into the terms of a lower determination.

In the whole range of Mechanics — Hegel writes — "bodies exist only as points; what gravity determines is only spatial interrelations of points. The unity of matter is only the unity of the place it seeks, not the unity of a concrete One. That is the nature of this sphere." And yet, on its highest level of development, Mechanics is able to transcend its own abstract character;

for, in its descriptive laws of the solar system — tracing a pattern of elliptical orbits about an energizing center — it comprehends the notion of what matter, as manifest motion, must really be in itself. In a startling anticipation of the vision of Niels Bohr, Hegel writes:

> What the solar system is as a whole, matter is now to be in detail . . . . The determinations of form which constitute the solar system are the determinations of matter itself and they constitute the being of matter. The determination and the being are thus essentially identical; but this is the nature of the qualitative, for here, if the determination is removed, the being, too, is destroyed. This is the transition from Mechanics to Physics (*PN*, § 271, *Z*, pp. 83-84).

The whole of Newtonian science is comprehended within the abstract range of Mechanics, excepting only the theory of light of the *Optics* — Newton's one major attempt to make the transition from Mechanics to Physics (in Hegel's sense of the terms). Newton had confidently imagined that, with the method of the *Principia*, he could easily make that transition, and then move on from Physics into Organics to complete his Natural Philosophy. But in Hegel's judgment, as in the judgment of Einstein and his peers, Newton's attempt to comprehend scientifically the phenomena of light was a failure, and foredoomed to be a failure because of the inadequacies of its analytical, decompositional method. Just as Newton decomposed the ellipses of Kepler's laws into rectilinear components, thereby depriving them of their qualitative identity, so he decomposed the fluid transparency of white light into colored corpuscles, which he declared to be primary and simple; and, with that, the qualitative, distinctive actuality of light slipped out of his scientific grasp.

Hegel was aware that Light — which for him as for Einstein was the first physical manifestation of matter — united qualitatively the characteristics of abstract corpuscular and wave motions; he knew also that light, in reflecting, refracting, and otherwise manifesting itself, shows all the colors of the entire universe, including those revealed in the dark when a prism is set up, just right, as a divider between light and dark. But, about the corpuscular and wave theories, Hegel held that they were both one-sided, and therefore inadequate approaches to the dialectical notion of light in its qualitative unity. Hegel writes:

> Light is an interesting theme to treat; for we think that in Nature we have only the individual, *this* particular reality. But light is the very opposite of this . . . . In thinking of light, we must renounce all conceptions of composition and the like . . . . The expression "bundles of rays" is merely one of convenience, it means nothing; the bundles are light in its entirety, which is only outwardly limited; it is no more divided into bundles of rays than is the Ego or pure self-consciousness. It is the same when I say: in my time or in Caesar's time. This was also the time of everyone else; but here I am speaking of it in relation to Caesar, and restrict it to him without meaning that he really had a separate ray or parcel of time. The Newtonian theory according to which light is propagated in straight lines, or the wave theory which makes it travel in waves, are, like Euler's aether or the vibration of sound, materialistic representations quite useless for the comprehension of light (*PN*, § 276, Z, pp. 93-94).

But the best, in this extraordinarily thorough anticipation of things to come in physical theory, is what follows — where Hegel rejects (as modern Quantum Physics rejects) the notion that the wave theory is superior to the corpuscular theory. According to the wave theory, he writes —

> the dark element in light [the color-producing element] is supposed to run through the movement in a series of curves which can be mathematically calculated; this abstract determination has been introduced into the theory, and is nowadays thought to be a great triumph over Newton. But this is nothing physical; and neither of these two ideas is in place, since nothing empirical obtains here. There no more exist particles of light or waved aether than the nerves consist of a series of globules, each receiving an impulse and setting others in motion (*PN*, § 276, Z, p. 94).

Hegel died, it is to be noted, more than a generation before the birth of the people who are usually honored in our catechisms of popular science for having discussed such matters for the first time. Also on the *speed* of light, Hegel anticipates the pioneers, writing:

> The propagation of light occurs in time, since, being an activity and an alteration, it cannot dispense with this moment . . . . The distances which light is supposed to travel involve time; for illumination, whether through a medium or by reflection, is a modification of matter requiring time (*PN*, § 276, Z, p. 94).

But the speed of light is not, according to Hegel, like the speed of other physically determinate manifestations of matter. In the sphere of *qualified* as distinct from abstract matter, light is primary — the first, and therefore *limiting* manifestation of matter in motion. The sun, says Hegel, does not pour out its light *incidentally* while serving as the central material point of the solar system. That system's orbital structure is the inner form of matter itself, as we have noted, and it is that circling about a center that shows itself physically as light. But, as each particle of matter is a microcosmic solar system, all matter is — for the eye that can discern its true, centralized orbital speeds — luminous. Again in a thoroughly Einsteinian vein, Hegel characterizes Light as the "self-contained totality of matter," explaining that, as an "existent, space-filling force," it is "absolute velocity, pure materiality which is everywhere present, real existence which remains within itself, or actuality as transparent possibility." "Light," he concludes, "brings us into the universal interrelation; everything exists for us in theoretical, unresistant fashion because it is in light." (*PN*, § 275, Z, p. 88).

Einstein has told us that it was as a consequence of the labors of Faraday, Clerk Maxwell, and Hertz, but particularly of Maxwell, in the study of light and electro-magnetic phenomena, that modern science generally abandoned the established view that Galilean-Newtonian mechanics could stand as the "basis of all physics." Attempts to solve the difficulties of application of the Newtonian principles to the newly-developed spheres led first to formulation of the field theory of electricity, then to the effort to base all physics upon the concept of field, and finally to the theory of relativity, which is the "evolution of the notion of space and time into that of the continuum with metric structure,"[15] which is in our view then qualitatively determined. "The general theory of relativity,"

Einstein has said with his usual respectful regard for the overthrown Titan of classical mechanics, "formed the last step in the development of the programme of the field-theory. Quantitatively it modified Newton's theory only slightly, but for that all the more profoundly qualitatively."[16]

Already in Hegel's day, the phenomena of magnetism, electricity, and chemism, together with those of light, were calling into being a unified science very different in principle from Newtonian mechanics. Scientific "law" in the mechanical sense means, he explains, "the combination of two simple determinations such that merely their simple interconnections constitute the whole relationship, and yet each must have the show of independence with regard to the other" (*PN*, § 270, *Z*, p. 72). But such a concept of law has, he insists, a very limited range — that of mathematical abstraction. It will not do in the study of bodies as they *actually* fall, or as they actually orbit around an energized center; but the inadequacy there may be obscured by assuming that the bodies in those qualitatively determined relationships are really nothing more than points in the geometric sense. It is otherwise, however, with the phenomena of light, magnetism, electricity, and chemism.

In magnetism, for instance, Hegel writes, "the inseparability of the two determinations is already posited"; consequently there is not a co-relationship of "law" in the mechanical sense (*PN*, § 270, *Z*, p. 72). Magnetic phenomena, he explains, are not gravitational phenomena which mathematical analysis can, for its arbitrary convenience, separate into inertial as well as gravitational components. "Magnetism," he writes, "differs from gravity in this, that it forces bodies into a quite different direction from the vertical." Motion in the sphere, or "field" of magnetism is not that of rectilinear attraction; but it is also "not rotary, not a curve upon itself, like the motion of the heavenly bodies, which is accordingly neither attractive nor repellent" (*PN*, § 313, *Z*, p. 171).

Summing up his case against scientific "reductionism" in this sphere, Hegel continues:

> In all higher forms [as contrasted with the forms of abstract mechanics] the individualized whole constitutes the third in which the determinations are conjoined, and

we no longer have the direct determinations of two things which are in relationship with each other.

Laws in the mechanical sense are possible for the planetary motions, he says, because those motions involve two distinct phenomenal elements — not to be confounded with the non-empirical centripetal and centrifugal forces. Those two phenomenal elements are "the form of the path and the velocity of the motion." But if such laws are to be comprehended in a higher principle so as to embrace the phenomena of light and magnetism as well, the "thing to be done," he concludes, "is to develop this from the Notion. This would give rise to a far-reaching science and the difficulty of the task is such that this has not yet been fully accomplished." (*PN*, § 270, *Z*, p. 72).

The men who have undertaken to develop that "far-reaching science" in our time have all started from the premise that it would have to be built up from the very bottom — from a rectification of the first "reductionist" error of classical mechanics, which consisted in its positing space and time as only externally interrelated in the phenomena of motion. Identifying the essential element in Einstein's labors of rectification, Bertrand Russell wrote:

> The scientific merit of Einstein's theory lies in the explanation, by a uniform principle, of many facts which are unintelligible in the Newtonian system. The philosophical interest lies chiefly in the substitution of the single manifold, space-time, for the two manifolds, space and time.[17]

How the original "reductionist" error came to be made, Einstein himself has explained as follows:

> The lack of definiteness which, from the point of view of empirical importance, adheres to the notion of time in classical mechanics was veiled by the axiomatic representation of space and time as things given independently of our senses. Such a use of notions — independent of the empirical basis, to which they owe their existence — does not necessarily damage science. One may however easily be led into the error of believing that these notions, whose origin is forgotten, are necessary and unalterable accompaniments to our thinking, and this error may constitute a serious danger to the progress of science.[18]

Literally billions of words have been written on this theme since Ernst Mach and then Einstein opened it up for the academic community of mathematical scientists. Yet in all that literary production, which still floods the markets today, there is, I am confident, no discussion of the reductionist error as profound or as philosophically consistent as Hegel's in the opening sections of his Mechanics, from which point he pursues the process of philosophical *rectification* up through the whole range of mechanics into those higher spheres of nature where to mathematize at all is to commit the gravest sort of reductionist error — unless one's purpose is avowedly reductionist and utilitarian.

In reviewing Hegel's approach to Newton in the *Philosophy of Nature*, we have started from the "difficulties" of the phenomena of light and electromagnetism only because it has been from that standpoint that our contemporary science, always working "reductionistically," has found its way back to the beginnings, ironically getting a reductionist satisfaction out of the effort to rectify the original reductionist error of Newton. Hegel pursued a "reductionist" course in his great intellectual voyage of discovery, the *Phenomenology of Mind*; but in his systematic exposition of the doctrine of Mechanics, as in all the philosophical sciences of his *Encyclopedia*, he reverses that course, working his way up from the most abstract to the most concrete conceptions.

V

Although we have the assurances of the greatest practitioners that, in mathematical science, intellectual insight and discursive reasoning (*nous* and *episteme*) come first and mathematization follows, many of us are still reluctant to believe that we are dealing with truly scientific thought when its utterance is not in equations. For those of us who feel that way, the best approach to Hegel's Mechanics is, as we have suggested above, through close study of the several hundred pages on "Quantity" and "Measure" in the larger *Science of Logic*, which bristle with formulas and constructions of the analytical calculus and geometry. Hegel was, as we noted, well trained in the higher mathematics. But, as a great philosopher in the Aristotelian tradition, he knows that the place of mathematically-shaped abstractions lies between the purely logical and the sensory, and that such shaped abstractions can be used meaningfully in natural science only after first principles (in mechanics, the principles of space, time, matter, and motion) have been logically determined in thought.

Early in the Mechanics, Hegel sums up the range of concepts he is about to explore. "Self-externality," he writes (linking the *Naturphilosophie* with what precedes it in his System),

> splits at once into two forms, positively as Space, and negatively as Time. The first concrete thing, the unity of these abstract moments, is Matter; this is related to its moments, and these consequently are related to each other, in Motion. When this relation is not external, we have the absolute unity of Matter and Motion, self-moving Matter (*PN*, § 253, Z, p. 28).

When mechanistic physics speaks of material "points" in Space (as Newton does), the concept of Time, Hegel explains, is incidentally introduced. For the mathematical point, having no dimension, is obviously a negation of Space, and that is precisely what Time is. And it is the point of Time in space that traces the "lines" of spatial dimensionality as its *loci*. Anticipating the need for the Riemann-Einsteinian advance, he observes:

> There is no *science of time* corresponding to the *science of space*, to geometry. The differences of time have not this *indifference* of self-externality which constitutes the immediate determinateness of space, and they are consequently not capable of being expressed when the Understanding has paralyzed it and reduced its negativity to the unit (*PN*, § 259, *Remark*, pp. 37-38).

Here is where Hegel observes that a science of *measures*, competent to deal with time in its negativity, as the moving-point of space, "would be the most difficult of all sciences."

Hegel then points out that, in its traditional meaning (philosophically defined by Aristotle), the term Place has always expressed "a posited identity of space and time." That is a profound as well as obvious observation. The moderns who speak of the *space-time continuum* for want of a suitable single word, might do well to consider the long historical development of the doctrine of Place — a doctrine which, according to Pierre Duhem, holds the future of natural science. In our ordinary usage, Hegel notes, a thing in "place" is understood to be a thing in space-time, here and now, or there and then. Zeno's paradox of motion, we are reminded, was defined as a space-time paradox of places. A thing at rest or in motion is in "place" always, even though, in motion, we distinguish (as Hegel says) "three different places: the present place, the place about to be occupied, and the place which has just been vacated" — in which distinction the "vanishing of the dimensions of time is paralyzed." Yet it remains clear in all of this, Hegel continues, that "there is really only *one* place, a universal of these places, which remains unchanged through all the changes; it is *duration*, existing immediately according to its Notion, and as such is Motion" (*PN*, § 261, *Remark*, Z, p. 43).

Zeno's paradox shows that rectilinear motion, out of one place into another, no matter how far extended, contains no *measure* of itself, and is therefore not really motion. Having no *measure* means that it has no time, which is the measure of motion. Curvilinear motion that returns to its former places, on the other hand, contains its own measure. The lines of a space-time continuum (as contrasted with the timeless space of Euclidean geometry) must, therefore, curve back on themselves. With "Einsteinian" insight, Hegel writes:

> This return of the line is the circle; it is the Now, Before, and After which have closed together in a unity in which these dimensions are indifferent, so that Before is equally After, and vice versa. It is in circular motion that the necessary paralysis of these dimensions is first posited in space. Circular motion is the spatial or subsistent unity of the dimensions of time . . . . it is motion in its essence, motion which has sublated the distinctions of Now, Before, and After, its dimensions or its Notion. In the circle, these are in unity; the circle is the restored Notion of *duration*, Motion extinguished within itself. There is posited *Mass*, the persistent, the self-consolidated, which exhibits motion as its possibility (*PN*, § 261, *Remark*, Z, pp. 43-44).

The so-called *mass*-point, in other words, is "circling motion" in itself. I doubt that anything more profound has been written in modern times on the abstract foundations of mechanics. To sum up, and hurry forward, we may say: Anticipating the language of Ernst Mach, Einstein, and Planck, Hegel defines space and time as positive and negative determinations of Motion, which, in its self-circling, is Mass. Time is the restless, ubiquitous point of space that negates dimensionality in itself while generating the same as "loci" of its Future and Past. Time gives "place" to the lines, planes, and volumes of space. And Hegel dares to conclude that "moving place" or, as we usually say, *loco*motion, is the sole constituent of Matter.

Every time-point is thus a mass-point circling in itself: an essentially *moving* place that tends restlessly to circle "out of place" and back into it. Thus this universal gravitation of time-points is simultaneously a moving away and a moving toward, self-repulsion from one center and attraction toward another. As Hegel expresses it: "Matter is both moments [repulsion as well as attraction] and their unity, centralized in a point, is gravity." Matter itself is "tending toward a center, but — and here is its other determination — a center located outside itself." More precisely: Gravity is not mere attraction, which is the tendency to negate spatial separateness and produce continuity. On the contrary, "gravity preserves both separateness and continuity" as moments of its concept (*PN*, § 262, pp. 44-47). And these moments, apprehended abstractly as repulsion and attraction, are destined to be narrowly determined as independent forces, centrifugal and centripetal (*PN*, § 269, pp. 62-65).

Those who take space and time abstractly, who conceive of "matter" as "occupying" space and as being "acted upon" by independent forces of "inertia" and "gravity" have, in other words, taken rectilinear uniform motion as simple, and accelerated and curvilinear motion as composed. From Hegel's standpoint these are to be reversed. And in what he has to say on this point, "there is undoubtedly [as Professor Findlay has said of his concept of light] a flavor of relativity-physics."[19] Hegel says:

That movement in general is movement that returns upon

itself may be concluded from the determinations of particularity and individuality in a body, which give it an internal focus of separateness together with a tendency to join a center outside itself. These are the determinations underlying the concepts of centripetal and centrifugal force; these are then taken abstractly as independent vectors which, brought to bear accidentally on the same inert body, give it the empirically observed motion. Thus you have the transformation of physical reality into lines that really serve only to facilitate mathematical expression (*PN*, § 270, *Remark*, pp. 68-69).

Before the development of a "field" theory of gravitation in our own time, Hegel's application of the dialectic to analysis of physical phenomena had no counterpart in the mathematical thinking of physicists or astronomers. But now even children are familiar with a concept of geometric space suffused with a time that varies with each point of space, and with pictures of the circling centers of atomic particles. In terms less rigorous than Hegel's but not inconsistent with them, Einstein has written:

We have two realities: *matter and field* . . . . But what are the physical criterions distinguishing matter and field? Before we learned about the relativity theory we could have tried to answer the question in the following way: matter has mass, whereas field has not. Field represents energy, matter represents mass . . . . From the relativity theory we know that matter represents vast stores of energy and energy represents matter . . . . the division into matter and field is, after the recognition of the equivalence of mass and energy, something artificial and not clearly defined . . . . What impresses our senses as matter is really a great concentration of energy into a comparatively small space. We could regard matter as the regions in space where the field is extremely strong . . . . There would be no place, in our new physics for both field and matter, field [in Hegelian terms, "moving place"] being the only reality. This new view is suggested by the great achievements of field physics, by our success in expressing laws of electricity, magnetism, gravitation in the form of structure laws, and finally by the equivalence of mass and energy.[20]

We noted in passing that it was on the basis of the field theory that the Einsteinians rejected the Newtonian principles of rectilinear inertial and gravitational motion, adopting a four-dimensional geometry in place of Newton's calculus to express mathematically their conception of an astronomical order in which inertial and gravitational mass are identified and the fundamental motion is curvilinear. And, while we cannot dwell on it, we should at least mention here that, at one point in his larger *Science of Logic*, Hegel speaks of the possibility of developing a four-dimensional space-time geometry to do justice to Kepler's laws. Such a geometry, Hegel says, "might prove powerful with regard to free movement, wherein one (spatial) side is governed by geometrical determination (in Kepler's law s^3:t^2), and the other (temporal) side by arithmetical determination." The mathematics of that geometry, Hegel suggests, might serve to comprehend the elliptical motions of planets in their uncomposed naturality, in a manner consistent with the Hegelian concept of matter and gravity (*SL* [J/S] 1, p. 324).

VI

Hegel, as we said, places Kepler's laws of planetary motions at the apex of the grand pyramid of Mechanics. On that apex, looking beyond itself, mechanistic science transcends the abstract, and the transition is made into the sciences of qualified matter. Just below that apex Hegel sets the Galilean laws of falling bodies.

Of these laws, Hegel says: "they are immortal discoveries which redound to the greatest honour of the analysis of the Understanding." Still, in themselves they are not enough. "The next step," he continues, requires "their *proof* independently of empirical methods." And such proof, according to the Newtonians, has already been supplied — furnished, allegedly, "by mathematical mechanics itself, so that even a science based on empirically-ascertained facts is not satisfied with the merely empirically *pointing out* (demonstration)." What Einstein and Planck and their peers have undertaken to do mathematically, beyond the sphere of the empirically verifiable, Newton also attempted to do; but, according to Hegel, his method was inadequate. Newton's "proof" of Galileo's laws, Hegel says, takes for granted what those laws describe: the empirically established fact of the uniformly-accelerated motion of a freely falling body. Newton's analytical treatment of that given fact consists, Hegel says,

> in the conversion of the moments of the *mathematical* formula into *physical* forces, into an *accelerating* force imparting one and the same impulse in each unit of time, and into a force of *inertia* which perpetuates the (greater) velocity acquired in each moment of time — determinations utterly devoid of empirical sanction and equally inconsistent with the notion (*PN*, § 267, *Remark*, p. 5 7).

In other words, Hegel indicates that Newton treats a heavy, falling body, which *naturally* gravitates toward a center outside itself, as if it were an inert body responding inertly to an external thrust or force — as if it were *not* itself essentially gravitational. "The motion of falling," Hegel writes, "forms the transition and middle term between inert matter and matter whose Notion is absolutely realized, that is, absolutely free motion." Inert matter is the abstraction of a single material point, conceived as having no time in itself. It will remain at rest, or, if moved, will move inertially as if it were at rest, the two being equally timeless and therefore not really distinguishable as rest and motion. On the other hand, "heavy matter in the motion of falling," Hegel writes, is at least "partly adequate to its Notion, namely, through the sublation of the Many, as the effort of matter to reach one definite place, as center." The next step in the determination of matter is that "falling *toward*" a center must also be seen as "repulsion *from*" a center — which is what the so-called fixed stars manifest in their "constellational" pattern. Though in themselves they are matter orbiting about an energized center, with respect to one another, they are simply held in a rigid equilibrium of attraction and repulsion. The stars, says Hegel, "belong to the sphere of dead repulsion . . . . Matter, in filling space, erupts into an infinite plurality of [luminous] masses, but this, which may delight the eye, is only the first manifestation of matter."[21]

Not in abstraction as inert, not in falling, not in the rigid equilibrium of stellar repulsion and attraction, but only in the absolute mechanics of universal gravitation — in the grand mechanics of the sun and planets, moons and comets — is the true Notion of matter realized.

As in his discussion of the Newtonian calculus and the concept of force, so here in his discussion of Newton's concept of universal gravitation, Hegel praises before he criticizes. "Universal gravitation," he writes, "must be recognized as a profound thought in itself, though it is especially by reason of the quantitative determinations bound up with it that it has attracted attention and credit." So far from criticizing the concept, Hegel takes it up as an essential moment of his system, which (it should be recalled) is, like Aristotle's, a system of gravitation, in which all components, those of the *Logic* and *Philosophy of Mind* as well as those of the *Philosophy of Nature*, are drawn together and sustained by a single principle that operates on or in them like a magnet on metal filings; or, better, like the command of a commander-in-chief to all his armies — a command that exists apart, perfectly, in the commander-in-chief, but which is also present in all the purposeful activities of the army on all levels. Hegel is more concerned than Galileo or Newton were with the *cause* of such universal gravitation; but, as we suggested earlier, he does not deny the right of empirical science to study the filings in a magnet field (or the moving multiplicity of nature as a whole for that matter) as if there were no underlying, magnetic mover.

The trouble with Newton's use of the notion of universal gravity in his treatment of Kepler's laws is the same we identified in considering his treatment of Galileo's laws. In Newton's "law," Hegel notes, "there are included, as we have shown, two moments" whose unhappy fate it has been "to be regarded as separate *forces*, corresponding to the forces of attraction and repulsion, more precisely determined as *centripetal* and *centrifugal* forces. These forces are conceived as *acting* on bodies, and as accidentally and independently brought to bear upon a third something" — the material point of the pattern of motion under study. "In this way," Hegel goes on, "whatever deeper meaning might have been in the thought of universal gravitation is again lost"; and he predicts that science will not be able to "penetrate into the theory of absolute motion so long as the much-vaunted discoveries of *forces* prevails there" (*PN*, § 269, Z, p. 63).

To make clear the line of Hegel's argument, we should remark here on the great cultural paradox that presents Newton to us as the fulfillment of a scientific development that is usually traced to him from the labors of Copernicus through those of Galileo and Kepler. That development from its inception aimed at creating a single physics, made up of a single set of principles, to displace the old Aristotelian double physics with its double set of principles (celestial and curvilinear, terrestrial and rectilinear). Galileo, as any serious student of his works must know, opted for unity on the basis of curvilinear motion, so that all apparent rectilinear motion would be either an optical illusion (like that of falling bodies, where the rotational movement of the earth is shared by body and observer, and therefore canceled out) or a resultant compounded of naturally curvilinear motions. Copernicus had abolished the entire realm of rectilinear motion by assigning celestial motion to the terrestrial orb. And Kepler, too, while laboring to eliminate the complexities of circles on circles in the Ptolemaic and Copernican systems, was none the less a champion of curvilinear physics. From Copernicus to Galileo and Kepler, the triumphant claim of science had been, therefore, that the physical universe is indeed One, and all celestial. But then came Newton to bring the whole business down with a Baconian thud: The universe is physically One, as required, but — according to Newton's doctrine — it is all earth, all rectilinear — so that all curves are either optical illusions or resultants of compounded, naturally rectilinear motions.

From Hegel's point of view both positions, the Galilean as well as the Newtonian, were one-sided abstractions of the Understanding — like the contradictory corpuscular and wave theories of light. Against both (and again in an Einsteinian vein), Hegel argues that the proper scientific course is to distinguish and preserve qualitative differences. Inert, falling, rigidly-fixed stellar, and the freely-moving matter of the solar system must be comprehended together in their qualitative differences. Altogether, Hegel concludes after a long discussion of principles,

There exist three motions: (a) mechanical motion which is communicated from outside and is uniform; (b) the partly conditioned and partly free motion of falling, where the separation of a body is still posited contingently but where the motion already belongs to the gravity itself; and (c) the unconditionally free motion, the principal moments of which have been indicated, the great mechanics of the heavens. This motion is a curve. In it, the positing of a central body by the particular bodies, and conversely, the positing of these by the central body, occur simultaneously. The center has no meaning apart from the periphery nor the periphery apart from the center. This puts to rout those physical hypotheses which start now with the center and now with the particular bodies, sometimes making the former and sometimes the latter the original factor. Both points of view are necessary, but, taken separately, they are one-sided. The diremption into different bodies, and the positing of the moments of subjectivity, is a simple act, a free motion, nothing external like pressure and thrust (*PN*, § 269, *Remark Z*, p. 64).

That is a summation worthy of Einstein or Planck. On the lowest, abstract level are the inert, unorganized material entities: their motion comes to them from the outside, is uniform, according to the pressure or thrust, but essentially random. Focusing by abstraction on the inert particle, we cannot know what *forces* may act on it from unknown sources not yet posited; focusing on posited forces, we cannot know what particles, if any, will be acted upon, here or there. But on the level of heavy, organized matter, the motion is not only random or mechanical, but also determined, by its organization around a center of gravity, as a weighing down of one organized mass toward other organized masses. Higher still, however, is the gravitational relation manifested in the organized equilibrium of the solar system — and that, as Hegel says, has nothing random or forced about it. On that level, he writes,

we must not speak of forces. If we want to speak of force, then there is but one force, and its moments do not, as two forces, pull in different directions. The motion of the celestial bodies is not any such pulling this way and that but is free motion; they go on their way, as the ancients said, like blessed Gods (*PN*, § 269, *Remark, Z*, p. 65).

That last phrase, it should be noted, was cited by Sir Arthur Eddington in *The Nature of the Physical World* to epitomize his own doctrine of the planetary movements, in the light of the Einsteinian general theory of relativity.[22] Einstein himself has observed that in the "translation of the law of inertia into the language of the general theory of relativity" we get a new law of motion which is not rectilinear at all, being the law of "a system of total differential equations, the system characteristic of the geodetic line" which curves back on itself. Einstein says further: "In place of Newton's law of interaction by gravitation, we shall find the system of the simplest generally covariant differential equations which can be set up for the g_{uv} tensor. It is formed by equating to zero the once contracted Riemannian curvature tensor ($R_{uv} = 0$)" — which means that all apparently rectilinear motion is henceforth to be understood as the segment of a vast curve.[23]

But from Hegel's point of view, this Einsteinian development is also one-sided. All that Hegel says against Newton's "proofs" would apply also, *mutatis mutandis*, to the Einsteinian-Riemannian formulas, were they offered as "proofs." The philosophic virtue of the latter, in comparison with the *Principia*, is their philosophic modesty. The Einsteinians acknowledge that their mathematical analysis, which permits them to speak of non-empirical clocks slowing down non-empirically and about non-empirical rulers shrinking, proves nothing. But, if more were claimed for that analysis, it could hardly expect to fare any better at the hands of another Ernst Mach than Newton's analysis has fared.

In his fullest commentary of the relation of Newton's mechanics to Kepler's laws, Hegel makes the following points:

1. It is a mere mathematical translation that turns the A^3/T^2 of Kepler's Third Law into a product (A/T^2 x A^2) of which one of the factors is the ratio of Newton's law of gravitation.

2. Newton's "demonstration" that a body moving around the central body in subjection to the law of gravitation pursues a *conic section*, does not, by any logical means, show the necessity for its being an *ellipse*. And the worst is that

> the conditions which make the path of the body a *specific* conic section are, in the analytical formula, *constants*, and

their determination is referred to an *empirical* circumstance, namely, to a particular position of the body at a
certain point of time, and to the *fortuitous* strength of an
impulse which it is supposed to have received in the
beginning; so that the circumstance which determines the
curve to be an ellipse falls outside the formula that is
supposed to be proved, and no one has ever dreamt of
proving this circumstance (*PN*, § 270, *Remark*, p. 66).

3. Newton's law of the force of gravity has only an empirical,
not a philosophical basis. There is, for instance, no *reason* given
as to why the centrifugal force manages to "overcome" the
centripetal force just when the latter ought, by definition, to be
the greatest (perihelion), and then manages to let itself be
"overcome" in turn just when the centripetal force ought to be
weakest (aphelion). The explanation is that, the empirical fact
being known in advance (as summed up in Kepler's laws), the
analytical calculus is conducted accordingly. One of the most
thorough analyses of the relation between Kepler's achievement and Newton's, in recent times, is that of Pierre Duhem in
his *Aim and Structure of Physical Theory*. Pursuing a course of
reasoning that comprehends Hegel's arguments, Duhem concludes:

> The principle of universal gravity, very far from being
> derivable by generalization and induction from the ob-
> served laws of Kepler, formally contradicts these laws. If
> Newton's theory is correct, Kepler'"s laws are necessarily
> false.[24]

VII

Summing up, we may say that the great value of Hegel's
criticism of Newton's celestial mechanics consists in its emphasis on the error of scientific "reductionism" upon which that
mechanics was founded — an error that still plagues theoretical
physics, obstructing its advance, and making impossible a
philosophically-integrated Natural Science. The popularity of
Einstein has made this part of Hegel's criticism more acceptable now than ever before. Yet hardly less impressive than his
criticism of Newton is Hegel's sustained polemic against the
pre-Darwinian advocates of an evolutionary origin of species,
which he conducts on the same grounds. Like the Newtonians

in Mechanics, Hegel argues, so the evolutionists in biology are "reductionist." They "decompose" the self-generative cycle of a species into two constitutive elements or vectors, one of which is the characteristic actuality of the species just below it in the unbroken chain of organic forms, while the other is a sort of fortuitous thrust (chance mutation) acting at right angles, so to speak, and thus deflecting the old species out of its old generative cycle into a new one. Summing up the lesson of his entire Philosophy of Nature from this standpoint, Hegel says:

> Now, here is what is really involved in this conception. What, speaking generally, we call inorganic nature is thought of as having an independent existence, while the organic is attached to it in an external fashion, so that it is a mere matter of chance whether or not the organic finds the conditions of existence in what confronts it . . . . The question is this: Is that the true concept of the inorganic, and do living things represent what is dependent? [On the contrary] this is the true relation: man is not an accident added on to what is first; the organic is itself what is first . . . . Regarded in this fashion, the universe is not an aggregate of many accidents existing in a relation of indifference, but is a system endowed, in its essential character, with life.[25]

Here we break off. The wealth of materials in Hegel's *Philosophy of Nature* that have a bearing on the theme of this paper is inexhaustive. As I have observed elsewhere, no scholar who has seriously occupied himself with the history of the sciences of celestial and terrestrial mechanics, and of inorganic and organic physics, can read Hegel on these subjects without a sense of awe; for that history, from its Greek origins down to the nineteenth century, lives in his pages. Those of us who have for decades poured over the sources, guided by Pierre Duhern and his peers, can hardly fail to recognize in Hegel an easy mastery of much of the relevant materials. For me, at any rate, the ten volumes of Duhem's *Le système du monde* serve as an historical commentary on Hegel's *Mechanik* and *Physik* which, in turn, serve to make philosophical sense out of the long development of scientific thought traced by Duhem through all its evolutions, revolutions, and involutions, through all its errors and aberrations, exhuming once-famous doctrines from long oblivion, showing how the science of each epoch is nourished by the systems of past centuries, indicating how often the scientific certainties of one proud age are laughed at as absurdities in the next, while as often today's absurdities are seen forcing themselves forward into acceptance as the high truths of tomorrow.

Duhem's history of science displays a *dialectical* development, and Hegel's *Philosophy of Nature* compels us to recognize the continuous presence of that dialectical past in contemporary empirical science. It is thus a work of permanent scientific as well as philosophic value.

NOTES

1. The translations cited here from Hegel's *Lectures on the History of Philosophy* have sometimes been adapted in accordance with the German text (Michelet, 1840).

2. Inscription on statue in the ante-chapel of Trinity College, Cambridge.

3. John N. Findlay, "Hegel and the Philosophy of Physics," in *The Legacy of Hegel: Proceedings of the Marquette Hegel Symposium, 1970*, ed. J. J. O'Malley, et al. (The Hague, Nijhoff, 1973), p. 83.

4. The translations cited here from Hegel's *Logic* have sometimes been adapted in accordance with the German text (Henning, 1840, 1955).

5. The translations cited here from Hegel's *Philosophy of Nature* have sometimes been adapted in accordance with the German text (Pöggeler, 1959; Michelet, 1847).

6. J. N. Findlay, *Hegel: A Re-Examination* (New York, Humanities Press, 1958, 1976), pp. 167-8.

7. The translations from Hegel's *Phenomenology of Mind* have been adapted in accordance with the German text (Hoffmeister, 1949).

8. Louis de Broglie, *Physics and Microphysics* (New York, Grosset and Dunlap, 1966), pp. 238-9.

9. *Ibid.*, p. 75.

10. See V. Cioffari, *Fortune and Fate from Democritus to St. Thomas Aquinas* (New York, 1935), *passim*, for a review of the commentary on Dante's Heisenbergian line (*Inf.*, IV, 136) epitomizing the doctrine of Democritus.

11. H. D. Anthony, *Sir Isaac Newton* (New York, Collier, 1961), pp. 140-141.

12. Tobias Dantzig, *Number: The Language of Science* (New York, Macmillan, 1954), pp. 234, 335.

13. Bertrand Russell, *The Scientific Outlook* (New York, Norton, 1932), p. 264.

14. Albert Einstein, *Out of My Later Years* (New York, Philosophical Library, 1950), P. 110.

15. Einstein, *Later Years*, p. 97.

16. Albert Einstein, *The World As I See It* (New York, Covici Friede, 1934), p. 57.

17. Bertrand Russell, "Introduction," in A. V. Vasiliev, *Space, Time, and Motion* (New York, Knopf, 1924), pp. xv-xvi.

18. Einstein, *Later Years*, p. 69.

19. Findlay, *Hegel*, p. 279.

20. Albert Einstein and L. Infeld, *The Evolution of Physics* (New York, Simon and Schuster, 1961), pp. 256-58.

21. *PN*, § 267, *Z*, p. 59; § 268, *Remark, Z*, pp. 61, 62.

22. Arthur Eddington, *The Nature of the Physical World* (Cambridge, Cambridge University Press, 1948), p. 147.

23. Einstein, *Later Years*, p. 80.

24. Pierre Duhem, *Aim and Structure of Physical Theory* (Princeton, Princeton University Press, 1954), p. 193.

25. *Hegel's Lectures on the Philosophy of Religion*, trans. E. B. Spiers and J. B. Sanderson (New York, Humanities Press, 1962), Vol. III, pp. 340-341.

TRUTH IN THE PHILOSOPHICAL SCIENCES OF SOCIETY, POLITICS, AND HISTORY

To the question "what is truth?" Hegel replies (with Socrates and Aristotle and most other systematic thinkers of the West) that it is a ratio. He holds that it is not simple but composed, and that, in the pursuit of knowledge, it comes not among the first things, but among the last. More precisely: truth for Hegel is neither a subjective idea in itself nor an objective thing in itself, neither a universal abstractly conceived nor a particular empirically apprehended, but an adequate linking-together in reason *(ratio)* of thought and thing, universal and particular.

The entire Hegelian system as we have it in the *Encyclopedia of the Philosophical Sciences* is unmistakably an analytical exposition of truth as a ratio. Its three major parts develop the truth of idea as *idea in itself* (Science of Logic), the truth of thing as *idea in its otherness* (Philosophy of Nature), and the truth of the adequation of idea and thing as *idea comes back to itself out of that otherness* (Philosophy of Mind).[1] Each of the parts, in turn, mirrors the structure of the whole; and so do the parts of the parts, down to the simplest constituent propositions, for every proposition or sentence capable of expressing even a modicum of truth is, according to Hegel, a linking together of subject and predicate, of particular and universal, of thought and thing.

The sciences that especially concern us here — the social, political, and historical sciences — are parts of a part of the Philosophy of Mind which, like the other two major divisions and the system as a whole, presents its contents first as idea

[First appeared in *Beyond Epistemology*. Ed. Frederick G. Weiss (Martinus Nijhoff. The Hague, 1974). Present text comes from *The Political Thought of G. W. F. Hegel* (Griffon House Publ., NY, 1978).]

(Subjective Mind), then as thing (Objective Mind), and finally as an adequate linking-together of idea and thing (Absolute Mind). The conclusion is hardly to be avoided, therefore, that in the least parts as well as in the whole of his system, Hegel quite deliberately sustains the classical definition of truth which, in its Latin form, survived into modern times as a copmmonplace of medieval philosophy: of truth which, in its Latin form, survived into modern times as a commonplace of medieval philosophy: *veritas est adaequatio intellectus et res.*

Immanuel Kant, it is important to recall, had rejected that traditional notion of truth. Or rather, in his celebrated *Critique of Pure Reason*, he had begun by granting it, but only to dismiss it at once as something trivial. And Hegel criticizes him for it, particularly in the *Science of Logic* (Johnston and Struthers, Vol. II, p. 227), where he defends the medieval commonplace as "a definition which is of great, and even of the highest value." Against Kant, he there argues that if the old notion of truth

> is recalled in connection with the fundamental assertion of transcendental idealism, namely, that cognition by means of reason is not capable of apprehending the things-in-themselves, and that reality lies utterly outside the Notion [Begriff], then it is clear immediately that such a reason, which cannot establish a correspondence between itself and its object (the things-in-themselves), is an untrue idea; and equally untrue are things-in-themselves which do not correspond with the Notion of reason, a Notion which does not correspond with reality, and a reality which does not correspond with the Notion. If Kant had kept the idea of an intuitive understanding close to this definition of truth, then he would not have treated this idea, which expresses the required correspondence, as a figment of thought, but as truth.[2]

Because he adhered to an untrue idea of what truth is, Kant was foredoomed to fail in his attempt to assess the capacity of human reason to arrive at truth. Hegel characterized as a "mark of the diseased state of the age," the general adoption of the "despairing creed that our knowledge is only subjective." The natural belief of ordinary men in all ages gives the lie to such a view. Rightly understood, truth is objective; rightly understood, thought coincides with thing. Hegel cites Dante's insistence (*Paradiso* iv, 124-30) that the human intellect is certainly capable of attaining truth, and that, indeed, nothing short of truth can satisfy it. The business of philosophy, he concludes against Kant, is precisely to confirm the old belief that it is "the characteristic right of mind to know the truth" and thus "to bring into explicit consciousness what the world in all ages had believed."[3]

In his *Science of Logic*, Hegel refers us specifically to his *Phenomenology of Mind* for a detailed analysis of the limitations of Kant's approach to the question of knowledge. Kant's basic defect, according to Hegel, was that he "neither considered nor investigated the truly speculative ideas of the older philosophers about the notion of Mind," taking his departure in this area exclusively from Hume's skeptical treatment of the rationalist metaphysical doctrine of the mind. In his *Phenomenology* of 1806, Hegel assumed that same vantage point, accepting the Humean and Kantian formulations of the problem of truth; but then he went on to rectify the Kantian errors, giving us a vivid account of the riot of thought through which the mind, driven by doubt, must pass in rising to the level of "insight into what knowing really is."[4]

Of the *Phenomenology of Mind* it has been correctly said that it is the germination of a living seed which absorbs and consumes its environment in preparation for its own systematic growth, which is yet to come. In the process of getting to know what knowing really is, the mind initially takes for granted "the existence of the concrete formations of consciousness, such as individual and social morality, art and religion." But to arrive at its goal, it must free itself of all that it has received or absorbed uncritically. Thus — Hegel explains in retrospect — the development of consciousness traced in the *Phenomenology* involves a sort of cultural unraveling "of the matter or of the objects properly discussed in the special branches of philosophy." What belongs in the ratio of truth of the complete system is "prematurely dragged into the introduction," and that makes the exposition intricate.[5]

Practically all the distinguishable sciences of the three parts of the *Encyclopedia* make an appearance of sorts in *the Phenom-*

enology of Mind – but not in the form of truth. Their vast cultural wealth is poured into the consciousness of the individual mind to nourish it the way food nourishes the individual body. Just as the body in its growth from the fertilized egg recapitulates the great chain of animal forms that are implicit in its nature, so the mind of the individual recapitulates the experience of the family, civil society, state, and period of history into which it is born. Through self-criticism, conscious Mind, which is initially a captive of its cultural environment, must emerge, finally, as Free Mind, ready for the logic of truth in its systematic form. There is no avoiding that preliminary illogical, almost riotous confrontation with the fullness of human culture, however; for a large part of the task of preparing the mind for genuinely philosophic science is precisely to unravel the complexities of existential experience, and thus "to show how the questions men have usually raised about the nature of Knowledge, Faith, and the like – questions which they imagine to have no connection with abstract thoughts – are really reducible to the simple categories which first get cleared up in Logic."[6]

The *Phenomenology of Mind* is not to be confounded, therefore, with the system of the *Encyclopedia*. The former is an existential treatise in the modern sense. Whoever takes up the question of knowledge as posed by Hume and Kant and their disciples in our own time is certain to find himself at one turn or another of the path of the *Phenomenology* – which is a preparatory work of Conscious Mind. The *Encyclopedia*, on the other hand, is the consummate work of Free Mind. It presupposes that Conscious Mind has become Free through insight into what philosophic truth really is: an *adaequatio intellectus et res*, developed into a universal whole, each part of which consists of a ratio of ratios, analyzable downward in its rational necessity to the least meaningful linking-together of the basic parts of speech.

I. The Hegelian-Aristotelian Perspective

Because the truth of the Hegelian system is the whole in its organic articulation, there can be no specially favored begin-

ning, no basic introductory science so completely true in itself
that it must stand first. The notion of a beginning in philosophy
has meaning, Hegel writes, "only in relation to a person who
proposes to commence the study, and not in relation to science
as science."[7] The system in its truth is a great "circle of
education" without beginning and without end — a circle that
freely turns upon itself, carrying its constituent sciences around
with it, each in its distinctive place, fixed there by a rational
necessity, each offering a distinctive approach (neither more
nor less valid than any other) to the truth of the whole.

Only Free Mind can know the whole truth in its freedom;
yet, paradoxically, it is only through knowledge of the truth that
Mind is made free. As often as he discusses what true knowledge is and what results from reason's absorption in it, Hegel
confronts this paradox. Repeatedly, he cites the Biblical admonition: "You shall know the truth and the truth shall make you
free." And almost invariably, he couples with it Spinoza's
paradoxical formulation of the ancient truth that freedom is
"insight into necessity." Hegel thus sums it all up in the opening
pages of his *Encyclopedia*:

> Truth is only possible as a universe or totality of thought:
> and the freedom of the whole, as well as the necessity of
> the several sub-divisions, which it implies, are only pos-
> sible when these are discriminated and defined. . . . Each
> of the parts of philosophy is a philosophical whole, a circle
> rounded and complete in itself. In each of these parts,
> however, the philosophical idea is found in a particular
> specificity or medium. The single circle, because it is a
> real totality, bursts through the limits imposed by its
> special medium, and gives rise to a wider circle. The whole
> of philosophy in this way resembles a circle of circles. The
> idea appears in each circle, but, at the same time, the
> whole idea is constituted by the system of these particular
> phases, and each is a necessary member of the organiza-
> tion.[8]

Like the satellite epicycles of the ancient and modern
astronomies, each science of the system of sciences has a
separate center of its own and a relatively independent progression of its own around that center. The ultimate moving

principle is that of the whole; but that is by no means an exclusive or restrictive principle. On the contrary, as Hegel writes, "genuine philosophy makes it a principle to sustain every particular principle."[9] Indeed, because its organic connection with the whole leaves it relatively free in its self-centered progression, every one of the specialized disciplines of the *Encyclopedia* has a tendency to "burst through" the limits of its special medium and extend its sway at the expense of its neighbors. The science of history, for instance, has always had an insatiable appetite for devouring neighboring disciplines, claiming that its sweep ought to encompass all that is humanly known or knowable. Similar claims have been advanced more recently by political science, sociology, economics, psychology, anthropology, and even bio-chemistry. Obviously it is only the systematic discipline of the whole, however arrived at, that can by rational necessity keep the constituent disciplines in place.

The organic conception here is far removed from the Kantian critical perspective. The premises of transcendental idealism with respect to the nature of mind and truth are abandoned in favor of the dialectical realism of Aristotle. Of this there can be no serious doubt. The staggeringly humble tribute to Aristotelian thought in the concluding lines of the *Encyclopedia*, where Hegel expresses his own loftiest thought in Aristotle's Greek, is well known. What needs to be stressed here is that the Hegelian system in its entirety — as distinct from the introductory *Phenomenology of Mind* – is essentially Aristotelian from its immediate approach to the question of knowledge to its full exposition of truth as Absolute Mind.

In his *History of Philosophy,* Hegel credits Aristotle with the initial logical insight into what knowing really is, praising him especially for the clarity of his distinctions in remarking how, even in its most abstract expression, truth is not something simple but a ratio. Aristotle had emphasized in his *De Interpretatione* (which is essentially a grammar of logic), that subjects and predicates and linking verbs, "as isolated terms, are not yet either true or false," for "truth and falsity imply combination and separation." Of the process of combination in thought, Aristotle had said further (in a very "Hegelian" vein): "Neither are 'to be' and 'not to be' and the participle 'being' significant of any truth, unless something is added, but imply a copulation, of which we cannot form a conception apart from the things coupled."[10]

It is on the insight so abstractly expressed here that Hegel constructs his grand "cycle of education." Ultimately, the "things coupled" in his *Encyclopedia* are all the constituent truths of all traditional disciplines of scientific knowledge, ranging from the abstract sciences of logic and mathematics, through the mechanical, physical, and organic branches of natural science, to the cycle of man-centered studies that culminate in the sciences of artistic making, religious behavior, and God-centered metaphysical speculation. Just as in the mathematical sciences, the goal is a formulation of truth as a set of mathematical ratios, so in the all-comprehending system of sciences, the goal is an all-comprehending philosophical ratio of ratios. Though he did not attain it himself, Aristotle had projected just such a goal for philosophy; and to realize it has been, according to Hegel, the proper task of philosophy ever since. Hegel is thus characterizing his own philosophic labors of a lifetime, as well as the limits of Aristotle's achievement, when he remarks in the *History of Philosophy* that

> the whole of Aristotle's philosophy really requires recasting, so that all his determinations can be brought into a necessary systematic whole — not a systematic whole which is correctly divided into its parts, and in which no part is forgotten, all being set forth in their proper order, but one in which there is one living organic whole, in which each part is held to be a part, and the whole alone is true. Aristotle, in the *Politics*, for instance, often gives expression to this truth.[11]

That his *Encyclopedia* is offered as a recasting of the Aristotelian philosophy, Hegel himself assures us quite explicitly in many places and perhaps most explicitly in his introduction to *the Philosophy of Mind*. There he says that "the books of Aristotle's *De Anima*, along with his discussions on the *psyche*'s special aspects and states [discussions pursued in *the Nichomachean Ethics, Politics, Rhetoric, Poetics, Metaphysics*, and related writings] are still by far the most admirable, perhaps even the sole work of philosophical value on this topic." And his conclusion is that "the main aim of a philosophy of mind can only be to reintroduce unity of idea and principle into the theory of mind, and so reinterpret the lesson of those Aristotelian books.[12]

Following Aristotle's lead, Hegel distinguishes three developmental phases, or functional aspects of Mind, to which the designations Subjective, Objective, and Absolute correspond. In its subjective development, Mind acts to rationalize, or assimilate to its own nature, an animal actuality, which is only potentially human. The Aristotelian leads for this phase are clearly indicated in the *De Anima*. In its objective development (and here Hegel follows closely the leads of the *Ethics* and *Politics*), Mind shapes for itself the rational, or *mindful* realities of family-life, civil society, and states, whose coming into being and passing away constitutes the course of history. Finally, in its absolute development (corresponding to the sphere of Aristotle's *Metaphysics*, Book X of the *Ethics*, the *Poetics*, and related passages of the *De Anima*), Mind transcends objective history, arresting time in the aesthesis of inspired art, overcoming mortality in the ecstasis of revealed religion, and assimilating itself to God (*nóesis noéseos nóesis* – thought thinking thought) in the experience of *sophia*, where the highest intuitive and discursive reasoning — the *nous* and *epistêmê* of Aristotle — are one.

It is important to keep in mind the essentially Aristotelian perspective in all of this, so that we may guard ourselves against the error of students of Hegel who don't know Aristotle and who insist on approaching the Hegelian system through Marx or contemporary existentialism: the error of imagining that Hegel is straying off on some needlessly obscure, tortuous new path of epistemological speculation, spurred on by his apparent mania for triads, at precisely those turns of his exposition where he means to be most respectful of the Aristotelian tradition.

II. *The Sciences of Objective Mind*

Within this broad Aristotelian design, Hegel distinguishes almost all the "disciplines" that have traditionally enjoyed academic status as sciences of human nature and conduct, and several that have acquired such status since his time. For most of the minor sciences, the definitions are necessarily brief in the *Encyclopedia*, in keeping with its character as a handbook; but many cursorily treated there are considered at length, with particularized discussions of methods of study and scientific validation, in the *Philosophy of Right, Philosophy of History, Philosophy of Fine Art, Philosophy of Religion,* and *History of Philosophy,* all of which are elaborations of the Philosophy of Mind.

From the standpoint of classification in the social or behavioral sciences, Hegel's broad distinctions of Subjective, Objective, and Absolute are very instructive. In his day they might have served, as he said, to re-introduce "unity of idea and principle" to a field where speculative chaos reigned. And one ventures to suggest that a general acceptance of them now might greatly facilitate the task of the many hard-pressed academicians who are today charged with regulating the seemingly endless, overlapping, proliferation of specialized disciplines in the field.

The sciences of society, politics, and history, strictly defined, make up the cycle of Objective Mind. But as they presuppose the "results" of the preceding sciences of Subjective Mind, it will be necessary, by way of introduction, to review cursorily the matter and form of those sciences.

Under Subjective Mind, Hegel distinguishes the sciences of anthropology, phenomenology, and psychology — all of which today qualify, on some one or another of the modern listings, as social or behavioral sciences. Anthropology is defined, in accordance with its etymological meaning, as the most general of the sciences of man. It focuses on the least common denominator of manhood: on the very *idea* – as Plato would say – of *anthropos;* or rather, in Aristotelian terms, on the characteristic act of manhood, through which the physical, self-nutritional, sentient, passionate, and emotional activities of an animal existence are "humanized."

The systematic science of phenomenology (not to be confounded with the "voyage of discovery" which prepares the mind for true science), presupposes the humanizing activities studied in anthropology. On its higher level, phenomenology traces the activities of Mind that transform animal awareness into thoroughly human consciousness, then into self-consciousness, and finally into that doubling, or "mirroring" of self-consciousness which Hegel calls Reason *(Vernunft)* in full potency, as distinguished from the mere Understanding *(Verstand)* of consciousness and self-consciousness.

Psychology takes up the activity of Subjective Mind where phenomenology leaves off, tracing its development, through self-analysis, on the levels of theoretic and practical reasons, to the level of potentially productive, or *willful* reason. As in the Freudian psychological self-analysis, so in the Hegelian, what emerges is the perfection of Subjective Mind as "Free Mind" — as mind become master in its own house (to use the renowned Freudian expression) and able, therefore, to overcome its subjectivity.

Anthropology, phenomenology, and psychology, thus defined, are introspective sciences of man. There are no objective "phenomena," no "evidences of things seen" to be "saved" by them. For validation of their measure of truth, scientists specializing in such fields must rely ultimately on subjective insight. In this respect, their relationship to the sciences of Objective Mind that immediately follow parallels the relationship of the Science of Logic to the Philosophy of Nature in the system as a whole.

Like the sciences of mechanics, physics, and organics that make up the Philosophy of Nature, the sciences of Objective Mind are objective in the strict sense. In both spheres the method of scientific study is therefore essentially the same. There are, on the one hand, external phenomena which must be taken for granted as empirically given, and, on the other, principles of thought, or organizing ideas, elaborated as hypotheses, that are not empirically given. The external phenomena are the "things," the hypotheses are the "thoughts" that must be adequately "linked-together," in reason, if the sciences of Objective Mind or those of the Philosophy of Nature are to have a valid ratio of truth in them.

It is, indeed, only the specific content or subject matter of the sciences of Objective Mind that distinguishes them from the natural sciences, in Hegel's scheme. Instead of testing the adequacy of their generalizing notions or hypotheses through direct observation of the characteristic motions of empirical phenomena on the level of mechanics, physics, and organics, they do so through direct observation of the phenomena of man, as he actually lives now, or has lived in the past, in family, civic, and political association with his fellows.

Again and again, in the *Philosophy of Right* and the *Philosophy of History* (which together cover the same ground as the section on Objective Mind in the *Encyclopedia*), Hegel reminds us of the obvious fact that the evidences of man's present and past existence as a social being have an objective authority for our consciousness at least as compelling as that of the "sun, moon, mountains, rivers, and the natural objects of all kinds by which we are surrounded."[13] Indeed, he insists that, since the aim of empirical science is to trace the operation of rational laws in the phenomena under study, the social sciences are specially favored in this respect. For it is the rational activity of man — the practical and productive reasoning of his Free Mind — that fashions the human institutions and institutional histories that are the proper objects of study in the theoretical sciences of Objective Mind. As Hegel explains in the Preface to the *Philosophy of Right*:

> So far as nature is concerned, people grant that it is nature as it is which philosophy has to bring within its ken . . . that nature is inherently rational, and that what knowledge has to investigate and grasp in concepts is this actual reason present in it; not the formations and accidents evident to the superficial observer, but nature's eternal harmony, in the sense of the law and essence immanent within it. The ethical world, on the other hand [the world of family, civil society, statehood, and history], is somehow not authorized (according to the bias of some) to enjoy the good fortune which springs from the fact that it is reason itself which has achieved power and mastery within that element and which maintains and has its home there. [While nature is assumed to be immanently rational] the universe of objective mind is thus supposed rather to be left to the mercy of chance and caprice, to be God-forsaken; and the result, from this standpoint, is that if the ethical world is

Godless, truth lies outside it, and at the same time, since even so reason is supposed to be in it as well, truth becomes nothing but a problem.[14]

Hegel very emphatically denies the view that the natural sciences — and particularly the mathematical sciences of celestial and terrestrial mechanics (astronomy and physics) — ought to be regarded as the sciences *par excellence* upon which all other sciences, and particularly the social sciences, ought eventually to pattern themselves. His arguments against such an assumption illuminate the seeming paradox of the fact that, when Sir Francis Bacon proclaimed a new beginning for natural science in the 17th century, he took his cue (as he acknowledges) from the founder of modern political science: Machiavelli. What Machiavelli had so successfully done with the science of politics, Bacon argued, ought to serve as a model for what obviously needed to be done for the advancement of a long-stagnated natural science. With profound insight into the making of states, Machiavelli had undertaken to trace the *laws of statecraft* as statecraft really *is*, rather than as, according to the moralists, it *ought to be*.

How can natural scientists apply Machiavelli's example in their field? How can the method of Machiavelli's political science be made to stand as a model for chemists and physicists? Bacon's brilliant suggestion is that chemists and physicists should hereafter apply themselves to the study of empirical phenomena that are, like states, man-made — phenomena to be produced by a *craft* which is of the same order, though on a much more primitive level, as Machiavelli's *statecraft*. That Baconian *craft*, through which natural science might hope to match Machiavelli's political science, is, of course, the craft of experimentation. Needless to say, scientific experiments as Bacon conceived them are man-made. And precisely because they are man-made, with human reason built into their minutest detail, study of them to ascertain their laws is much more rewarding than the study of empirical phenomena that are not man-made.

Experimental science — the glory of the modern world — is thus, from Hegel's point of view, a very specialized part of the social or behavioral sciences: a specialized part that is accurate in its results, from a logical mathematical point of view, to the measure of its relative emptiness. An experiment with a lever in a laboratory, for instance, is man-made in the same sense that the new state of Israel is man-made. And it is no doubt true that a Ben Gurion, who has actually experimented with the making of states, is probably much better able to comprehend the truth of the science of politics as Hegel expounds it, than the average experimenter with levers, who fails to recognize the *social* nature of experimental science, is able to comprehend the truth of the science of mechanics.

Giambattista Vico had of course made the same point in his *Scienza Nuova*. What mankind has itself made men can know better than they can know the natural things that God, or chance, has made. And this is true for Hegel as for Vico, ranging upward from the least artifacts of primitive peoples through all the utilitarian products that serve human ends in civil society, to all the things of fine art, religious worship, and high philosophy that constitute the grandeur of history's great states, empires. and world civilizations.

The same Free Mind of man that "makes" a controlled experiment in a physics laboratory has, needless to say, also made the laboratory itself, as well as the "Advanced Institute" of higher learning that envelops it, and the surrounding college town, civil society, and political order apart from which the pursuit of science is an impossibility. Free Mind is, as we noted, the perfection of Subjective Mind, or Mind which, through psychological self-analysis, has overcome its subjectivity and is able, therefore, to objectify, or make actual, what it implicitly is.

Free Mind first manifests itself objectively, writes Hegel, through the assertion of a universal, willful claim on all it surveys; and the disciplined study of that characteristic act of Mind as Will is distinguished by Hegel as the science of Abstract Right, or theory of Law — first of the philosophical sciences of Objective Mind. In asserting its willful claim on everything, Free Mind acts as if it knew no bounds — as if it had actually heard the God of *Genesis* say to it: "Be fruitful, and multiply, and replenish the earth, and subdue it: and have dominion over the fish of the sea, and over the fowl of the air, and over every living thing that moveth upon the earth." But, as in *Genesis,* so in the Hegelian system, Free Mind, in solitary possession of but a single body, finds that it cannot go it alone objectively. In attempting to exercise its claim on all things, it is again and again frustrated and forced, eventually, to seek a compensatory satisfaction in self-righteous, moral alienation from the objective world. The science that focuses on this retreat of Free Mind back into itself is the science of Morality.

Together, Hegel's sciences of Abstract Right and Morality give us an updated recasting of Aristotle's *Ethics,* the conclusion of which is that the individual as person and moral subject cannot realize his individual ends in isolation. Only lately have Right and Morality come into their own as objects of lively if not yet disciplined study in the modern curriculum of the social sciences. But in America, at any rate, they have come in with a vengeance, on the heels of the Negro Civil-Rights movement. It is a matter of newspaper headlines that, after years of fiercely asserting an abstract personal right, the American Negro has experienced an objective frustration that has constrained him to seek a compensatory satisfaction in self-righteous, moral alienation from the objective world. Negroes and the social scientists who study their moral frustration have had to learn the hard way — which is to say, empirically — the ancient truth that Free Mind, whether in a black or a white body, has a better chance of realizing its ends in the objective world if it enters it as a family member.

The "results" of Free Mind's experience in Abstract Right and Morality are the notions of right and wrong, of good and bad, of what ought and ought not to be. And these results are the presuppositions of the further development of the sciences of Objective Mind which are outlined in the *Encyclopedia* and elaborated in the *Philosophy of Right* under the headings: Family, Civil Society, and State.

These sciences, which are "social" in the strict sense, provide us with what is unquestionably an updated, Aristotelian *Politics.* Man, Aristotle had tried to demonstrate, is by nature — not by convention — a political animal. And his capacity to speak is perhaps the most distinctive sign of his political nature, in that, while mere voice (such as many animals possess) suffices to indicate pain and pleasure, it requires speech to "indicate the advantageous and the harmful, and therefore also the right and wrong."[15] In words that express Hegel's view as well, Aristotle had thus marked, in this respect, the transition from ethics to politics:

> For it is the special property of man in distinction from the other animals that he alone has perception of good and bad and right and wrong and the other moral qualities, and it is partnership in these things that makes up the family-unit or household and the state.[16]

As in Aristotle, so in Hegel, politics in its broadest sense, as distinguished from the personal ethics and subjective morality of the individual, begins with *economia* – the science of the family unit. From a cultural standpoint, it is regrettable that modern derivatives of the ancient Greek word have not retained its original significance. Our English word "economics," for instance, hardly serves any longer to give us an adequate idea of the original thing. A new content has crept in, gradually crowding out the old, which is now left to fend for itself academically, without benefit of a scientific-sounding name. To identify precisely what he means, and thus avoid cultural confusion, Hegel uses the prosaic designation "die Familie"; but it should be noted that in so doing he is, in effect, following the example of the learned 15th century humanist Leon Battist' Alberti who, in reviving the ancient study of *economia* as Xenophon had perfected it, called his book simply *Della Famiglia.*

In Marriage — first of the three moments of family life distinguished by Hegel — the "I-thou" personal relationship of man and woman, drawn together to perpetuate the species, becomes a "we" relationship with a distinct personality of its own. That "we" is strengthened in its unity through external embodiment in a Family Capital — second moment of the notion — which is not "yours and mine" but "ours." But full objectivization of the bond that unites husband and wife comes only with realization of the third moment — the generation and rearing of children, "in whom the parents can see objectified the entirety of their union . . . . For, while in their goods, their unity is embodied only in an external thing, in their children it is embodied in a spiritual one in which the parents are loved and which they love."[17]

Under the rearing of children, Hegel gives us a brief but very suggestive "science of education" which is further developed in the discussions on Civil Society and the State. As a function of the family, education has a negative as well as a positive aspect. On the positive side, its object is to instill ethical feelings that will enable the child "to live its early years in love, trust, and obedience"; whereas, on its negative side, its object is to raise the child out of its original state of dependence "to self-subsistence and freedom of personality and so to the level where he has the power to leave the natural unity of the family." Once educated to freedom of personality (within the "we" experience of family life), the child claims recognition as a person in his own right, and the unity of the original family is on the point of dissolution – an inevitable dissolution that becomes total in the death of the parents.[18]

Dissolution of the family, which may be gradual, eventually leaves the surviving members on their own in the network of "I-thou" relationships that make up Civil Society. They move into Civil Society as individuals, but, if they are products of well-ordered families, they already have in themselves the "we" experience of true community. They are ready in themselves, in other words, for the organic partnership of marriage and the formation of another family unit, at the same time that, as individuals, they are competing and cooperating with their fellows for the satisfaction of their personal needs. The experience of voluntary cooperation in Civil Society coupled with experience of family membership prepares human beings, finally, for fully-conscious participation in the "we" relationship of political community, upon which the objective subsistence of family life and the civil relationships ultimately depend.

In a famous *"addition"* to the *Philosophy of Right,* Hegel observes that Civil Society *(bürgerliche Gesellschaft)* is a distinctly modern development, in the sense that "only in the modern world have all the various elements or determinations of the idea received their due."[19] In this connection, Hegel notes that the ancient Greeks lived their lives almost exclusively as family members and as citizens or dependent subjects of a tightly regulated political community. Public law penetrated deeply into the privacy of family life, leaving virtually no middle ground for a "private" individual or associational existence independent of the characteristic ties of family and state. Separation from the former resulted almost simultaneously in full absorption by the latter. From the point of view of Greek social science, therefore, economics (in its original sense) and the science of politics exhausted the field.

Only in the modern world have family and state come to be separated, objectively, by a vast middle-ground where many human beings born out of wedlock, or separated from their parents in childhood, can manage to live their entire lives without conscious experience of membership in the social orders of family or state. For the ancients, that middle ground was but an abstract, psychological moment of social alienation; whereas, in the modern world, it is precisely there that Objective Mind has fashioned for itself the complex life of Civil Society, which has, in turn, called into being an entire cycle of new sciences whose focus of interest is *more* than economic, in the ancient Greek sense, at the same time that it is also always *less* than political. Defining the limits of this distinctive associational achievement of the modern world, Hegel writes:

> Civil Society is the realm of difference that separates family and state, mediating between them, even though in point of time its formation comes after the state, which its own objective existence presupposes as a necessary condition. If the state is represented to us as a unity of persons which is only a contractual arrangement or partnership, then what is really meant is only civil society. Unfortunately, many modern social theoreticians appear at present to be incapable of conceiving any other theory of the state than this.[20]

Cautioning readers against the tendency of his contemporaries to confound state and civil society, Hegel repeatedly stresses that the state no less than the family is an organic union; that its citizens as citizens are not in an 'I-thou" relationship with one another, but, rather, like family members, they constitute a substantive "we" that they tend to love and value more than they value their individual existences. In Civil Society, on the contrary,

> each member is his own end and everything else is nothing to him. And yet, because each must of necessity enter into relationships with others to realize his ends, those others, who would otherwise be objects of indifference, become indispensable means. Through this utilitarian linkage with others, each member's particularized pursuit of a particular end is universalized, its satisfaction being attainable only in the simultaneous attainment of satisfaction by others. Because the particularity of interests that constitute it are thus inevitably universalized, the whole sphere of civil society becomes an arena of mediation of opposites, where there is free play for every idiosyncrasy, every talent, every accident of birth and fortune, and where waves of every passion gush forth, regulated only by reason (Objective Mind) glinting through them.[21]

Already in Hegel's time, the new science that traced the characteristic acts of mind glinting through the intricate web of human relations in civil society bore the compound name of Political Economy [Staatsökonomie] — suggesting a fusing, or even a confusing, of the traditional sciences of family and state. Of Political Economy, Hegel writes:

> This is one of the sciences which have arisen out of the conditions of the modern world. Its development affords the interesting spectacle (as in Smith, Say, and Ricardo) of thought working upon the endless mass of details which confront it at the outset and extracting therefrom the simple principles of the thing, the Understanding effective in the thing and directing it. It is gratifying to find, in the sphere of needs, this show of rationality lying in the thing and working itself out there; but if we look at it from the opposite point of view, this is the sphere in which the Understanding with its subjective aims and moral fancies vents its discontents and moral frustration.[22]

It is in the competitive self-seeking of individuals in civil society that the personal moral frustration considered in depth by Hegel under the heading Morality actually takes place — a frustration that is relieved, in fact, only through entry into marriage or through the conscious assumption of rights and responsibilities of citizenship. But, while moral frustration is

inextricably woven into the fabric of Civil Society, the science
that studies the complex web of that fabric is nevertheless, in
Hegel's judgment,

> a science that does honor to thought because it finds laws
> in a mass of accidents. It is fascinating to see how action
> is linked with action, and how such linked actions fall into
> groups, influence others, and are helped or hindered by
> others . . . . It has a parallel in the science of planetary
> motions which, while always appearing complex and
> irregular to the eye, are nevertheless governed by
> ascertainable laws.[23]

Hegel expresses great admiration for the achievements of
specialists in the "dismal" new science and is not surprised that,
absorbed as they are in the excitements of studying a social
creation of their own era, many of them should be inclined to
ignore the social realities of family life and state that had
absorbed the entire interest of their predecessors since the
days of Plato and Aristotle. His concern is not to belittle the new
discipline, but rather to guard its legitimacy, together with that
of the traditional social sciences, by carefully distinguishing the
characteristic acts of human association that are the primary
object of study in each.

The paragraphs of Hegel's *Staatsökonomie* in which he
outlines the "laws" of the internal dialectic of Civil Society have
had a tremendous historical impact. His analysis of how that
dialectic results in the formation of social classes and special
interest groups that compete to universalize their interests
fascinated Karl Marx. And, at the point where Marx's powers
of concentration apparently failed — which is to say, where the
dialectic of civil society results in the formation of "service"
institutions for the regulation of civil rights, the "policing" of
civil disorders, and for the ultimate resolution of internal
conflicts through external expansion — it was Lenin's turn to
be fascinated.

Surely worthy of comparison with the scientific achievement of a Kepler or Newton is the economy of thought with
which Hegel was able to formulate the "law of social dialectic"
in three pages of his *Philosophy of Right*. First he reviews the
lessons of the English *laissez-faire* economists, noting how the

untrammeled internal development of civil society results in an over-production of industrial goods and population, and thus in large-scale unemployment. Then he considers the social consequences of such combined over-productivity and under-employment, observing that

> when the standard of living of a large mass of people falls below a certain subsistence level — a level regulated automatically as the one necessary for a member of the society — and when there is a consequent loss of the sense of right and wrong, of honesty and the self-respect which makes a man insist on maintaining himself by his own work and effort, the result is the creation of a rabble of paupers. At the same time this brings with it, at the other end of the social scale, conditions which greatly facilitate the concentration of disproportionate wealth in few hands.[24]

If the wealthier classes, or charitable foundations, attempt by direct means to guarantee the old standard of living of the unemployed, regardless of whether they work or not; or if (despite the fact of over-production) make-work schemes are introduced; the result — according to Hegel — is the same: "The evil to be removed remains and is indeed intensified by the very methods adopted to alleviate it. We have thus the seeming paradox that, despite an excess of wealth, civil society is not rich enough, i.e., its own resources are insufficient to check excessive poverty."[25]

In all the pages of *Das Kapital,* Marx succeeds in adding nothing essential to Hegel's brief formulation. And, as for the Hobson-Leninist extension of the Marxist doctrine in the theory of capitalist imperialism, here is Hegel's brief summation:

> The inner dialectic of civil society then drives it beyond its own shores to seek markets, and so the necessary means of subsistence, in other lands which either lack the means of which it has a superfluity, or are generally backward in industries . . . . The far-flung connecting-link of the sea affords the means for the colonizing activity — sporadic or systematic — to which the mature civil society is driven and by which it supplies to a part of its population a return

to life on the family basis in a new land and so also supplies itself with a new demand and field for its industry.[26]

Hegel, incidentally, insisted that all colonies founded by the modern European states would inevitably gain independence, and that their independence would prove to be "of the greatest advantage to the mother country, just as the emancipation of slaves turns out to the greatest advantage of the owners."[27]

It should be noted here that Marx and Lenin (though the latter in theory only) pursued the line of reasoning of Hegel's contemporaries who confounded civil society and the state. For Marx, the only social reality in the modern world was civil society. The development of capitalism, he held, had reduced the old institutions of family and state to the status of instruments, or tools, for the selfish satisfaction of individual, group, or class interests in the competitions of civil society.

But Hegel had analyzed that "new economic" view of modern society long before it was explicitly advanced by the authors of the *Communist Manifesto* as a revolutionary revelation; and he had rejected it, even as he rejected by anticipation, the related view of John Dewey, and Arthur F. Bentley which now prevails in the American academy: the view that the patterned activities of classes, interest groups, and "service" institutions in civil society are the sole characteristically political activities, and that political science therefore wastes its time when it looks beyond interest groups, etc., for a higher form of political reality.

In Hegel's judgment, all such Marxist or "systems-analysis" views of society illustrate the error of what has lately come to be called scientific "reductionism." Aristotle had written against such reductionism as applied to politics in the opening pages of his treatise on the subject, where he said that those who insisted that a political community differed only quantitatively from other forms of human association were wrong. Hegel, in fact, explicitly supports Aristotle's polemical demonstration that *politeia* is not an extended family, nor an elaborated employer-employee relationship, and certainly not a master-slave or exploiter-exploited class relationship; that it is on the contrary a qualitatively distinct community of free and equal human beings united in pursuit of the highest conceivable earthly ends of free men.

In strictly Hegelian terms, *politeia* is the objective reality Free Mind must fashion for itself if it is to realize all its potentialities —potentialities that cannot be realized in any associations, however large or small, of family-members as such, or civil-society burghers as such, but only in a more perfect union, or *we* relationship, of free and equal citizens.

Hegel thus accepts literally Aristotle's definition of *politeia* as the "government of men free and equal" and of political science as the science of such government.[28] He departs from Aristotle only to deny (but it is a very large *only*) that any human beings are by nature, rather than voluntarily, slaves. He affirms, on the contrary, that, through the extension of Christianity and the development of civil society, it is now possible for all human beings, including emancipated slaves and their descendants, to be educated up to equality in freedom; if not perfectly, as individuals, at least in the form of that politically shared willingness to die rather than endure enslavement, which characterizes the free life of sovereign states, large or small, in the modern world.

But how do the burghers of civil society overcome the tendency of its internal dialectic to "polarize" them into a rich few and a pauperized many? How is the so-called inevitable contradiction of modern capitalist society to be intentionally resolved so as to make a more perfect political union come into being instead? Hegel's answer is: through voluntary association in what be identifies as the "corporations" of civil society. By corporations, Hegel means every possible voluntary associa- tion of producers of goods and services, whether on the ownership, management, or wage-earning level. Here is the part of the Hegelian social and political theory that fascinated Benedetto Croce and Giovanni Gentile. It was a theory resem- bling Hegel's notion of a "corporation" society, to serve as the basis of a "corporate" state, that those philosophers advanced as an answer to the Marxist-Leninist anti-political, revolution- ary doctrine. But far more faithful to the Hegelian view in this respect (precisely because of its emphasis on the satisfaction of the individual in the resultant political community) is the corporate ideal of Herbert Croly's *Promise of American Life.*

The terms in which Croly argues for the continued "combination of capital," to be accompanied by "completer unionization" of labor, and the development of a "responsible concentration" of political power in government, "in order to maintain the balance," is strictly Hegelian, in form as well as content. And that Croly thesis, which so greatly influenced Theodore Roosevelt, is perhaps most Hegelian where its author concludes: "An organic unity binds the three aspects of the system together; and in so far as a constructive tendency becomes powerful in any one region, it will tend by its own force to introduce constructive methods of organization into the other divisions of the economic political and social body."[29]

In explaining how membership in business corporations, labor unions, and governmental agencies prepares burghers for integration in the free life of political community, Hegel observes that it is only in the absence of such associations that the polarization of society into a minority of rich capitalists and a majority of pauperized, unemployed workers can occur. "Unless he is a member of a corporation," Hegel writes,

> an individual is without rank or dignity, his isolation reduces his productive activity to mere self-seeking. . . . We saw earlier that in fending for himself a member of civil society is also working for others. But this unconscious compulsion is not enough; it is in the Corporation that it first changes into a conscious and thoughtful ethical mode of life. Of course corporations must fall under the higher surveillance of the state, because otherwise they would ossify, build themselves in, and decline into a miserable system of castes. In and by itself, however, a corporation is not a closed caste; its purpose is rather to bring an isolated trade into the social order and elevate it to a sphere in which it gains strength and respect.[30]

The corporation thus becomes for its members a kind of family; and Hegel, in fact, concludes his discussion of Civil Society with the observation that "as the family was the first, so the corporation is the second ethical root of the state," the two serving as the only securely fixed points "round which the unorganized atoms of civil society revolve."

Yet it would be completely erroneous to assume that political community, or the state in its proper sense, develops out of the dialectic of civil society. "Actually," Hegel writes, "the state as such is not so much the result as the beginning. It is within the state that the family is first developed into civil society, and it is the Idea of the state itself which disrupts itself into the two moments" out of which by scientific analysis, we seem to "deduce" its existence.[31]

By the time the state in its actuality is made the object of study in Hegel's *Philosophy of Right,* it is clear that the method of exposition to that point has been strictly Aristotelian. The whole has been analyzed into its constituent elements so that the organic connection and dependence of the parts on the whole may be displayed. Aristotle had said plainly enough that, while individual human beings form and perpetuate families and states through their common intercourse, the state is nevertheless, in the order of nature, prior to the family and the individual. In what is perhaps his most brilliant brief summary of the dialectic of the progression of sciences in this sphere, Hegel distinguishes the several sciences according to their objects of study:

> We begin with something abstract, namely, with the Notion of Will; we then go on to the actualization of the as yet abstract will in an external existent to the sphere of formal right; from there we go on to the will that is reflected into itself out of external existence, to the sphere of morality; and thirdly and lastly we come to the will that unites within itself these two abstract moments and is therefore the concrete, ethical will. In the ethical sphere itself we again start from an immediate, from the natural, undeveloped shape possessed by the ethical mind in the *family;* then we come to the *splitting* up of the ethical substance in *civil society;* and finally, in the State, attain the unity and truth of those two one-sided forms of the ethical mind. But this course followed by our exposition does not in the least mean that we would make the ethical life later in time than right and morality, or would explain the family and civil society to be *antecedent* to the State in the *actual* world. On the contrary, we are well aware that the

ethical life is the foundation of right and morality, as also
that the family and civil society with their well-ordered
distinctions already presuppose the existence of the State.
In the *philosophical* development of the ethical sphere,
however, we cannot begin with the State, since in this the
ethical sphere has unfolded itself into its most concrete
form, whereas the beginning is necessarily something
abstract. For this reason, the moral sphere, too, must be
considered before the ethical sphere, although the former
to a certain extent comes to view in the latter only as a
sickness.[32]

Briefly put, one may say that *abstract right* with its positing
of the will in external things, *morality* with its subjective justification, the ethical life of the *family* with its immediate bond of
love, and *civil society* with its mediated bonds of need, are
moments analyzable out of the actuality of the life of the *state.*
The *persons* of abstract right, the *subjects* of morality and
conscience, the *members* of families, and the *burghers* of civil
society enter the life of the state as *citizens;* to constitute a new
whole qualitatively different, as we have stressed, from all other
human associations. As to what characteristically unites citizens in a true state, Hegel writes: "Liberty and equality are
indeed the foundation of the state." But he hastens to add that
they are the foundation which is "as the most abstract, so also
the most superficial, and for that reason the most familiar."[33]

The State is the perfection of Objective Mind in the same
sense that Free Mind is the perfection of Subjective Mind. Free
Mind overcomes the original subjectivity of mind through
psychological self-analysis. Similarly, the State overcomes its
absorption in the processes of civil society (where classes
attempt to use its powers to advance class interests) by the self-
constituting processes of rational law.

States have a constituted actuality that can be studied
objectively. One can observe empirically how the constitution
of one's own state — whether Athens, Sparta, Rome, England,
the United States, or China — actually functions from day to
day. A comparative study of such constitutions — comparative
"systems-analysis," we would call it today — leads to knowledge
of the essential structure of a political community as such. But

each state has, of course, an historical development of its own that can be studied in itself as well as comparatively. The Athenian constitution, for example, was originally a despotic rule of one man, but there took place a gradual devolution of power, through a dozen or more political crises, from the rule of one through the rule of few and then of many; whereas the Spartan constitution, with its carefully separated and balanced powers, hardly changes at all in a comparable interval of time. Systems-analysis and constitutional histories were the basis upon which Aristotle founded his *Politics* – but only after having reviewed the theories of politics advanced by his predecessors in the field. And Hegel does the same. As T. M. Knox correctly remarks in his notes to the *Philosophy of Right,* according to Hegel,

> a study of positive law [systems-analysis] and history must precede the philosophy of right. The philosopher tries to see the meaning of the facts which the historian collects, and to discover the necessity at the heart of their contingency. It is important to notice that Hegel brought to the writing of this book an extensive study of the facts whose inward and moving principle he here professes to expound, and thus he is very far from attempting [to] deduce the philosophy of the state by a *priori* thinking.[34]

One "scientific" approach to the study of states Hegel very explicitly eschews. And that is the prescriptive approach, the aim of which is to construct a theory of the state as it "ought to be," so that statesmen (or youthful "idealists") may set about reconstituting their actual states on the scientist's model. His own object, he says, is the same as that of the astronomer studying the phenomena of the heavens, which is certainly not to teach men how the heavenly bodies "ought to move." "To consider a thing rationally," writes Hegel, "means not to bring reason to bear on the object from the outside and so to tamper with it, but to find that the object is rational on its own account."[35] This is true not only of the purely observational sciences, but also of those founded on experimentation. The experimenter certainly tampers with things in putting his experiment together; but once the experiment has been "made," his task is simply to describe and formulate the rational law implicit in it, without further tampering.

So it is with the study of the man-made state: its rationality has been built into it in the course of history by the generations of men who made it. The state is infinitely more complex than a man-made experiment in a laboratory, but it is, as we noted before, of the same order. Even in the laboratory, the scientist discounts unessential factors and speaks of "other things being equal." Similarly of the object of study of political science, Hegel says: "The state is no ideal work of art; it stands on earth, and so in the sphere of caprice, chance, and error; and bad behavior may disfigure it in many respects. But even the ugliest of men, or a criminal, or an invalid, or a cripple, is still always a living man. The affirmative, life, subsists despite his defects, and it is this affirmative factor [other things being equal] which is our theme here."[36]

According to its "ratio of truth," the state is known first as rationally constituted in itself (Constitutional Law), then as constituted for others (International Law), and finally as adequately linking its domestic and foreign relations in the unity of its role in World History. The state, Hegel repeatedly stresses, is the actuality of concrete freedom. It is free *in itself* and also *for others*. Its internal freedom is so articulated, constitutionally, as to guarantee maximum subjective freedom (diversity in civil society) with maximum objective freedom (unity of purpose in foreign relations). "Sovereignty" is the historical term for the constituted freedom of a politically united people. In its domestic aspect, sovereignty is the effective unity of the citizens, as producers and consumers of the commonwealth, expressed through the legislative processes; and of the wisdom of the "Civil" servants, or public-oriented elites, who in the process of administering the law take notice of the difficulties and unanticipated needs that inevitably arise.

But it is in its foreign-relations aspect that the constituted freedom of a politically united people — its sovereignty — is fully manifest. Hegel's words on this aspect of the subject have a tremendous bearing on the question of knowledge as it pertains to political science; for what is at issue here is the reality of statehood as it has been historically defined. The basis of all Right, Hegel says, is "personality"; and hence the imperative of Right is: "Be a person and respect others as persons."[37] States emerge historically to give every man's personality its due, to realize the freedom of personality in its fullness, equally for all, as far as possible. In the more perfect union of a state, the freedom of personality takes on the individuality of the whole. And Hegel says of it:

> Individuality is awareness of one's existence as a unit in sharp distinction from others. It manifests itself on the level of the state as a relation to other states, each of which is autonomous *vis-a-vis* the others. This autonomy embodies mind's actual awareness of itself as a unit and hence it is the most fundamental freedom which a people possess as well as its highest dignity . . . . Those who talk of the "wishes" of a "collection" of people to renounce its own political center and autonomy in order to unite with others to form a new whole, have very little knowledge of what a "collection" is or of the feeling of selfhood which a nation possesses in its independence.[38]

The contemporary world has heard so many voices — especially in the academy — cry out against this traditional notion of sovereignty that it has been a relief in recent years to hear the statesmen of the new state of Israel proclaim it at the top of their lungs, often against the combined self-deluding ignorance of what in the Old Testament is termed the gentiles, or "other" nations. The Israeli people have, of course, saved and planned for almost 2,000 years to make a place for themselves in this world — an objective place where, as Free Minds, they can live and govern themselves autonomously. During that interval, they have enjoyed all kinds of freedoms elsewhere, especially in England, France, and the United States; but for the Jews who think of themselves as essentially Jews, wherever they may happen to live in the world, those lesser freedoms — the freedoms of civil society — have never sufficed. The freedom they have sought, and now hope to realize in Palestine, is that sovereign freedom of autonomous statehood that Hegel characterizes as "the most fundamental freedom which a people possesses as well as its highest dignity."

The realization of freedom in autonomous states that face one another in the world like individualized personalities in civil society makes up, according to Hegel, the course of world history. World history "contains" the histories of individual states, even as the states "contain" the development of their constituent families and groupings of civil society which, in turn, "contain" the lives of their individual members.

The philosophical science of history, therefore, presupposes all that has gone before in the exposition of the sciences of Objective Mind. But here it is the coming to be and passing away of states in their *relations* with one another that is the distinguishably new object of scientific study. The method, however, remains the same; and in his lectures on the *Philosophy of History*, Hegel once again cites the practice of astronomers to justify his own scientific procedure. The astronomer doesn't come to the study of celestial phenomena with a blank mind. He comes to it with a mind full of the best ideas of mathematics and mechanics. Similarly, the serious social scientist doesn't come to the study of civil society, or the state, with a blank mind. And just as the concepts of Mind, Freedom, and Will are presupposed in the scientific study of family life, civil society, and statehood, so the concepts of statehood and related concepts (tribe, people, nation) must be presupposed in the scientific study of the so-called facts of history which cannot of themselves constitute an academic discipline. Against the naive notion of "facts" that can write themselves up into a science on a *tabula* rasa, Hegel observes:

> That a particular distinction is in fact the characteristic principle of a people is the element of our study that must be empirically ascertained and historically demonstrated. To do this requires, however, that we bring to the task not only a disciplined faculty of abstraction but also a long familiarity with the Idea. One must have what you may call, if you like, *a priori* knowledge, or long familiarity with the entire sphere of principles to which the specific principle in question belongs — just as Kepler (to name only the most celebrated scientist of this sort) must have been acquainted *a priori* with ellipses, cubes, squares and concepts of their interrelationships, before he could discover from the empirical data those immortal laws which are determinations of that sphere of representa-

tions. A person ignorant of such elemental concepts and distinctions will fail to understand — let alone discover — such laws no matter how long a time he spends contemplating the sky and the motions of celestial bodies.[39]

In his extended discussion of methods that makes up the introduction to his *Philosophy of History,* Hegel distinguishes Original History, Reflective History, and Philosophical History, showing how the facts, or things of the first, are to be adequately linked together with the thoughts or principles of the second in the truth of the third. As Professor J. N. Findlay correctly sums it up: "The Hegelian Philosophy of History therefore builds on the original histories which constitute the source-material for the past, and also on the more reflective histories which subject this source-material to various critical tests . . . . It only differs from both [in that] its aim is . . . to discover in past States different stages in the developing consciousness of Right, to discover a *line* of development running through all such stages, and to show, further, how events which seem unconnected with this development have none the less contributed to it."[40]

The developing consciousness of Right in history is, of course, the development of freedom. It is in becoming aware of history as the work of Free Mind that the individual mind, first, and then the mind of a people acting together, becomes fully free. The longing for realized freedom is the motive power of human conduct on all levels of the world of Objective Mind, but particularly on that of universal history. "When individuals and nations have once seized upon the abstract idea of freedom itself," Hegel says, "it has more than any other thing, boundless power, just because it is the very being of Mind, its very reality."[41]

But universal recognition that Mind is free in its essential being has been slow in coming. Whole continents have known nothing of genuine freedom; and even the Greeks and Romans mistook it for something attached to specially privileged races or to be acquired through privileged education. Only with the spread of the Judeo-Christian religion did the idea take root that freedom is the essential characteristic of manhood. Man, Christianity teaches, is intended inherently for the highest freedom — which is oneness with God. And through that teaching, Christianity has realized in its adherents — first in Europe but eventually elsewhere as well —an "ever-present sense that they are not and cannot be slaves"; so that, "if they are made slaves, if the decision as regards their property rests with an arbitrary will, not with laws or courts of justice, they would find their very substance outraged." This will for freedom, Hegel concludes, "is no longer an urge demanding satisfaction; it is very character itself — its being, without urgings, become spiritual consciousness."[42]

In the ancient history of the Far and Near East, the political freedom of states (the united willingness of citizens to die rather than suffer enslavement) was a reality only in the head of state: the single person who exercised such freedom in behalf of his subjects. Thus in the Ancient East, as also in its fossilized modern continuations, only one person in each free state was actually free. In the history of the classical world, on the shores of the Mediterranean, political freedom was much more widely experienced; many in the free states of Athens, Sparta, and Rome were personally free — though not yet all. In modern history, quite uniquely, freedom has at last become a recognized possibility, and is rapidly on its way to becoming an actuality, for all. As Hegel foresaw, all the traditionally enslavable peoples of the world — not only in Black America but in Black Africa and Yellow Asia as well — are rapidly becoming genuinely free through their newly asserted, manifest willingness to die rather than suffer enslavement.

III. The Political and Historical Moments of Truth

But it is not when political freedom first becomes possible —as in the backward, newly emerging nations of the world — that the truth of the social, political, and historical experience of man can be known. The awakening and flowering of scientific knowledge is itself deeply rooted in the course of history. It has its proper places and times, its propitious moments of truth, in politics as well as history. We noted earlier that the completed system of philosophical sciences has no privileged beginning. But the same cannot be said of the *impulse* to philosophize. An individual may conceivably begin to pursue true knowledge in a scientific manner with respect to any conceivable object of knowledge, whether mathematical or astronomical, biological or psychological, economic or socio-logical, etc.; but he can in fact do so only if he happens to have been reared in a society sufficiently advanced politically to assure him the leisure without which a scientific pursuit of knowledge is neither desirable nor possible.

In the opening pages of his *History of Philosophy,* Hegel cites Aristotle's words on the subject, agreeing that the desire to know, as an end in itself, becomes a pressing need only when "almost all the necessities of life and the things that make for comfort and recreation have been secured."[43] The possibility of satisfying such a need, even more than its awakening, presupposes the actuality of a politically advanced society with a considerable history behind it. Doubt, or wonder in the Aristotelian sense, which animates the need to philosophize, is not excited into being simply by man's awareness of his natural environment. The hungry man does not "wonder" about the food he needs to eat, any more than he wonders about the "nature" of the beast who attacks him when he is out hunting or about the nature of the pleasure he gets in gratifying his hunger or his sexual appetite. Before the wonder that leads to science can be awakened, the animal cravings must have disappeared, and so must the immediate fears; and in their place, as Hegel expresses it, "a strength, elevation, and moral fortitude of mind must have appeared, passions must be subdued and consciousness advanced to the point that its thinking is free and not self-seeking."[44] It is the point in the cycle of the sciences of Subjective Mind where, as a conse-quence of self-analysis, Mind is at last free to overcome its subjectivity.

Self-analysis of that sort is not possible among primitive peoples. The beginnings of true science are thus reserved for advanced societies; and even in advanced societies, one par-ticular phase of historical development is much more suitable for such beginnings than any other. Hegel emphasizes that, for a genuine awakening of scientific curiosity,

thought must be for itself, must come into existence in its

freedom, liberate itself from nature and come out of its immersion in sense-perception; it must, as free, enter within itself and thus arrive at the consciousness of freedom. If we say that the consciousness of freedom is connected with the development of philosophy, this principle must be a fundamental one in the people among whom philosophy begins . . . . Connected with this on the practical side is the fact that actual freedom develops political freedom (so that, objectively,) philosophy appears in history only where and insofar as free institutions are formed.[45]

In other words, the mind that can freely philosophize is the same Free Mind which, after experiencing the moral frustration of attempting to press claims of abstract personal right, realizes itself in the actualities of family life, civil society, statehood, and the universal history of states. Free men constitute states, states make history; and it is in the course of the universal history of states — from the founding of the first historical states in the great river-valley civilizations of the ancient Far and Near East down through the ages of ancient Greece and Rome and of the medieval and modern peoples — that Mind frees itself from temporal things to become Absolute in Art, Religion and Philosophy. In Hegel's words:

It may be said that philosophy first commences when a race [broadest extension of family-life] has largely left its concrete mode of existence [constituted statehood], when separation and change of class have begun [expansion of civil society], and the community is approaching its decline . . . . This holds good throughout all the history of philosophy . . . . Thus in Athens, with the ruin of the Athenian people, the period was reached when philosophy appeared . . . . In Rome, philosophy first developed in the decline of the Republic. [And] it was with the decline of the Empire that the height and indeed the zenith of ancient philosophy was attained in the systems of the neo-Platonists at Alexandria.[46]

The questioning of experience that results in the flowering of science and philosophy is the same questioning that consumes the social order by undermining its authority. For that reason it can be said that, while in the experience of any one person, wonder may rise to the level of systematic doubt at any point around the great circle of knowledge, historically it has awakened first within the range of the social, political, and historical consciousness of man. Excited by doubt, Mind invariably brings its quest for truth to focus, first of all, on its own social environment: which is to say, on the "institutions and forms of government of the people among whom it makes its appearance; their morality, their social life and capabilities, customs and enjoyments; their attempts and achievements in art and science; their religious experience; their wars and foreign relations; and lastly, the origin and progress of the states arising to displace them."[47]

When animated by doubt, when pursued questioningly, mind "subverts" what it studies. That was the charge raised against Socrates by the Athenian democracy; and it was a valid charge. But, as Hegel represents it, in condemning Socrates the Athenians were really condemning themselves. For Socrates was, in fact, the Athenian Mind itself committed to self-criticism. In every age of intense philosophical study, the studying mind and the historical actuality which it studies mirror one another, and are indeed one. On this theme Hegel says in the *History of Philosophy*: "Mind takes refuge in the clear space of thought to create for itself a kingdom of thought in opposition to the world of actuality, and Philosophy is the reconciliation following upon the destruction of that real world — a destruction which thought has begun."[48]

Hegel's philosophical sciences of society, politics, and history are thus mirrors of a dissolving world. Thought consumes its own objectivization of itself in space and time as objectively inadequate. True philosophy, like true art and true religion, transcends the realities of politics and history. It is utterly wrong, therefore, to try to make a secular optimist out of Hegel. What optimism is to be found in his philosophic system pertains to a sphere beyond history, and therefore beyond the associational life of family, civil society and statehood that makes up the pattern of history.

"Passions, private aims, and the satisfaction of selfish desires are the most effective springs of action in history," writes Hegel, "because they respect none of the limitations which Right and Morality would impose, and because they exert a more direct influence over men than the artificial and tedious discipline that tends toward order and self-restraint, law and morality." Yet, when we read the record of history and note the evil and ruin that such passions, aims, and desires have wrought, when we contemplate the "miseries that have overwhelmed the noblest nations and polities, and the finest examples of private virtue," we experience, Hegel writes, "mental torture, allowing no defense or escape but the consideration that what has happened could not be otherwise; that it is a fatality which no intervention could alter." It is out of a history that "excites emotions of the profoundest and most hopeless sadness" that we pass into the sphere of Absolute Mind."[49] The transition is the flight of Minerva's owl — which is possible only after the long day's task is done. Philosophy's backward glance on the wreckage of political history is a tragic theodicy.

One must stress the pessimism of the Hegelian doctrine of Objective Mind to avoid the popular error that would make of him an idolator of statehood and the historical process. The state is for Hegel, as for St. Augustine and the Founding Fathers of the United States, a necessary evil. Men initially build up the edifice of human society, he says, to gratify their passions; but they end up "fortifying a position of Right and Order against themselves." [50] The passionate aims of individuals are checked and balanced in the rationality of states; and the self-centered interests of states are checked and balanced in the hard trials of universal history. That history is by no means a theater of happiness. On the contrary, its periods of happiness are no more than blank pages, signifying nothing.

To make a worldly optimist out of Hegel, one must either decapitate him, denying his doctrine of art, religion, and God-centered philosophy, as Croce and the fascist humanists generally have done; or turn his entire doctrine upside down, as Marx and the materialist humanists have done. Right side up and whole, Hegel must rank with St. Augustine among the profoundest worldly pessimists of Christendom, even as he must rank with Aristotle — *il maestro di color che sanno* — among the greatest of systematic philosophers who have concerned themselves with the sciences of society, politics, and history.

NOTES

1. *The Logic of Hegel* (Part I of *Enzyklopädie*), trans. William Wallace (Oxford, 1892), pp. 28-29 (§18). This work is hereafter cited as *HL;* translations adapted slightly in accordance with German text (Henning, 1840, 1955).

2. *Hegel's Science of Logic*, trans. W. H. Johnston and L. G. Struthers (London, 1951), Vol.II, p. 227.

3. *Hegel's Philosophy of Mind* (Part III of *Enzyklopädie*), trans. W. Wallace and A. V. Miller (Oxford, 1971), p. 180 (§ 440). This work is hereafter cited as *PhM*; translations adapted slightly in accordance with German text (Boumann, 1958).

4. *The Phenomenology of Mind*, trans. J. B. Baillie (London, 1931), p. 90; adapted slightly (Hoffmeister, 1949).

5. *HL*, p. 59 (§ 25).

6. *HL*, *ibid.*

7. *HL*, p. 28 (§ 17).

8. *HL*, pp. 24-25 (§ 14, 15).

9. *HL*, *ibid.*

10. *The Basic Works of Aristotle*, ed. Richard McKeon (New York, 1941), p. 41 (adapted in accordance with Bekker, *De Interpretatione*, 16^b 19-25).

11. *Hegel's Lectures on the History of Philosophy*, trans. E. S. Haldane and Frances H. Simson (London, 1955), Vol. II, p. 223. This work is hereafter cited as *HPh*; translations adapted slightly in accordance with German text (Michelet, 1840).

12. *PhM*, p. 3 (§ 378).

13. *Hegel's Philosophy of Right*, trans. T. M. Knox (Oxford, 1956), p. 106 (§ 146). This work is hereafter cited as *PhR*; translations adapted slightly in accordance with German text (Gans 1833, 1952), making use also of the translation by S. W. Dyde (London, 1896).

14. *PhR*, p. 4 (Preface).

15. *Aristotle's Politics*, trans. H. Rackham (Camb., Mass. and London, 1950), p. 11 (1253^a).

16. *Ibid.*

17. *PhR*, pp. 264-5 (note to § 173).

18. *PhR*, pp. 117-118 (§ 175)

19. *PhR*, pp. 266-7 (note to § 182).

20. *PhR*, p. 266 (note to § 182).

21. *PhR*, p. 267 (note to § 182).

22. *PhR*, pp. 126-7 (§ 189).

23. *PhR*, p. 268 (note to § 189).

24. *PhR*, p. 150 (§ 244).

25. *Ibid.*, § 245.

26. *PhR*, pp. 151-2 (§ 246, 248).

27. *PhR*, p. 278 (note to § 248).

28. *Aristotle's Politics, op. cit.*, p. 29 (1255^{b20}).

29. Herbert Croly, *The Promise of American Life* (Indianapolis, 1965), p. 395.

30. *PhR*, pp. 153, 278 (§ 253 and note to § 255).

31. *PhR*, p. 154 (§ 255) and p. 155 (§ 256).

32. *PhM*, p. 130 (§ 408).

33. *PhM*, p. 265 (§ 539).

34. *PhR*, p. 306.

35. *PhR*, p. 35 (§ 31).

36. *PhR*, p. 279 (note to § 258).

37. *PhR*, p. 37 (§ 36).

38. *PhR*, p. 208 (§ 322).

39. *Hegel's Philosophy of History*, trans. J. Sibree (New York, 1956), p. 64. Translation adapted slightly in accordance with German text (Lasson, 1930).

40. J. N. Findlay, *Hegel: A Re-examination* (New York, 1962), p. 334.

41. *PhM*, p. 239 (§ 482).

42. *PhM*, p. 240 (§ 482).

43. *HPh*, Vol. I, p. 51.

44. *HPh, ibid.*

45. *HPh*, Vol. I, pp. 94-95.

46. *HPh*, Vol. I, pp. 52-3.

47. *HPh*, Vol. I. p. 53.

48. *HPh*, Vol. I. p. 52.

49. *Hegel's Philosophy of History, op. cit.*, pp. 20-21.

50. *Ibid.*, p. 27.

PART THREE

◇◄◄◄◄►►►►◇

LAW, GOVERNMENT, AND POLITICAL PHILOSOPHY

MAITLAND ON ENGLISH LAW

Frederic William Maitland (1850-1906) was recognized in his own lifetime as the greatest historian of English law; his claim to that title has not been effectively challenged since. He was a brilliant undergraduate in moral sciences at Trinity College, Cambridge University, from 1869 to 1872, before studying for the Bar at Lincoln's Inn. In 1876 he entered the law chambers of Benjamin B. Rogers, who later said of him: "He had not been with me a week before I found that I had in my chambers such a lawyer as I had never met before . . . . his opinions, had he suddenly been made a judge, would have been an honor to the bench."[1]

Even while serving as a barrister, Maitland's attention was more and more to be attracted to historical studies. In 1884, after publication of his learned *Pleas of the Crown for the County of Gloucester*, he obtained a readership at Cambridge University. *Justice and Police* appeared the following year. But it was publication of his *Bracton's Note Book*, in which he showed Bracton to be the "crown and flower of English medieval jurisprudence," that established his reputation as a master of the sources of early English legal history. *Bracton's Note Book* appeared in 1887. The following year Maitland was elected into the Downing Professor-ship of the Laws of England at Cambridge.

During the remaining eighteen years of his life, Maitland's pen poured out "a flood of books, articles, and reviews . . . of a sustained high quality and, at times, brilliance unequaled in English historiography."[2] A master of the sources, he wrote always with "that firmness of hand which nothing but original research can give."[3] His health was frail and in 1889 he con-

[From *Justice and Police* by Frederic William Maitland. AMS Press, New York, 1974.]

fided to a friend: "Many things are telling me that I have not got
unlimited time at my command."[4] By 1898, he was constrained
to spend his winters in the Canary Islands. He was 56 when he
died there on December 19, 1906. But by then he had amply
earned the right to be ranked among the very greatest scholars
of the modern era. He had achieved in the field of English legal
history what Aldoph von Harnack achieved in the history of
Christian dogma, Eduard Meyer in the history of the ancient
Near East and Greece, Theodor Mommsen in the history of
Rome, Erich Caspar in the history of the Papacy, Hegel and
Windelband in the history of philosophy and Otto von Gierke
(to whom Maitland owed much) in the history of fellowship law
(*Genossen-schraftrecht*).

Maitland was a lawyer first and then an historian. By
combining in himself the two professions, he did inestimable
service for both. "In an age of great historians," wrote Sir
William Holdsworth of Cambridge University, "I think that
Maitland was the greatest."[5] He labored over the legal documents of medieval England to make them available in critical
editions for future scholars. But he had a marvelous capacity to
give life to dead letters, to make the eras glimpsed through
those documents come alive for modern readers. And his
literary style was of an excellence matched — if it was matched
at all — only by the best pages of Edward Gibbon, Thomas
Macaulay, and Winston Churchill. Maitland's two masterpieces of historical writing are *The History of English Law Before
the Time of Edward I*, a massive two-volume work published in
1895 with the collaboration of Sir Frederick Pollock, and his
brief but brilliant and controversial *English Law and the Renaissance* (1901), in which he argues that England might not have
become a bastion of civil liberties under the common law had
not its lawyers fought off the mounting influence of continental
Roman law in the age of Henry VIII.

If we consider that Maitland's chief scholarly labors were
focused on the history of English law from the Norman
conquest in 1066 through the reign of Elizabeth I, his little
volume on *Justice and Police*, which focuses on Victorian England, ranks as an exception. It was not written for scholars. He
was commissioned to write it as part of a popular series entitled

The English Citizen, His Rights and Responsibilities; and, as he explains in a brief preface, the assignment fell to him only because a colleague originally charged with writing it had been unexpectedly called away.

Justice and Police gives a non-technical account of the actual system of justice and law enforcement in England at the time it was written — between 1884 and 1885. Yet the author's mastery of the history of English law enforcement is manifest throughout. And its historical perspective is what makes the work especially valuable for those of us who — with concerns of our own about justice and police — read the book now in a distant time and place. By accurately tracing the pattern of the past in this vital sphere of law and order, Maitland was able also to anticipate the pattern of a future which has become our present.

By coupling *police* with *justice* in the book's title, Maitland sought explicitly to narrow the precise meaning of the latter word. "By the *Justice and Police* of a country," he explains, "are meant those institutions and processes whereby that country's law is enforced; whereby, for example, those who are wronged obtain their legal remedies, and those who commit crimes are brought to their legal punishments."[6] Those institutions and processes are themselves defined by law. But such law constitutes only a small part of the entire body of law in the "domain of English justice," which includes, in addition, the "rules defining crimes and the punishments of those who commit them, rights and the remedies of those who are wronged." What comes specifically under *justice* and *police* is the "body of rules defining how and by whom, and when and where rules of the former kind (about punishments and remedies) can be put in force."[7]

Expressed as briefly as possible, what Maitland supplies in this book is an account of how English law "becomes a coercive power." It is a matter worthy of study by enlightened citizens because, as Maitland observes, it will profit us precious little "that our law about rights and remedies, crimes and punishments, is as good as may be, if the law of civil and criminal procedure is clumsy and inefficient."[8] Clumsy and inefficient are words frequently used in contemporary America to characterize the disorder that now prevails in our procedures of civil and criminal justice. Our courts are jammed, our police are pilloried, and swarms of known criminals under indictment freely roam our streets. Maintland's development of his keen observation on this point thus talks directly to a major problem of our time.

The book develops its subject under two basic divisions which are already clearly defined in Maitland's preliminary statement that the "main objects of justice are to afford remedies for the infringement of rights (civil justice), and to insure the punishment of crime (criminal justice)."[9] We have there the fundamental distinction between remedial justice, which is concerned with the rights of the victim of injustice, and penal justice, which is concerned with the rights of society in the punishment of a perpetrator of injustice. Whenever that distinction is drawn historically, it tends to give rise "to two different systems; there will be criminal cases and civil cases, a criminal procedure and a civil, perhaps criminal courts and civil courts."[10]

These are matters, definitions and distinctions of great moment for all those who are concerned with criminal justice in the United States today. There has been great ideological pressure since the end of World War II to re-interpret the traditional meaning of *justice and police*. The inclination of academicians ignorant of the history of law and legal processes has been to minimize the importance of remedies for the wronged and punishment for criminals in favor of so-called crime prevention and the "rehabilitation" of convicted criminals. Traditionally, the tasks of prevention and rehabilitation were not parts of justice and police. Prevention and correction, it was understood, were exalted tasks of an ideal character — tasks reserved for eminent statesmen, priests, rabbis, philosophers, or educators with charismatic gifts. The history of law must frown disdainfully on the naiveté or malice of the legislation that has changed our prisons into "correction facilities" and our guards into "correction officers."

The main burden of justice and police is to provide remedies for persons wronged and punishments for perpetrators of crimes. In the case of a civil wrong, the law stresses remedies; punishment is meted out to the wrong-doer only if no adequate remedy is otherwise available to the person wronged. In the case of a crime, the law stresses punishment; remedies for the victim are secondary, for it is the social order itself which is threatened by crime, and the threat is effectively allayed only when society as a whole — rather than an individual victim — feels vindicated in the process of according the criminal his social due through just punishment. Maitland thus illustrates the distinction:

> A civil action is one thing, a criminal prosecution quite another . . . . Of course, though a wrong is often no crime, and a crime is often no wrong, still there are many acts which are both wrongs and crimes. A man may be guilty of high-treason or many other crimes against public order without giving any one a cause for civil action; and even of crimes which are classed as offences against property, many can be committed without any one being injured; the forger is punished though he has not defrauded any one. On the other hand, the notice-board which tells us that "Trespassers will be prosecuted" is, if strictly construed, a wooden falsehood; a mere trespass on the land of another may be the subject of a civil action, but not of a criminal prosecution. Still, very often the same act is both a crime and a wrong. An assault is a case in point, and so is a theft. The defamatory libel that is a wrong is, at least very generally, a crime also. But, with a few exceptions, the rule holds good in England that no remedy or redress can be had in criminal proceedings . . . though the crime be a wrong, the person wronged has no exclusive or peculiar title to prosecute the offender.[11]

That paragraph exemplifies the main virtues of Maitland's style and the quality of his judgments and learning. With wit and precision he points out that society, not the individual wronged personally, exacts punishment of the criminal. In other writings, Maitland is at pains to show how, with the strengthening of the social order, punishment of criminals tends invariably to become more lenient and humane, whereas when respect for law and order declines, or is non-existent, the reverse obtains: punishment for crime becomes of necessity brutal, revengeful, and even exemplary, all of which makes it an effective deterrent, but the opposite of just. The point is that an orderly society can "afford" to be lenient with criminals on the grounds that it is not threatened to its foundations even by the most heinous of individual crimes. But when a nation's laws, police, courts, and prison guards are subject to ridicule; and when a decadent intelligentsia busies itself with writing apologies for criminals as "victims" of the social order; then, sooner or later, society must revert to using criminal justice procedures for self-defense, while frightened citizens in turn resort to taking the law in their own hands for self-protection until the public institutions of justice and police resume their traditional responsibilities.

From our vantage point in the United States today, the most interesting portions of *Justice and Police* are Chapters X through XIV which review the process of criminal justice from the marshalling of a police force (constabulary) to maintain social order, through the official acts of arrest, court examination, summary jurisdiction, prosecution, the structure of the criminal courts, and the criminal trial and its consequences. The American reader has only to be sure he has understood the English terms to see that we are concerned here with matters of utmost importance for our time. He can learn from it the folly of burdening our system of law enforcement with tasks it cannot conceivably perform — such as crime prevention and the rehabilitation of criminals. In any event, it is imperative that we begin to take the history of our institutions seriously before history brusquely passes us by. In Maitland's words: "Today we study the day before yesterday, in order that yesterday may not paralyze today, and today may not paralyze tomorrow."[12]

NOTES

1. Cited by Robert L. Schuyler in "The Historical Spirit Incarnate: Frederic William Maitland," *The American Historical Review*, LVII, é, Jan., 1952, p. 305.

2. Warren O. Ault, "The Maitland-Bigelow Letters," *Boston University Law Review*, XXXVII, 1957, p. 286.

3. Sir Edward Fry, review of the *History of English Law before Edward I*, in *English Historical Review*, X, 1895, p. 760.

4. *The Letters of Frederic William Maitland*, ed. by C.H.S. Fifoot, Cambridge, Mass., 1965, p. 60 (letter dated 12 March 1889, to Paul Vinogradoff).

5. See Schuyler, *opus cit.*, p. 332.

6. Below, p. 1.

7. Below, p. 2.

8. *Ibid.*

9. Below, p. 12.

10. *Ibid.*

11. Below, pp. 13-14.

12. *The Collected Papers of Frederic William Maitland*, Cambridge, 1911, III, pp. 438-39.

Major biographical and critical studies of Maitland include: *Frederic William Maitland*, by H.A.L. Fisher, Cambridge, 1910; *Frederick (sic) William Maitland and the History of English Law*, by James R. Cameron, Normon, Oklahoma, 1961; *Maitland: A Critical Examination and Assessment*, by Henry E. Bell, Cambridge, Massachusetts, 1965. Cameron's book has extensive bibliographies.

CESARE BECCARIA'S
ON CRIMES AND PUNISHMENTS

*If at one time it seemed likely that the historical spirit (the spirit
which strove to understand the classical jurisprudence of Rome
and the Twelve Tables, and the Lex Salica, and law of all ages
and climes) was fatalistic and enimical to reform, that time
already lies in the past. . . . Now-a-days we may see the office of
historical research as that of explaining, and therefore lighten-
ing, the pressure that the past must exercise upon the present, and
the present upon the future. To-day we study the day before
yesterday, in order that yesterday may not paralyze to-day, and
to-day may not paralyze tomorrow.*[1]

Frederic W. Maitland

I. REPUTATION

Historians of criminal law agree, almost without exception,
that the "glory of having expelled the use of torture from every
tribunal throughout Christendom" belongs primarily to Cesare
Beccaria.[2] His treatise *On Crimes and Punishments* (*Dei Delitti e
delle Pene*), newly translated here, is generally acknowledged to
have had "more practical effect than any other treatise ever
written in the long campaign against barbarism in criminal law
and procedure.[3]

The work was originally published anonymously in Tuscany
in 1764. Almost at once, as if an exposed nerve had been
touched, all Europe was stirred to excitement. The first English
translator, writing eighteen months after its original appearance, noted that the work had already passed through six
editions in Italian, that several French editions had appeared,

[From *On Crimes and Punishments*, translated with an Introduction by
Henry Paolucci. The Library of Liberal Arts, Bobbs Merrill Educational Publishing, Indianapolis, 1963.]

and that "perhaps no book, on any subject, was ever received with more avidity, more generally read, or more universally applauded."[4] The French translation of 1766, by the Abbé Morellet, had been the vehicle for rapid diffusion of the work through all the enlightened salons, coffee-houses, and courts of Europe. In Paris, d'Alembert, Helvetius, Buffon, d'Holbach, and the visiting Hume praised it enthusiastically. Voltaire, who later graced it with an elaborate commentary, hailed it as "le code de l'humanité."[5] Frederick II of Prussia expressed his admiration by complaining, in a letter to Voltaire, that Beccaria "has left hardly anything to be gleaned after him" in the sphere of criminal law.[6] Maria Teresa of Austria and the Grand Duke Leopold of Tuscany publicly declared their intention to be guided by the book's principles in the reformation of their laws, while Catherine the Great of Russia called upon its author to reside at her court and attend to the necessary reforms in person.[7]

In England, it was Beccaria's treatise, as Sir William Holdsworth states, that "helped Blackstone to crystallize his ideas."[8] Upon reading it Jeremy Bentham was moved to write: "Oh, my master, first evangelist of Reason . . . you who have made so many useful excursions into the path of utility, what is there left for us to do? — Never to turn aside from that path."[9] Across the Atlantic, John Adams took inspiration from the book for his defense of the British soldiers involved in the Boston Massacre of 1770; and long after the trial, many of those who had been present recalled vividly, as John Quincy Adams later reported, "the electrical effect produced upon the jury and upon the immense and excited auditory, by the first sentence with which he opened his defense, which was [a] citation from the then recently published work of Beccaria."[10]

In the midst of such widespread approbation, the slight adverse criticism the work initially attracted proved to be of little consequence. The Church of Rome had placed the treatise on the Index in 1766, condemning it for its extremely rationalistic presuppositions.[11] But in Beccaria's own Milan the representative of Austrian despotic rule, Count Firmian, personally defended the author against charges of sacrilege and political subversion, and the Austrian government itself was moved to honor him by assigning him a professorial chair in the Palatine schools of Milan.[12] By that time, however, critics frustrated in their attacks on Beccaria's work were already redirecting their efforts to the less formidable task of impugning his character.

II. CHARACTER OF THE AUTHOR

Cesare Beccaria was born on March 15, 1738, of an aristocratic Milanese family that had long ceased to exercise political functions commensurate with its title. After eight years of what he later called "fanatical education,"[13] under the Jesuits of Parma, he studied, without distinguishing himself, at the University of Pavia, where he received a degree in 1758. In 1761, encouraged by his friends Pietro and Alessandro Verri, he boldly contracted a marriage which his father had sought by every possible means to prevent. But the experience of attempting to earn a living, and the specter of poverty, soon unsettled his resolve. In a melodramatic scene staged by his resourceful friends, he and his frightened bride humbly begged and obtained parental forgiveness and support. Young Beccaria's resentment against the authority of the aristocratic paterfamilias — an authority which he would inherit upon his father's death — was later movingly expressed in several passages of his celebrated treatise.

The Verri brothers also encouraged Beccaria in his intellectual exploits. For the elder brother, Pietro, ten years his senior, young Cesare came to feel, he later said, "the same enthusiasm of friendship that Montaigne felt for Étienne de la Boétie.[14] He was everything Cesare dreamed of being. After a rebellious youth of wild love affairs and heated family quarrels, Pietro had successfully launched himself on a literary career, only to interrupt it suddenly by enlisting in the Austrian army. He attained the rank of captain and distinguished himself for bravery in the campaigns of the Seven Years' War against Prussia. When he returned to Milan in 1760, he undertook, with his younger brother Alessandro, to initiate a program of political, social, and literary reforms. With the young Milanese intelligentsia rallying around them, they formed a society later known as the "academy of fists," dedicated to waging relentless war against economic disorder, bureaucratic petty tyranny, religious narrow-mindedness, and intellectual pedantry. To propagate their ideas they eventually established a periodical, *Il Caffé*, modeled on Joseph Addison's *Spectator*.

It was as a member of this avant-gardist "academy of fists" that Beccaria first took up his pen in behalf of humanity. The heated discussions that animated the Verri house, where the reformers regularly met, fascinated his attention. Under Pietro Verri's guidance, he began to read the enlightened authors of France and England: Montesquieu, first of all, then Helvetius, who taught him the principle of "utility," then d'Alembert, Diderot, Buffon, Hume — "illustrious names," he later wrote, "which no one can hear without emotion."[15] He was an avid reader and an attentive listener. But, except for occasional outbursts of compassion and irrepressible indignation when the discussion turned on the sad tale of man's inhumanity to man, he said little, and wrote only when his friends assigned a topic, elaborated the subject matter, and literally pieced his fragmentary utterances together for him. His first publication, a treatise "On Remedies for the Monetary Disorders of Milan in the Year 1762," was thus written at the suggestion and with the constant prodding of Pietro Verri, who had expert knowledge of the subject, and who, when the work was attacked soon after publication, personally took up the burden of defending it.

On Crimes and Punishments was composed with similar prodding and assistance. Pietro Verri, Beccaria gratefully acknowledged in a letter to the Abbé Morellet, "gave me the strength to write; and I owe it to him that the manuscript of *On Crimes . . .* which he generously transcribed for me in his own hand, did not end up in the flames."[16] When a rumor began to circulate that the work was not really Beccaria's, Pietro took care to define very precisely his role in its composition. "I suggested the topic to him," he conceded, "and most of the ideas came out of daily conversation between Beccaria, Alessandro, Lambertenghi, and myself." But the book itself, he asserted unequivocally, "is by the Marquis Beccaria." Admittedly young Cesare "knew nothing about our criminal system" at the time the topic was suggested, but what he lacked his friends were eager and able to supply. Alessandro Verri had assumed the official post of "protector of prisoners" in Milan, and therefore had firsthand knowledge of penal practices. Pietro had already begun to compile materials for a history of torture, and had a host of details on the tip of his tongue. Beccaria — Pietro's account continues — "began to write down some of his ideas on loose pieces of paper; we urged him on with enthusiasm, stimulating him so much that he soon got together a great quantity of them. After dinner we would take a walk, discuss the errors of criminal jurisprudence, argue, raise questions, and in the evening he would write. But writing is so laborious for him, and costs him so much effort that after an hour he collapses and can't go on. When he had amassed the materials, I wrote them out, arranged them in order, and thus made a book out of them."[17]

Because of Beccaria's fear that he might be prosecuted for it, the book thus shaped by enthusiastic collaboration was originally issued anonymously. But once it was clear that the Milanese political authorities welcomed the treatise, anonymity was discarded. The happiest result of the publication was, of course, the attention it drew from the Parisian intelligentsia. After the French translation appeared, the Abbé Morellet, writing in the name of the Encyclopedists, invited Pietro Verri to visit Paris with Beccaria so that due honor might be accorded the author of *On Crimes and Punishments*. Unfortunately, Pietro could not accept; his recent appointment as head of a commission charged with revising the provincial laws obliged him to remain in Milan. Beccaria, fearful of the impression he would make, in person and alone, at first refused to budge. But Pietro was master. As he had regulated Beccaria's marital affairs, as he had directed his reading and writing, so he assigned him the task of journeying to Paris to receive the honors of the world. On October 2, 1766, accompanied by Alessandro Verri, Beccaria took his departure, following his escort, it is said, not like a hero on his way to a triumph, but like a condemned prisoner on his way to the gallows.

Halfway there, he threatened to turn back, "By God," Pietro Verri wrote to spur him on, "I owe you the candor to tell you a truth in writing that I might not have the heart to tell you face to face, and it is that there is a puerile side to your character that greatly detracts from the esteem to which you are entitled .... This European trip is certain to cure you, and it is the only thing that can cure you."[18]

In Paris, Beccaria was indeed received with adoration. The most famous personalities of the day escorted him from salon to salon, where he was honored as a great benefactor of humanity. But he made a very bad impression. Morellet thus represents the fiasco in his *Mémoires*:

> ... he arrived somber and anxious, and one could hardly get a word out of him. His friend, on the contrary, a personable fellow, gay, and of ready wit, soon attracted to himself the solicitudes and attentions of society. It was this, finally, that completely turned poor Beccaria's head. After having spent but three weeks or a month in Paris, he went home alone, leaving us, as a pledge, the count Verri. Toward the end of his sojourn he was so irritated mentally and emotionally that he would close himself up in his room at the hotel where ... I often went to keep him company, trying, without success, to calm him.[19]

Before it took place, Pietro Verri exerted every possible pressure to prevent Beccaria's homeward flight. "You must not forget," he wrote, "that, having attracted to yourself the regard of mankind ... , you cannot hope that the act of timidity you contemplate will remain hidden." He warned Beccaria that some people would say he was an effeminate, childish imbecile, without backbone, "incapable of living away from his mother." Others would think he fled because Paris had slighted him, and "all sorts of things are bound to be said about your character which I can darkly foresee and which you can imagine as well as I, if you reflect on it."[20]

But for once Beccaria asserted his independence. Instinctively he realized that he was not able, as a man, to live up to the reputation of the book. Hoping to salvage that reputation, and eventually his own as author, he chose to disappoint the expectations of the "academy of fists" and to alienate his dearest friend by taking flight.

Once home, Beccaria never ventured forth again. In Milan, where he could not conceal the truth about himself, there was much ridicule and gossip. And yet, he was the gainer. Enjoying the patronage of the Austrian government, he lapsed into an Epicurean indolence. From 1768 until his death in 1794 he occupied a series of public offices that were all more or less sinecures; but isolated as he was from his old friend he was not able, in all that time, to produce a single writing worthy of public attention.

Abroad, however, especially in France and England, a legend began to shape itself about his name. Admirers of his book, ignorant of the political situation in Milan, interpreted Beccaria's long silence romantically, as evidence of cruel suppression at the hands of a tyrannical and bigoted government. "Athens," an English admirer wrote, "would have honored him; Rome would have given him a triumph; in Italy he is silent." A French translator concluded: "If he who at twenty-six could write the immortal *On Crimes and Punishments* had lived in a land of freedom, we would have had other masterpieces, and posterity would not have to regard with astonishment the silence in which Beccaria kept himself for the rest of his life."[21]

While Beccaria lived, such a legend could not have gained credence in Italy. But after his death, Pietro Verri, who survived him by three years, prepared a way for its eventual cultivation. With the man himself no longer present to embarrass the cause, "Citizen Verri," on December 13, 1797, called upon the municipality of Milan to erect "a monument of recognition to the immortal Beccaria."[22] Thus the man who might have been the most devastating witness against him undertook to silence public criticism — and very nearly succeeded. Except for the scruple of scholars, Beccaria would be remembered today, everywhere in the world, not only as a literary champion of the cause of humanity but also as one of its heroic, long-suffering martyrs.

III. STYLE AND CONTENT

Much has been written about the style of the work. In the late eighteenth century, a number of neo-classical purists denied that it had a style in the strict sense. For instance, Giuseppe Baretti, the distinguished literary critic and friend of Samuel Johnson, did not hesitate to describe it as a "wretched little thing bastardly written."[23] Some critics who knew the complex story of its composition — how a mass of ideas from the French rationalists had been hastily scribbled by Beccaria, transcribed and reordered by Verri, drastically revised by subsequent editors and translators, especially by Morellet, whose paragraphing and reordered sequence Beccaria willingly adopted as an improvement over the original — argued that *On Crimes and Punishments* ought not to be considered as the work of an individual author with a distinctive personality and style of his own. And yet even a cursory reading of its pages suffices to discredit such an allegation. His friends no doubt supplied the ideas and what little logical sequence is to be found in it, but, as Pietro Verri remarked, "the poetry of the work is Beccaria's very own."[24]

That there is poetry in the treatise critics of the romantic era readily acknowledged. Ugo Foscolo, rejecting the neo-classical standards, characterized its style as "absolute and secure,"[25] and subsequent scholars have remarked that while the writing is uneven in parts the effect of the whole borders on the sublime. Many of its sentences, especially those in which the author offers to display his mastery of "geometric" reasoning, are hopelessly involuted. Clauses are strung together in a maze of complexity, as if the author were attempting to express involved thought with maximum precision, when in fact he is merely trying to veil his juridical and historical ignorance, which was notorious. Sympathetic translators often presume to break up such sentences, hoping thereby to resolve the riddle of their meaning. But the result is invariably disastrous. Syntactical simplification merely lays bare the emptiness of arguments that Beccaria's involuted language manages to conceal. Stylistically, moreover, the labored passages serve admirably to throw the truly eloquent sequences into high relief. In Chapter XIV, for instance, after a painfully long and complicated discussion of the utility of offering impunity to criminals who agree to give evidence against their companions, Beccaria suddenly interrupts himself to exclaim: " . . . but I torment myself uselessly trying to overcome the remorse I feel in authorizing the inviolable laws, the monument of public trust, the basis of human morality, to countenance treachery and dissimulation."

The style is, in other words, that of an impassioned plea —
a style suitable for a work pertaining to the practical and
productive spheres of juridical discourse rather than to the
theoretic. As employed by Beccaria, its object is not to demonstrate what the law *is*, but rather to incite men to *make* it what
the author thinks it *ought to be*. Bentham has carefully drawn the
distinction, contrasting two basic kinds of juridical writing —
the expository, concerned with ascertaining what the law is,
and the censorial, treating of what it ought to be. Beccaria, he
has asserted emphatically, "may be styled the father of *Censorial
Jurisprudence*." Montesquieu had indicated the direction, but
his own *Spirit of the Laws* was, according to Bentham, "a work
of mixed kind," part expository, part censorial. Before
Montesquieu, of course, "all was unmixed barbarism."[26]

In his introductory statement "To the Reader," Beccaria
warns those who would criticize him that he means to proceed
in the "geometric spirit," establishing what ought to be in the
sphere of law by systematic deduction from a set of self-evident
principles which his reader must be intelligent enough not to
expect him to prove. He is aware that his principles cannot be
induced by studying things as they are, especially not in the
sphere of criminal procedures, where gross error, ignorance,
and malice have reigned for centuries. But that is their virtue,
not their vice.

According to Beccaria, the fundamental principle that
ought to govern the entire sphere of legislation is self-evidently
that of "the greatest happiness to be shared by the greatest
number." This principle has never actually determined the laws
of men, but enlightened thinkers, he says, have always acknowledged its primacy and have already made use of it to discover
the various subordinate principles that ought to regulate
industry, commerce, foreign affairs, and the relations between
sovereigns and their subjects. One area not yet effectively
explored in the light of that principle is that of crimes and
punishments. "Few persons," Beccaria writes, not in the least
attempting to conceal his practical intent, "have studied and
fought against the cruelty of punishments and the irregularities
of criminal procedures, a part of legislation that is as fundamental as it is widely neglected in almost all of Europe." To

study and to fight against the present situation amount to the same, in Beccaria's judgment, for he believes that the situation is sustained entirely by ignorance. To focus light upon it is to destroy it.

In the first chapter Beccaria raises the basic questions he means to explore:

> But what are to be the proper punishments for such crimes?
> Is the death-penalty really useful and necessary for the security and good order of society? Are torture and torments just, and do they attain the end for which laws are instituted? What is the best way to prevent crimes? Are the same punishments equally effective for all times? What influence have they on customary behavior?

These problems, he urges, must be analyzed with "geometric precision." To discover the principles that ought to govern such an analysis Beccaria directs his readers to "consult the human heart," where nature itself has imprinted them.

Political community, Beccaria's heart tells him, is, or rather, ought to be the result of an accord entered into by men in order to guarantee for themselves the maximum enjoyment of personal liberty. Each individual willingly sacrifices to the political community only so much of his liberty as "suffices to induce others to defend it." Laws are, or ought to be, simply the necessary conditions of this "social contract," and punishments under the law ought to have no other purpose than to defend the sum of sacrificed shares of liberty "against private usurpations by individuals." Punishments aiming at any other end are "useless" and by their very nature unjust.

These rationalistic ideas of majoritarian hedonism, social contract, and utility were commonplace enough in Beccaria's time. The novelty of his book consists in his censorial application of them. His presentation proceeds as a kind of trial. From the beginning it is clear that, in the author's judgment, a terrible crime has been committed against humanity. The principles that ought to govern all human relations have been and are still being violated in a most barbarous manner. Under accusation before the court of world opinion are almost all the rulers, legislators, jurists, magistrates, policemen, and jailers of the past and present. It is useless to argue against the impassioned author that he misrepresents many of the juridical theories and practices brought under accusation. It is of no concern to him that the principles he professes are inadequate to embrace in any meaningful way the facts of Western legal experience; that no nation, past or present, was ever formed by a social contract; that law is not and never has been merely a bond of equals, as the social contract theory assumes. Neither is it of concern to him that, in the attempt to realize the greatest happiness of the greatest number, utility itself may dictate the necessity of torture, severity of punishments, and even the death penalty. What is of concern to him he has plainly stated in words that limit precisely the use to which the doctrine of his book can properly be applied. Recognizing the censorial force of the words, John Adams made use of them, before a hostile court, to open his defense of the British soldiers implicated in the Boston Massacre:

> . . . if, by defending the rights of man and of unconquerable truth, I should help to save from the spasm and agonies of death some wretched victim of tyranny or of no less fatal ignorance, the thanks and tears of one innocent mortal in his transports of joy would console me for the contempt of all mankind.[27]

IV. HISTORICAL SIGNIFICANCE

Beccaria's *On Crimes and Punishments* played a significant role, historically, in the final phase of the long struggle between the hereditary aristocrats of Europe and the great monarchic families bent on destroying the independent authority of the so-called intermediate powers. Basing their rule on the ever increasing wealth and numbers of the rising bourgeoisie, the great monarchs gradually succeeded in depriving the aristocratic class of its political and military functions, if not of its leisure. No longer able to justify their privileged status by their willingness and ability to fight, ambitious noblemen took to the pen. Some labored, by means of words, to validate old feudal claims, recognition of which their ancestors had extorted by violence. Others, resigning themselves to a courtier's life, attempted to justify on historical or rational grounds the prerogatives of absolute monarchs. Still others courted the rising bourgeoisie, hoping to establish themselves as a new aristocracy of intellect and sensibility by defending the "rights of men and inviolable truth" against all the oppressive forces of darkness.

Beccaria's treatise was a contribution to the third of these aristocratic causes. In the interests of mankind, its author appealed to the enlightened rulers of Europe to use all their coercive power to crush the petty tyrannies of aristocratic privilege and bureaucratic abuse. In its immediate sense, the appeal seemed, indeed, to serve the cause of monarchs against the intermediary powers. But its ultimate effect was to precipitate the ruin of both. Throughout Europe the revolutions that swept away aristocratic privilege did not cease until they had swept away monarchic pretensions as well. And they proved to be viciously brutal revolutions, in some instances, precisely because enlightened monarchs had encouraged the propagation of works that exaggerated the evils as well as the powers of the *ancien régime*.

To what extent Beccaria's work exaggerated the evils of criminal procedure in his day his own grandson, Alessandro Manzoni — Italy's greatest novelist and one of her greatest poets — troubled himself to demonstrate in his *Storia della Colonna Infame*. Illustrating at length a passage on torture in his novel *I Promessi Sposi*, Manzoni acknowledges that Beccaria's "little book, which was rather an overflow of spontaneous inspirations than a work of premeditated study, prompted, and I am on the verge of saying, commanded the reform" of criminal law.[28] But then he proceeds to review the evidence marshalled in justification of its severe indictment of the past. For that purpose he examines Pietro Verri's *Osservazioni sulla Tortura*, posthumously published in 1804,[29] in which one may read for oneself the materials that were drummed into Beccaria's ears when Verri was priming him to write on crimes and punishments.

Manzoni stresses particularly the misrepresentation of the juridical ideas of the preceding ages, defending at length the jurists Claro and Farinacci, who are so pointedly maligned in the opening paragraphs of Beccaria's treatise. He shows that

Verri, followed by Beccaria, attributed to them doctrines the very opposite of what they taught. He observes that they were, in fact, men no less compassionate than the humanitarian rationalists who criticized them; that they had labored long, not merely with words, but with the full weight of their juridical authority, to check the ever-lively tendency of law-enforcers to apply inordinate physical and psychological pressures in their efforts to maintain public order. In language permeated by the "historical spirit," defended by Frederic Maitland, Manzoni thus places the radical reform movement in historical perspective:

> That is how it usually happens with human reforms which are only gradually accomplished (I speak of genuine and just reforms, not of all things that have taken the name): to the men who first undertake them, it seems a great deal to modify the situation, to correct it in various parts, to subtract and add. Those who come later, often much later, finding the situation still bad (as it is), are likely to dwell on the latest contributors, condemning as authors those whose names are most recently connected with it, simply because they have given it the form in which it currently lives and prevails.[30]

Beccaria, according to Manzoni, was one of those who came much later. Having exaggerated the number and strength of his enemies, he was filled with wonder, understandably, at the apparent efficacy of his words. But students of history ought not to perpetuate his exaggerations, for it is simply not true that the criminal procedures Beccaria attacked were as vicious as he made them out to be; neither is it true that the system of law he boldly challenged "had on its side," as some of his admirers assert, "all authority living and dead." Old, and undermined in many parts as it was, that husk of ancient law "would have fallen eventually," so Manzoni concludes, "even under the blows of less spirited assailants . . . . But at an earlier time such a triumph would have been impossible: in the vigor of youth, error is stronger than genius."[31]

NOTES

1. Frederic William Maitland, *The Collected Papers of Frederic William*

Maitland (Cambridge, 1911), III, 438-39.

2. See Leon Radzinowicz, *A History of English Criminal Law* (New York, 1948), I, 277-83; James Anson Farrer, *Crimes and Punishments, Including a New Translation of Beccaria's "Dei Delitti e delle Pene"* (London, 1880), pp. 3, 46; Coleman Phillipson, *Three Criminal Law Reformers* (London, 1923), pp. 32-34, 100-02.

3. Harry Elmer Barnes and Howard Becker, *Social Thought from Lore to Science* (Washington, 1952), I, 551-52.

4. Cesare Beccaria, *An Essay on Crimes and Punishments*, tr. unknown (London, 1767), Preface of the Translator, pp. iii-iv.

5. See Cesare Beccaria, *Des dèlits et des peines*, tr. J. A. S. Collin de Plancy (2nd edn.; Paris, 1823), p. xviii.

6. Voltaire, Francois-Marie Arouet, *Oeuvres complètes*, ed. L. Moland (Paris, 1877-85), L, 265.

7. On Beccaria's influence, see Phillipson, *Three Criminal Law Reformers*, pp. 83-106.

8. Cited by Radzinowicz, *History of English Criminal Law*, I, 346.

9. MSS. University College, London, No. 32. Cited in Élie Halévy, *The Growth of Philosophical Radicalism* (London, 1928), p. 21.

10. John Adams, *The Works of John Adams* (Boston, 1856), II, 238-39n.

11. See article on Beccaria in *Enciclopedia Cattolica* (Vatican City, 1949), Vol. II, col. 1126.

12. See Phillipson, *Three Criminal Law Reformers*, pp. 14, 21.

13. See Marcello T. Maestro, *Voltaire and Beccaria as Reformers of Criminal Law* (New York, 1942), p. 52.

14. Beccaria, *Opere*, ed. Sergio Romagnoli (Florence, 1958), II 867.

15. Maestro, *Voltaire and Beccaria*, p. 52.

16. Beccaria, *Opere*, II, 867.

17. Carlo Casati, *Lettere e Scritti Inediti di Pietro e Alessandro Verri* (Milan, 1879-81), I, 189-90.

18. Beccaria, *Opere*, I, xxxiii.

19. Abbé Morellet, *Mémoires* (Paris, 1823), I, 167-68.

20. Beccaria, *Opere*, I, xxxi.

21. Beccaria, *Des délits et des peines* (Paris, 1823), p. xxvi.

22. See Piero Calamandrei's introduction to Cesare Beccaria, *Dei Delitti e delle Pene* (Florence, 1950), p. 61.

23. *Ibid.*, p. 46.

24. *Ibid.*, p. 61.

25. *Ibid.*, p. 49.

26. Jeremy Bentham, *A Fragment on Government*, ed. F. C. Montague (London, 1891), p. 105, n. 2.

27. See John Adams, *Works*, II, 238. The source in Beccaria's treatise is Chapter I, Introduction (p. 10).

28. Alessandro Manzoni, *Tutte le Opere di Alessandro Manzoni*, ed. Alberto Chiari and Fausto Ghisalberti (Milan, 1959), II[1], 969.

29. Pietro Verri, *Osservazioni Sulla Tortura*, in *Scrittori Classici Italiani di Economia Politica*, Parte Moderna (Milan, 1804), XVII, 191-319.

30. Manzoni, *Opere*, II[1], 695.

31. *Ibid.*, II[3], 683.

THE KISSINGER LEGACY

The war in Vietnam was, in a sense, a theorists' war par excellence. The strategists of the late nineteen-fifties were only slightly interested in the question of which country or countries might be the scene of a limited war . . . . Kissinger had warned in his 1957 book that the policy he was proposing would require 'a public opinion which had been educated to the realities of the nuclear age.' . . . One might say that the plan was to pay for nuclear peace with limited war . . . and that it was in the very nature of the doctrine that it had to be presented misleadingly to the public and the world. For to explain the policy fully would be to undermine it.

Jonathan Schell
The Time of Illusion (New York, 1976)

Kissinger's war began as a theorist's war with the publication of *Nuclear Weapons and Foreign Policy* (New York, 1957), and it remained a theorist's war — a textbook war — until its author was appointed to the post of Special Assistant to the President for National Security Affairs by President-Elect Richard M. Nixon, on December 2, 1968.

After that, Henry A. Kissinger — young Harvard theorist and Rockefeller Brothers Foundation research-director — quickly found opportunities to turn theory into practice. He rose rapidly from the status of mere coordinator of National Security Council deliberations to that of chief White House military strategist and tactician for a very real war. Rising higher still, he had the extraordinary experience, as Secretary of State, of receiving in his very own hands a presidential letter of

[From *Kissinger's War: 1957-1975*. Published for The Walter Bagehot Research Council by Griffon House Publ., NY, 1980]

resignation, the first ever submitted in American history.

With the man who originally appointed him driven from office, Henry Kissinger went on to exercise a virtual monopoly in the conduct of America's side of a war which had already become for him an almost total fusion of theory and practice. That was the time of the Ford-Rockefeller *interregnum* – a period more than two years during which the top elective posts of the American Government, both the Presidency and the Vice-Presidency, were occupied by non-elected appointees. Then it was that Secretary Kissinger, still holding his cards very close to his chest, maneuvered spectacularly to bring the war to a close.

The end came abruptly in April 1975, while the American Embassy in Saigon was in full operation. Henry Kissinger had decided not to "panic the natives" by signaling the precipitous and total flight of the American presence he had designed. Thus, American newsmen were on hand to photograph the efforts of many local clients of our Government to cling to the landing-gear of the "last" American helicopters fleeing from the scene. Even so, it could not be said that the war had ended haphazardly. Certainly Henry Kissinger gave none of us the impression that, as its supreme theorist and strategist, he had lost control of the war. On the contrary, those who knew his "theory" of limited war in the nuclear age, could see at once that he had obviously brought the thing to an end quite in accordance with the theoretic prescriptions of 1957, not the least of which was, in his own view, the following:

> A doctrine of limited war will have to discard any illusions about what can be achieved by means of it. Limited war is not a cheaper substitute for massive retaliation. On the contrary, it must be based on an awareness that with the end of our atomic monopoly it is no longer possible to impose unconditional surrender at an acceptable cost . . . . The argument that neither side will accept defeat, however limited, without utilizing every weapon in its arsenal is contradicted both by psychology and by experience. There would seem to be no sense in seeking to escape a limited defeat through bringing on the cataclysm of an all-out-

war, particularly if all-out war threatens a calamity far transcending the penalties of losing a limited war. It simply does not follow that because one side stands to lose from a limited war it could gain from an all-out war. (1957 ed., pp. 123-124)

I. The War in Theory: Kissinger's Apprenticeship

In early January 1969, shortly after Kissinger's appointment to the office his Harvard-MIT colleagues McGeorge Bundy and Walt W. Rostow had held under Presidents Kennedy and Johnson, the Council on Foreign Relations published a second, abridged edition of *Nuclear Weapons and Foreign Policy*. Gordon Dean had written a publisher's foreword for the original edition and he here supplied a revision of the same in which he summed up the reasons for the "immediate and profound impact" the book had previously made "both here and abroad." A first reason, he said, was that it had "succeeded in articulating with great clarity the fears and reservations that many Americans had been feeling about certain of our postwar policies and failures — especially about our reliance on massive retaliation." Another was that "readers found in Dr. Kissinger a first-rate intelligence which had succeeded in cutting through many false assumptions and contradictions in our policies to propound a fresh conception." But, speaking for those who had originally employed young Henry Kissinger to write the book for them, Gordon Dean had not hesitated to conclude:

> Finally, the book carried added weight, perhaps, because it was the outgrowth of a study conducted by the Council on Foreign Relations, which called together a panel of exceptionally qualified individuals to explore all factors involved in the making and implementing of foreign policy in the nuclear age. Thus, although the book is the work of an individual, Dr. Kissinger had the benefit of the wisdom and experience of experts and men of affairs in all relevant fields, such as government, diplomacy, science, engineering, the military services, and weapons production.

The immediate impact of the book in 1957 had been to

establish Henry Kissinger as the leading academic critic of the way President Eisenhower, with Richard M. Nixon as his Vice-President and John Foster Dulles as his Secretary of State, had brought the Korean War to an end in 1953. Eisenhower had campaigned for the Presidency the year before on a pledge that he would quickly end the stalemate in Korea. Truman's administration had failed to convince the aggressors, "in advance," that their aggressions would not be a profitable operation; "a wholly new Administration" was required "to bring the Korean War to an early and honorable end," because the "old Administration cannot be expected to repair what it had failed to prevent."

After the July 27, 1953 Truce Treaty was signed, and he was asked "what it was that had brought the Communists into line," President Eisenhower had replied without equivocation: "Danger of an atomic war. We told them we could not hold it to a limited war any longer if the Communists welched on a treaty of truce. They didn't want a full-scale war or an atomic attack. That kept them under some control."

At about the same time, in his "historic" address of January 12, 1954, before the Council on Foreign Relations, Secretary Dulles formulated the national security principle that had guided Eisenhower in terminating the Korean war. The containment policy inherited from the Truman administration, Dulles had said, remained in force; but with this difference: henceforth potential aggressors would have our assurances in advance that their aggression would backfire on them, that we would strike back to contain it, not necessarily on the spot, to their perceived advantage, but "at places and with means of our own choosing . . . reinforced by the further deterrent of massive-retaliatory power."

That was the Eisenhower-Dulles policy against which Kissinger had purportedly written his *Nuclear Weapons and Foreign Policy*. Between 1957 and the 1960 election, Nixon had often spoken in defense of what Kissinger criticized; and, as it became clear that Nixon would be the leading Republican presidential contender after Eisenhower, the Democratic contenders began to identify him with the massive retaliation policy and attack him for it. Professor Paul Peeters very ably documented the phenomenon at the time in *Massive Retaliation: The Policy and its Critics* (Chicago, 1959), where we read:

> No author is more frequently quoted by critics of massive retaliation than Henry Kissinger, and none has bothered less about understanding what he criticizes . . . . If Senator Kennedy quotes Mr. Kissinger about our alleged "Maginot-line reliance upon massive retaliation," it is because, with Kissinger, he identifies massive retaliation with overwhelming air-atomic superiority, a misconception for which there is no excuse whatever.

Perhaps if the United States had been at war somewhere in 1960, as it had been in 1952 and would be in 1968, Richard Nixon might have won the Presidency that year. During John F. Kennedy's three years as President, at any rate, it was not the Eisenhower-Dulles strategy for handling limited wars but one very like Kissinger's — advanced and implemented by McGeorge Bundy, Walt Rostow, and Robert McNamara — that was operative. By then Henry Kissinger had in fact written a second important book on the subject, *The Necessity for Choice* (New York, 1960), refining his earlier doctrine. In 1957, he had argued that, in waging a limited war, a threat to use tactical nuclear weapons might be admissible, provided the enemy were assured that it would not lead to our employment of strategic nuclear arms, or other means of all-out war, simply to avoid limited defeat. In 1960, on the contrary, he argued that nuclear weapons of any kind, tactical or whatever, had no place at all in his refined doctrine of limited war. To be truly limited in his sense of the term, a war would have to be fought exclusively with conventional weapons, he explained, from beginning to end, since it would be virtually impossible to authorize our field commanders to use tactical nuclear weapons, and then expect them to pull back intentionally, and lose, if the enemy persisted in his resistance. Kissinger therefore argued in 1960 that no nuclear weapons, not even such as might have a force yield *less* than conventional weapons, should be in the possession of any American unit committed to combat in a limited war. Summing up his "reversal" on this position since 1957, Kissinger wrote:

Some years ago this author advocated a nuclear strategy. It seemed then that the most effective deterrent to
any substantial Communist aggression was the knowledge that the United States would employ nuclear
weapons from the very outset. [That was, of course, the
Eisenhower-Dulles view rejected by Kissinger;
Kissinger's nuclear strategy proposed to go as far as to
use the *threat* of tactical nuclear weapons, not massive
retaliation, as a last resort.] The need for forces capable of fighting limited nuclear war remains. However, several developments have caused a shift in the
view about the relative emphasis to be given conventional forces as against nuclear forces . . . .

To be sure, troops can be trained to use both nuclear
and conventional weapons. They should be aware of
the elementary forms of protection [!] against nuclear
attack. But once committed to combat, the units actually engaged in military operations must choose one
mode of warfare or the other . . . . If nuclear weapons
become an integral part of the equipment of *every* unit,
it will be next to impossible to keep a war conventional
regardless of the intentions of both sides. Even if the
plan is to employ nuclear weapons as a last resort (and
"in a manner to minimize damage") this becomes
empty when the responsibility of defining a last resort
becomes too decentralized. A regimental or even a
divisional commander should not be the judge. Lacking the over-all picture, he will always be tempted to
utilize all weapons available to him. When he is hard-
pressed, it would require superhuman discipline not to
employ arms which he believes would solve his difficulties.

That was the Kissinger limited-war doctrine of 1960, which
he further refined in several chapters of his *Troubled Partnership*
(New York, 1965) and in his introduction to a book of "read-
ings," titled *Problems in National Strategy*, published that same
year. Basically, for all its apparent complexity, Kissinger's
doctrine differed from the limited-war facets of the containment and massive retaliation policies in only one essential
respect. As Acheson and Dulles defined them, limited wars

were to be fought so as either to stop the aggressor on the spot or, by striking him elsewhere with means and at times of our own choosing, to compel his withdrawal to his starting point. Kissinger's limited war, on the other hand, was to be fought in such a way that, if the enemy refused to give up his local aggression, we could always be in a position to let our side lose — rather than threaten escalation as Eisenhower had done to end the Korean war.

President Kennedy's limited-war strategists, who later served President Johnson, fully accepted the Kissinger version of the limited war doctrine. Yet, as the subsequently published *Pentagon Papers* prove, they never quite succeeded in getting their Presidents to accept the notion that, in Vietnam, losing might after all be preferable to winning. As late as March 17, 1968, just weeks before his announcement that he would not seek a second elective term, President Johnson pounded a lectern before a large audience to say: "Your President has come here to ask you people, and all other people of this nation to join us in a total effort to win the war. Make no mistake about it — I don't want any man in here to go home thinking otherwise — we are going to win!"

Those words of a beleaguered President — faced by a "dump Johnson" movement led by Allard Lowenstein and fully supported by the Eastern intelligentsia — had been rather a cry of defiance against what was for him an inexplicable yet determined effort within his own administration to drive him out of office by means of the war. And at the same time, the Republican Party strategists were predictably trying to take maximum political advantage of the intense opposition the incumbent Democratic President was facing in his own party. With that, we are plunged into the midst of the extraordinary presidential campaign of 1968, when Richard M. Nixon emerged from the political graveyard to gain the Republican nomination and win the November national election.

That he was preparing himself for a comeback, despite his narrow defeat for the Presidency in 1960 and his landslide loss by more than a million votes in the California gubernatorial race of 1962, the former Vice-President had clearly signaled to attentive king-makers in 1966, right after the midterm congressional elections. The results in 1966 clearly presaged what the consequences of the internal Democratic party divisions might be for Johnson in 1968. In many parts of the country, anti-war Democratic liberals and Republican conservatives bent on defeating Democrats by hook or crook had joined forces to oust Democratic incumbents or defeat Democratic aspirants who openly supported "Johnson's war" in Vietnam. And Nixon did not blush at the time to indicate his availability as a candidate for high office ready to "serve" just such a coalition in 1969. Without mincing words he had said on November 11, 1966: "The peace party always wins. I know my party. If the war is going on in '68, there is no power on earth can keep them from trying to outbid the Democrats for the peace vote."

That Nixon statement was widely publicized. I. F. Stone's weekly Washington Newsletter ran a banner headline on it, and then placed ads in the major newspapers, including the *New York Times* and *Washington Post*, calling attention to I. F. Stone's readiness to draft Nixon, if need be, as the Republican candidate to stop Johnson in 1968. Stone wrote: "Many of us will see a Republican victory again — as in 1952 — as the only way to end an Asian war. The price will be the end of that progress on the home front which began under Kennedy and took on real momentum under Johnson before he made his error in February 1965, in the skies over North Vietnam. Even another interlude of social stagnation and lackluster leadership will not be too high a price to pay for peace if Johnson does not change course."

By the start of the 1968 campaign, Nixon was talking like Dulles and Eisenhower before the end of the Korean war. In one of his set speeches, he would typically identify the long-drawn-out Vietnam war as another "Democratic" war, like the Korean war, which could only be ended by a speedy return to the peace-strategy of General Eisenhower. "How do you bring a war to conclusion?" Nixon would ask rhetorically. "I'll tell you how Korea was ended . . . . Eisenhower let the word go out—let the word go out diplomatically — that he would not tolerate this ground war of attrition. And within a matter of months they negotiated."

It was candidate Nixon's way of saying that, while he would

never have gotten us into the Vietnam war in the first place —
fighting the enemy on his own terms on his own grounds — he
would follow the example of his old commander-in-chief in
getting us out. He would let the enemy know that he would not
keep the war limited for their convenience, but would respond
with means and at places and times of our own choosing —
reinforced by the further deterrent of massive retaliation.

Nixon had apparently returned in principle to the Dulles
doctrine against which Henry Kissinger had launched his
Nuclear Weapons and Foreign Policy in 1957. Why would he then,
just a few months later in 1968, turn to the author of that book
to fill the post that McGeorge Bundy and Walt W. Rostow had
held under Presidents Kennedy and Johnson? Coral Bell, in her
highly sympathetic, pro-Kissinger study of *The Diplomacy of
Detente: The Kissinger Era* (New York, 1977), put the question
this way: "How did it happen that Mr. Nixon, who as vice-
president seemed to out-Dulles Dulles in his readiness for war
in the 1954 Vietnam crisis, and who held the angry 'Kitchen
Debate' with Khrushchev in 1959, chose a National Security
Advisor of Kissinger's well-known views ten years later?"

Professor Bell surmises that it was a case of opposites trying
to "use" one another. At any rate, Nixon's seeming acceptance
of Kissinger's "concept of detente," she writes, "may have been
rather more a tactic than a strategy: that the cold warrior of Mr.
Dulles's time was still lying in wait behind the artful web of Dr.
Kissinger's detente diplomacy." But finally Kissinger got the
upper hand. Nixon may well have intended to use Kissinger's
concepts as a cover while preparing to follow the Dulles-
Eisenhower strategy in the end. Yet, as Bell puts it, "in his final
phase of weakness he had to accept them." And that provided
Kissinger with the one thing he could never have supplied for
his doctrine on its own, or with the help of his patron Nelson
Rockefeller: a conservative, hard-line anti-Communist cover.

Nixon's "credentials as a tough-anti-Communist," Professor Bell concludes, "operated as a sort of protective coloration
or camouflage for policies that would probably have raised
great alarm and resistance on the Republican right and in
'Middle America' if they had been sponsored by a liberal
Republican, like Rockefeller, and still more if they had been

sought by a Democrat. Even the eventual necessity of accepting the departure of American troops from Vietnam without victory might have been almost an impeachment matter for a different kind of President."

II. Back Door to Nixon

Walter Lippmann had justified his active support of Nixon straight through the re-election campaign of 1972 on the grounds that only such a man could have made the Kissinger reversal of the Cold War a reality without a tremendous "Middle America" backlash. In his interview with Ronald Steel, his biographer, published on October 16, 1971, we read: "Only Nixon, among the available public men, could have made such a reversal . . . . The theory when I was young and just learning about politics was that you always got Conservatives to do the liberal things, and liberals to do the conservative things. In Nixon's case it's very dramatic because he was such a violent and unscrupulous anti-communist, but nevertheless it's in the correct order of political progress that it's happening."

In the end — in his weakness — President Nixon tried desperately to give his intellectual critics the impression that he had really been playing the Lippmann role quite intentionally, that he had started *right off* as President with the intention of managing a Disraelian turnabout in the American political party system. He said, finally, that he was a "Disraelian"; but that was only after his top Harvard domestic policy advisor "Pat" Moynihan had given him a biography of Disraeli to read. Kissinger, on the other hand, had said quite frankly to a *Time* cover-story reporter before he took office in January 1969: "If I were in nineteenth-century Great Britain, I might be a Disraeli conservative in domestic affairs but not in foreign policy." As paraphrased by the *Time* reporter, Kissinger's own clarification of that self-characterization reads: "Disraeli was an unabashed imperialist. Kissinger, by contrast, believes that U. S. power must not be spread too thinly, especially in politically underdeveloped areas that Americans little understand."

In those days, Kissinger's views were so well-known, as Professor Bell says, especially in the academy, that, to explain why President-elect Nixon might have turned to him, the *Time* cover-story reporter inserted this purposively ambiguous comment: "A superficial reading of some of his works makes him seem like a hawk, but intelligent doves regard him as Richard Nixon's most astute appointment." What could not have been anticipated in January 1969 or October 1971 (when Lippmann rejoiced in the Kissinger-Nixon association) was that Kissinger could conceivably survive without *Nixon as his cover* – so as to avoid the risk of a Nixon reversion before America's self-inflicted defeat in the Vietnam "limited war" could be presented to a confused public (which had given Nixon a conservative landslide victory in 1972) as a *fait accompli*.

Professor Coral Bell acknowledged (in the book from which we have already quoted) that "there were a good many riddles and ambiguities in the relationship between Mr. Nixon and Dr. Kissinger," and adds that there "will perhaps continue to be even after both men have written their memoirs." That is certainly true. President Nixon's memoirs, to be sure, only compound the riddles and ambiguities; for the ex-President seems eager now to claim Kissinger's national security and foreign policy "triumphs" as his very own – as against the charge that he had really functioned finally (with respect to what Lippmann took delight in) only as some far-fetched Trilby to Kissinger's Svengali. But Kissinger's memoirs are something else. He comes close to telling us, in the first chapter of *The White House Years*, that he used *no* Disraelian maneuver to get himself hired by Nixon. He comes close to telling us that *he did not use* a most authoritative *conservative* advocate to facilitate the passage from Rockefeller to Nixon in 1968.

In a subsection of the first chapter titled "Nelson Rockefeller," Kissinger tells us of his bitter disappointment over Rockefeller's repeated loss to the "Nixon forces" of the Republican Party, which took its final toll in 1968. "I attended the gallant press conference in which Rockefeller conceded to Nixon," he writes, "and I was sick at heart." A few sentences later, we are in a subsection titled "The Phone Call," where we read: "Some months after that depressing day – with Richard Nixon now President-elect – I was having lunch with Governor Rockefeller and a group of his advisers in New York City in his small apartment on the fourth floor of the Museum of Primitive Art. It was Friday, November 22, 1968 . . . . In this splendid setting we were discussing what attitude Rockefeller should take toward a possible offer to join the Nixon cabinet and what Cabinet position he should seek if given a choice."

Kissinger observed that Nixon would "almost surely carry out his announced intention to act as his own Secretary of State," and therefore urged Rockefeller to aim for Secretary of Defense, in which post he would be able to "implement his decades-long interest in national security." Given the example of Robert McNamara, it was likely, too, Kissinger had added, that "the Secretary of Defense could play a major role in the design of foreign policy." And then it happened. "We were debating these considerations in a desultory fashion," writes Kissinger, "when we were interrupted by a telephone call from the office of the President-elect." Who but the President-elect would be putting in a call to that exquisitely decorated Rockefeller apartment "designed by the architect Wallace Harrison, who had also built Rockefeller Center"? Kissinger at this point lets his old patron down gently.

"It was a poignant reminder of Rockefeller's frustrating career in national politics," the ex-Harvard professor writes, "that the caller was Nixon's appointments secretary, Dwight Chapin, who was interrupting Rockefeller's strategy meeting to ask me — and not Rockefeller — to meet with his chief. In retrospect, it is clear that this phone call made our discussion pointless. But we returned to it as if nothing had happened. No one at the lunch could conceive that the purpose of the call could be to offer me a major position in the new Administration."

Obviously Rockefeller had not been pressing the President-elect to give his man Kissinger a major position in the new Administration. Had Kissinger himself, perhaps, made a back door bid on his own? Had he been expecting such a call, having told the appointments secretary's staff where he might be reached? "I did not know the President-elect," he writes. "My friend William F. Buckley, Jr., the conservative columnist, had told me for years that Nixon was underestimated by his critics, that he was more intelligent and sensitive than his opponents assumed. But I had no opportunity to form my own judgment until after the 1968 election." Acting for Rockefeller at the Republican National Convention in Miami, Kissinger had earlier that year met members of the Nixon campaign staff, but only to "make sure," as he says, that the Republican platform planks on Vietnam "took account of the hopes for a negotiated settlement." It had been the convention victors' small concession to the vanquished, he adds, "which we in the Rockefeller camp — with little enough to celebrate — welcomed as a moral victory."

Was that all the contact that preceded what Kissinger calls "The Phone Call"? No. There had been one more thing. Kissinger had agreed in a general way that both the Humphrey staff and the Nixon staff could get answers on specific questions in the area of his expertise, if they wished. But in any event, he hastens to add, "only one question was ever put to me by the Nixon organization." And here comes the second and only other reference to William F. Buckely, Jr. in the Kissinger memoirs.

> Early in October 1968, Bill Buckley introduced me to John Mitchell, then Nixon's campaign manager. Mitchell asked me if I thought the Johnson Administration would agree to a bombing halt in Vietnam in return for the opening of negotiations before the election. I replied that it seemed highly probable that the North Vietnamese wanted a bombing halt on these terms, and that they would seek to commit both candidates to it. Therefore I believed that Hanoi was likely to agree to it just before the election. I advised against making an issue of it. [To make an issue of it would have been in conflict with the Rockefeller platform plank on the "hopes for a negotiated settlement."] Mitchell checked that judgment with me once or twice more during the campaign. At one point he urged me to call a certain Mr. Haldeman if I ever received any hard information, and gave me a phone number. I never used it.

III. The Buckley Passport

In his *United Nations Journal: A Delegate's Odyssey* (New York,

1974), William F. Buckley, Jr. — who shows himself on the back jacket-cover in a group picture, standing behind Secretary of State Kissinger on the day when they both inaugurated their State Department careers at the United Nations General Assembly, where Kissinger spoke and Buckley, with many other staff members, listened — tells us about his having "introduced Kissinger to John Mitchell," or rather, to intermediaries who provided the actual service. At the Miami Republican Convention, before the nomination, Kissinger had tried to negotiate a deal with Buckley to rally conservative support for Rockefeller, in the event that Rockefeller won. In Buckley's words: "My responsibility, Kissinger urged, was to demonstrate to American conservatives that the country would be better off with Rockefeller as President, than with a Democratic President." Buckley's response was that Rockefeller could not conceivably win the nomination unless Goldwater supported him *in advance*, which he would never do.

Then came the October intervention to which Kissinger refers. Kissinger "asked to lunch with me," writes Buckley. "He had a few ideas he thought would be interesting to Nixon, in framing his foreign policy speeches. But these ideas he must advance discreetly, as he would not wish to appear, having just now left the dismantled Rockefeller staff, to be job-seeking." Buckley called Frank Shakespeare at the Nixon Headquarters and recited Kissinger's qualifications. Shakespeare called them to the attention of "Len Garment and John Mitchell, neither of whom," as Buckley puts it, "had heard Kissinger's name before. They were impressed . . . and said they would introduce him to Nixon, except that Nixon was out of town campaigning. Kissinger's drafts were cordially received."

Kissinger has told us of the results of his contacts with John Mitchell. But he has said nothing about his final drive to reach Nixon through Buckley. That occurred, Buckley tells us, in late November — no doubt shortly before that November 22, 1968 advisory lunch in Rockefeller's Museum of Primitive Art apartment. "I was lecturing in Los Angeles," Buckley tells us, "and was staying with friends in Pasadena" — which, by normal standards, would have made him relatively inaccessible. Yet "Kissinger reached me by phone." This time there was no talk of proceeding discreetly. As Buckley recalls, Kissinger was concerned by what might happen to the limited war in Vietnam during the final weeks of the lame-duck Johnson incumbency. "Nixon must be told," Kissinger had said, "that it is probably an objective of Clifford to depose Thieu before Nixon is inaugurated. Word should be gotten to Nixon that if Thieu meets the same fate as Diem, the word will go out to the nations of the world that it may be dangerous to be America's enemy, but to be America's friend is fatal."

That biblically-phrased petition of late November 1968 moved the editor of *National Review*. He now intervened decisively. "I telephoned New York," Buckley writes. "A personal meeting was set up between Kissinger and the President-elect, and a week or so later, my phone rang." The caller said: "You will never be able to say again that you have no contact inside the White House." Thus, it was not as "Rockefeller's man" but as "Buckley's man" that Kissinger received "The Phone Call" at Rockefeller's apartment from Nixon's appointments secretary, Dwight Chapin, asking him "— and not Rockefeller — to meet with his chief."

IV. The Clark Clifford Connection

From the standpoint of national-security ideology, rather than that of sheer political ambition, it may be said that Kissinger's last-minute warning, sponsored by Buckley, about the possible collapse of the war in Vietnam before Nixon's inauguration represented a desperate effort on Kissinger's part to "save" his kind of war from being aborted before its "strategic" lessons had been fully learned by the American people. Clark Clifford, to whom Kissinger referred in his urgent late-November call to Buckley, had replaced Kissinger's friend Robert McNamara as Defense Secretary on March 1, 1968. Long before that, McNamara had begun to compile his long "white paper" on the war, later called the *Pentagon Papers*. He had called in Henry Kissinger himself, as *Time* magazine later reported, to structure the project. McNamara's replacement by Clifford signaled the start of an all-out drive to "win in Vietnam."

As he later explained in detail in his much-publicized *Foreign Affairs* article of July 1969, Clifford had taken office on March 1, 1968, "with one overriding immediate assignment — responding to the military request to strengthen our forces so that we might prosecute the war more forcefully." The military in the field had called for some 206,000 additional troops, beyond the 525,000 level already being maintained there. And Clifford was directed, as his "first assignment, to chair a task force named by the President to determine how this new requirement could be met. We were not instructed to assess the need for substantial increases in men and materiel; we were to devise the means by which they could be provided."

The military request had not been something out of the blue. The military had known from the beginning what it would cost to "contain aggression" in Vietnam, given the restraints imposed upon them by the post-1961 limited war doctrine, to which Kissinger had contributed so much theoretically. Kissinger had said, for instance, that "any limited war must have some sanctuary areas," and that the old concept of destroying "enemy communication and industrial centers" would have to be greatly modified, if limited wars were to be kept limited in his sense. As against the massive-retaliation of striking "at places of our own choosing," Kissinger had proposed that, in his kind of limited war, "each side could be required" to list the towns and industrial and transport-communications centers, as well as bases that were vital to its viability as a society, and those "would then be immune from attack."

The restrictions placed on the American fighting forces in Vietnam had been from the beginning — under President Kennedy — of that order; and the Diem regime had balked at them, till it was overthrown in 1963, because comparable restraints certainly had not been and would not be imposed on Hanoi by Peking or Moscow. The combined American and Diem forces in the South had the charge of securing the integrity of South Vietnam without pursuing the enemy into his Laotian, Cambodian, and North Vietnamese sanctuaries ["the danger of misunderstanding is least," Kissinger had written, "if the sanctuary follows national boundaries"] without mining his harbors, and without destroying his great industrial stores or manufacturing centers. Had such political restraints not been imposed, President Johnson's escalation of the troop level during 1965 would have resulted, no military man doubts, in a complete collapse of the enemy's war effort in the south before the year was over. As for functioning under those restraints, "sound estimates of the cost and requirements were available," Hanson Baldwin would later write in *Strategy for Tomorrow*, "*before* the first U. S. combat troops were committed in March, 1965. Both the Army Chief of Staff and the Marine Commandment are on record in the early months of 1965 as estimating that victory in Vietnam would require 500,000 to 800,000 men and take years of effort."

Were those estimates ever passed on to President Johnson by the defense establishment he had inherited from the Kennedy administration? Hanson Baldwin writes: "It is hard to believe that the President received those estimates." Had Johnson received them, Baldwin continues, it is inconceivable that he would have "announced a major build-up of combat forces in Vietnam" in the summer of 1965 only to let it be altogether undermined "by the nation's failure to mobilize its reserve forces." And he concludes: "The military had anticipated and prepared for mobilization; again it is difficult to believe that the President fully understood the inevitable consequence of his failure to utilize rapidly and decisively the nation's might. Somewhere between the responsible heads of the armed forces in the Pentagon and the Commander in Chief communications broke down or meanings were obscured."

In late 1967 and early 1968, the estimates Hanson Baldwin speaks of finally reached President Johnson. As a direct consequence he asked Clark Clifford to replace McNamara and work out ways for finally bringing the troop level up to the figure the military had requested from the outset. But, as Clifford later put it in his *Foreign Affairs* account of what happened to him during his first weeks in office, despite his most strenuous efforts to get his inherited task force to "stay with the assignment of devising means to meet the military's requests, fundamental questions began to recur over and over." What followed in his retrospective account are several pages of the kind of arguments against escalation of a limited war to a force level to secure victory that Kissinger advanced in his *Nuclear Weapons and Foreign Policy* and in *The Necessity for Choice.*

Clifford finally lost patience. He had helped to draft the official text of the Acheson-Truman doctrine of containment. How, he wanted to know from his inherited experts, are we going to contain the enemy aggression, finally? And it is here that he gives us what is surely one of the most startling revelations in American national -security history. "When I asked for a presentation of the military plan for attaining victory in Vietnam," he writes, "I was told that there was no plan for victory in the historic American sense." What was the point then of having fought to this point? What was to be gained by further fighting? Clifford, as he made clear, despised the academic notion of war fought merely to "lengthen the step," as Kissinger had said, between the stark "alternatives of surrender or all-out war." He rejected flatly the Kissinger notion of wars which, while they gave our "native belligerency" an outlet for a while, could nevertheless be rigorously scaled down to serve the very limited aims "of obtaining a breathing space for negotiations and of bringing home to the opponents the risk of all-out war."

In Vietnam, obviously, the "breathing space" that Kissinger's kind of war provided had served to persuade only the American public at home — not our military men in the field, and least of all the North Vietnamese — of the risk of all-out war. Clifford was told that, instead of any plan to defeat the enemy in any sense, the idea was to keep the present level of resistance constant in the hope that the enemy "would find it inadvisable to go on." Clifford then asked: "Does anyone see any diminution in the will of the enemy?" The consensus in that task force inherited from the Kennedy days was that "there appeared to be no diminution in the will of the enemy" and that, on the contrary, it was the great mass of Americans that was tiring of the war. That was the turning point for Clifford. "After those exhausting days," he then says, "I was convinced that the military course we were pursuing was not only endless, but hopeless." He had started with the overriding immediate assignment of strengthening our forces so that we might prosecute the war more forcefully; he had learned after a few days that the war had been architected during the Kennedy years on the Kissinger model so as to preclude so much as a *plan* for victory in the historic American sense; and so, he had quickly concluded, the time had come "to disengage."

Had Clifford been converted from hawk to dove? No. Rather, he had seen at once that the Vietnam war had been structured as a war we allegedly "could afford to lose," so as to "educate" us as a nation to the futility of the containment and massive-retaliation varieties of war which specified no fail-safe force levels of American local resistance. Eisenhower had threatened to generalize the war in Korea in order to contain the aggressor. If that was really out of the question in Vietnam, then the best thing, Clifford concluded, is to end the killing as quickly as possible, write the war off as a mistake, and gird ourselves to fight a proper kind of war in the proper place.

That is the advice Clifford gave President Johnson late in March 1968, and Johnson did not know what to make of it. He had hoped Clifford would say: Let's supply the troops requested; let's escalate to win. Pulling out would sound like surrendering! And his Harvard-MIT advisers who shared Kissinger's view of the utility of *some* fighting as a fail-safe alternative to starker choices agreed. Johnson was advised not to escalate to victory and not to pull out. And that was the *status quo* national-security policy he bequeathed to his Republican successor. The Kissinger-style limited war was thus destined to survive the collapse of the Johnson Presidency.

Johnson seemed to hope, during the nine months after his decision not to seek re-election, that his successor would be a tough Republican who would "clean the rascals out" of the national security and defense department establishments. But his successor had, before his inauguration as President, heeded the advice of the man who had come to him so highly recommended by "America's leading conservative journalist," if not by its leading capitalist-liberal Republican politician. With Henry Kissinger by his side at the Hotel Pierre in the weeks just prior to his inaugural address, Richard Nixon soon found himself maneuvered into saving Kissinger's war for Kissinger himself to handle in its long drawn-out final phase. That war, as we know, was then destined to end not like the Korean war, with our client-state's territory cleared of the enemy, but in a quite opposite fashion. And the end, as we saw it on TV in April 1975, came only after 26,000 additional American soldiers had died, after 200,000 more had been wounded, and after the spirit of the American people back home had been broken. We say nothing here of the price paid by the Vietnamese.

V. Nixon's Inaugural: The Pledge to Negotiate

According to Raymond Price, principal writer of Nixon's inaugural address, the sentence in that address which Henry Kissinger particularly urged on the President-elect was the one that reads: "After a period of confrontation, we are now entering a period of negotiation." Kissinger had submitted a three-page draft of what he titled his "Proposed Foreign-Policy Section of Your Inaugural Address." His cover-memo made clear that his overriding concern was that some statement of commitment to the Rockefeller plank of the Party Platform — the plank on the hope of a negotiated settlement in Vietnam — be included. "Some version of the underlined sentences on page three," he had written, "should be in for the reasons we have discussed. I shall be happy to explain the grounds for the other passages."

Raymond Price writes of this in *With Nixon* (New York, 1977), where he is at pains to indicate just what influence Kissinger had been able to exert on the Nixon administration even before actually assuming office. "In passing the Kissinger material along" to Price, as principal speech writer, "Nixon explained to me," Price writes, "that [the underlined sentences in Kissinger's draft] had been worked out with Soviet representatives as a public signal to confirm private indications he had given that he really did want an 'era of negotiation.' But that — or some version of it — was the only part of the Kissinger material that was sacrosanct." In Kissinger's draft, the under-lined sacrosanct sentences read: "To those who, for most of the post-war period, have opposed and, occasionally, threatened us, I repeat what I have said already: let the coming years be a time of negotiation rather than confrontation. During this administration the lines of communication will always be open."

That was the tiny seed out of which the great tree of the "detente reversal" of twenty-five years of American cold-war policy was to grow. The lines of communication between the White House and the Kremlin were to become so open during the Nixon-Kissinger years that the continuing war in Vietnam took on an aspect altogether unprecedented in military history. Between 1969 and 1975, the United States transformed its war effort in Vietnam into what has been aptly characterized as "one of the most savage retreats in modern history." Kissinger wanted the retreat, to be sure; but he wanted it to be savage, as he repeatedly said, to prevent a "Middle America" backlash on the home front. That was the cover for all-out detente with Moscow.

In *The Time of Illusion* (New York, 1976) — a remarkably impartial book to be discussed at length later in these pages — Jonathan Schell (a journalist of impeccable liberal-intellectual credentials) says at one point: "If the President was going to risk American credibility by withdrawing from the war . . . it would have to be accompanied by many awesome displays of unimpaired resolve." Displays, he specifies, "such as the invasion of Cambodia" when half our troops were out, "the mining of the ports of North Vietnam" when almost all our troops were out, and later, "the carpet-bombing of North Vietnam in the Christmas season of 1972" when the so-called peace accords, or terms of only lightly-disguised American surrender, were about to be initialed by Kissinger and Le Duc Tho in Paris.

All that while, Kissinger was pursuing Soviet-American detente, the crowning moment of which was the Moscow Summit meeting of May 1972. General John D. Lavelle, commander of all U. S. air operations in Southeast Asia had just been relieved of his command and stripped of two of his four stars for having conducted "unauthorized" strikes against staging areas for mass invasions from the North which Kissinger's strategy had declared to be "immune from American attack" while detente negotiations were going on with Moscow. Jonathan Schell thus represents the apparent paradox for us: "For a moment, as President Nixon proclaimed that 'America's flag flies over the ancient Kremlin fortress' while Americans were dying in Southeast Asia in an attempt to counter the Kremlin's influence, the fighting in Vietnam came to look like something without precedent in military history: a war in which generals on the opposing sides combined into a joint command."

Mr. Schell, it appears, had read Kissinger's theoretic accounts of how limited wars ought to be fought in the nuclear age only after the Vietnam war had taken its full toll at home as well as abroad. Thus he could say: "In the framework of Kissinger's thinking, it made perfect sense to move toward the summit, and so toward peace, in the sphere of direct relations with the Soviet Union, while simultaneously moving toward . . . intensified war in the sphere of Vietnam." *In Nuclear Weapons and Foreign Policy* Kissinger had argued that, since "the goal of war can no longer be military victory, strictly speaking, but the attainment of certain specific political conditions which are fully understood by the opponent . . . it will be necessary to give up the notion that direct diplomatic contact ceases when military operations begin. Rather, direct contact will be more than ever necessary to ensure that both sides possess the correct information about the consequences of expanding a war . . . . If our military staffs could become clear about a doctrine of limited war, we could then use the disarmament negotiations to seek a measure of acceptance of it by the other side."

With even greater frankness he had added elsewhere in the same 1957 volume: "A limited war can remain limited only if at some point one of the protagonists prefers a limited defeat to an additional expenditure of resources or if both sides are willing to settle for a stalemate in preference to an assumption of increased risk." Such are indeed the matters to be discussed by cold-war adversaries in the nuclear age when their leaders meet in summit conferences. Kissinger made that one of the central arguments of his 1960 volume *The Necessity for Choice*. His kind of limited war, as contrasted with the open-ended varieties of limited war comprehended in the massive retaliation and containment policies, he wrote in 1960, "is based on a tacit bargain not to exceed certain restraints. One side's desire to keep the war limited is of no avail unless the other cooperates: it takes two to keep a limited war limited . . . .It is often argued that, if both sides could agree on anything as complicated as limited war, they would probably agree on keeping the peace in the first place. But this is essentially a debating point . . . .Limited war is not a substitute for constructive policy. It does offer the possibility — not the certainty — of avoiding catastrophe."

Kissinger there reminds his readers that "if we reject the concept of limited war," as he defines it, then "our only options will be surrender or all-out war." And "since surrender will not be our national policy," he adds, "it is important to get our choices straight. Limited war is palatable only when compared with even starker alternatives." But that, in his view, puts large demands on policy makers. If they are not to go astray, as Acheson and Dulles went astray, they must stand with him in the conviction that, to be certain of avoiding catastrophe in a limited war, we "must enter it prepared to negotiate and settle for something less than our traditional notion of complete victory."

It is not difficult to understand, after reading the passages just cited from his books, why Kissinger should have been so anxious to prevent a unilateral, unnegotiated American withdrawal from the fighting in Vietnam — such as Clark Clifford had urged on Johnson in 1968. From the standpoint of Kissinger's limited-war theory, the controlled fighting must be continued until the risks of escalation are sufficiently appreciated, at least by one side, to make it ready to accept defeat if the other side won't settle for a stalemate. Clifford's proposed unilateral retreat would have returned the United States to precisely where it had been in the very first stages of its involvement in Vietnam back in the mid-1950s. That fighting had to continue, according to Kissinger, until the Soviet-American detente he had been negotiating was signed, sealed, and institutionalized; and then, with Soviet intervention, motivated by its desire to enjoy the advantages of detente, Hanoi would be forced to settle; or, if that couldn't be brought about even with Soviet intervention, then we would wisely settle, accepting limited defeat — in the spirit of Kissinger's *Necessity for Choice* — rather than risking the survival of mankind once more with another massive-retaliation threat, like that of Eisenhower in 1953.

VI. What Price Kissinger?

But how exactly did Henry Kissinger's ascendancy over Richard Nixon starting in January 1969 actually affect the conduct of our limited war in Vietnam? General William C. Westmoreland, who commanded our forces in Vietnam from 1964 to 1968, and then continued in service as Army Chief of Staff through 1972, has suggested that it is a question warranting at least as much in-depth investigation by our Congress as the Watergate scandal and at least as much news media curiosity as was shown in the public exhibition and endless discussion of the *Pentagon Papers*. We know all about Nixon's doings in the White House with regard to almost all matters except those that fell under Kissinger's care. Has that been because of news media respect for the alleged "confidentialities of foreign relations"? Jonathan Schell reminds us of the absurdity of such a suggestion by drawing this contrast: "The underground record of the executive branch in foreign policy during the Kennedy and Johnson years was made known through publication of the Pentagon papers, but the underground record in foreign affairs of the Nixon Administration remains mostly undivulged."

That contrast is the theme of a later chapter in this book. Here we want to consider briefly General Westmoreland's complaint against the congressional and news media persistence in trying to sweep the facts about a national disgrace of the proportions of our conduct of the war in Vietnam — especially since 1969 — under a rug, as he put it.

As an interested party, even, in some measure, as a responsible party, General Westmoreland has called our government's "handling of the Vietnam episode," especially since the Tet offensive of 1968, "a shameful national blunder." In an article dated March 26, 1978, Westmoreland acknowledges that military intervention in Vietnam had been from the very beginning a blunder from the military standpoint. The military had told their commander-in-chief exactly that, at the very start — though, in keeping with their oath, they responded loyally to White House orders. But what added national *shame* to the blunder, in his view, was what happened after 1968 — which is to say, after Henry Kissinger entered the White House with Richard Nixon.

Bad as things were, down through 1968, President Johnson at least had not contemplated subjecting our troops to a slow withdrawal, punctuated by virtually meaningless military ventures that could serve no real military purpose when most of our troops had already been withdrawn. That came with Kissinger in 1969 when, in the General's words, "the United States resorted to a withdrawal strategy, and omitted any demand for a *quid pro quo* from Hanoi." That made a shameful end to the war inevitable. And he concludes: "Our country, once an honorable ally, had betrayed and deserted the Republic of Vietnam after we had enticed it to our bosom. It was a shabby performance by the United States. That unhappy experience should not be swept under the rug and forgotten."

Is Henry Kissinger to remain *forever* immune from serious news media and congressional scrutiny? It is inconceivable that any other public figure of such notoriety could have gotten away with blocking public access, in our day, to the records of "telephone conversations that Kissinger conducted from his White House and State Department offices," simply by removing them *illegally*, for safe-keeping, to "the late Nelson A. Rockefeller's estate in Pocantic Hills, N. Y. and later donating them to the Library of Congress under a deed that bars public access." The Supreme Court has ruled that, had the transcripts of the phone conversations not been removed illegally from the White House and the State Department offices, they would have been accessible, to be sure; but, the only public recourse now is for the White House and State Department to charge Kissinger with theft and get the courts to convict him and *then* order restoration. The whisper against that in public corridors and major editorial offices has been: Lese Majesty. Kissinger's connections apparently make him "to powerful to be hurt by public action."

But Kissinger's long time friends are something else. Many of them fear that, with his Disraelian efforts to get himself another "conservative" presidential sponsor, he may be going too far. It is the fate of Disraelians out of office that what they say — no longer contradicted by their deeds — has to be taken literally. If Kissinger fails to push himself back into high office, his "cavorting like a hawk," his "playing tough," to ingratiate himself with right-wing Republicans is apt to ruin things he supported in the past with his Disraelian deeds. Some of his long-time friends have therefore been conducting preemptive strikes against him, and revealing "secrets" in the process, to secure a hold on him for the future.

Typical of this is the book *Uncertain Greatness: Henry Kissinger and American Foreign Policy* (New York, 1977), by Roger Morris. Roger Morris had been a member of Kissinger's innermost circle of aides during the first year and a half in the White House. At the time he wrote his book, he was director of humanitarian policy studies for the Carnegie Endowment for International Peace. His concern in the book is plainly to protect the cause of peace in the nuclear age, which Kissinger had so "ably served" in practice, from the consequences of his play-tough rhetoric to attract a new conservative Republican prospective presidential employer. He finds an opportunity to do that very typically in a passage where he explores the reasons for Alexander Haig's rapid rise in Kissinger's service from lowly staff-colonel to four-star general.

"Kissinger," Morris writes, "needed Haig to provide reassurance, as well as to act as a litmus test on the right in a government where Kissinger was unlikely to be attacked successfully from the left. For the most controversial policies Kissinger planned — initiatives in arms control and ending the war — he would be, he believed, most vulnerable to criticism. Haig the decorated combat veteran, the leathery soldier of stern opinions, would help clothe those actions. Jealous of the relationship as well as of Haig's power, Helmut Sonnenfeldt would joke in acid terms that Kissinger the German-Jewish immigrant kept on Haig, the all-American colonel from Philadelphia, to testify at some imagined right-wing trial, if Henry went too far with detente."

But, as Professor Coral Bell has observed on another level of discourse, the "eventual necessity of accepting the departure of American troops from Vietnam without a victory" — the fail-safe ending to the war that Kissinger's limited war doctrine forced on the country — might indeed "have been an impeachment matter for a different kind of president." Impeachment proceedings were finally started against Nixon, but not for the "impeachment matters" to which Coral Bell refers.

The chapters that follow are a month-by-month account of the Kissinger legacy. (The first was written in March 1975.) Kissinger's doctrine of limited war, as Jonathan Schell so aptly put it, was supposed to "provide the United States with an effective means of promoting its interests and ideals at levels of violence below the brink of nuclear war; instead, it provided the notorious quagmire in Vietnam into which the United States poured its energy and power uselessly for more than a decade . . . and precipitated a wave of disrespect for a particular President which resulted in his forced resignation from office." The consequences of Kissinger's theory of war as applied to Vietnam are here examined in detail in all their dramatic implications. The pattern that emerges is a grim account of the Kissinger strategy as it was carried into practice. I have traced the theoretic formulations of that position in my earlier book, *Who is Kissinger?* and in related articles, many of which were published on the *New York Times* "Op-Ed" page between 1971 and 1974. Here I have carried the examination into the final phase of the process: Kissinger's prolonged effort to keep a "fixed fight" in Vietnam fixed to the end, while gaining time to prepare the home front for what he has called the "much more difficult task of living in dignity when impotent."

[Ed. note: *Kissinger's War: 1957-1975* is currently in reprint. Copies may be ordered from The Bagehot Council/Griffon House Press, Inc., 1401 Pennsylvania Ave., Wilmington, DE 19806.]

EUROPE AFTER 1992:
AN END TO NATIONHOOD
AS HISTORICALLY DEFINED?

"Europe 1992" is the latest rallying-cry of the common market countries of Western Europe. In its suitably ambiguous brevity, the phrase can mean many things at once. Certainly it is forward-looking. It points ahead to a Europe that is yet to come, still to be made, that those heeding the cry must help to make. Yet it is backward-looking, too, since it calls for change: from things as they are in the twelve market countries to things as they ought to be. And there is an unmistakable sense in the sound of it that the changes for which support is being rallied have been delayed too long.

What is to be changed? The year that "Europe 1992" specifies inevitably calls to mind the approaching quincentenary of Columbus' first landing on an uncharted island in the Western Hemisphere. Whether intentionally or not, the cry thus invites comparison and contrast between what Europe has been for the past five hundred years and what it may become after 1992. Europeans do not need to be pointedly reminded that, for too many generations past, especially in the less industrialized areas of the market, the only cry of real hope for millions had been "America! America!" — as if their continent belonged entirely to the past, with no real future of its own on the horizon. Now, at last, there is the promise of "Europe 1992" — a chance for the people of Europe to finally reach out and take their future back into their own hands. Momentous internal transformations, its propagandists assure us, are in process. By the end of 1992, if things work out as planned, they say, the world should indeed be witnessing the start of a new

[From *The World & I*, Vol. 4, No. 12, Dec. 1989]

"Age of Europe," to be inaugurated by a series of "bold ventures into the unknown," the results of which may prove to be as world shaking in their impact — though not in the same way — as those of the great European Age of Dis-covery inaugurated by Columbus' voyages five hundred years ago.

I. Europe As A Fatherland of Middle-Sized Powers

We know what eventually became of the two continents that Columbus unintentionally opened up to European conquest and development. Yet it was Europe itself, not the new Americas, that underwent truly radical internal changes in the decades immediately following 1492. For the old continent at that time finally became what it had been trying to become, without much success, all through the Middle Ages. It became, as the distinguished French diplomat Jean Laloy has aptly put it, the "fatherland of middle-sized powers," the "place where such powers were born."[1]

The usual term for the political unit distinguished by Professor Laloy as "middle-sized" is the traditional nation-state. In Europe's long history, states made up of many nations, like the Soviet Union, the Hapsburg, or Ottoman empires, have tended to be very large. At the same time states made out of fragments of a single nation, such as the divided Italian and German peoples before the 1860s, have tended to be relatively small. But Laloy speaks of Europe as the fatherland, or *birthplace*, of such powers. He very well knows that it was something else *before* it finally gave birth to such powers after a centuries-long labor in the womb of their "mother," the universal medieval church.

Laloy quotes Voltaire on how the family came to "function," as its early members approached maturity. It functioned, the master of enlightenment says, like a democratically run household in which all the members ranked as "juridically equal," because the "father" was no tyrant. The father, who had originally called himself a "holy" emperor of some kind, left the more mature members in charge, most of the time, to decide "family affairs" by what amounted to "majority rule"; or, when

that didn't work, by "coming to blows," and then making up, on
the assumption that the "better side always wins." In Voltaire's
words, as cited by Laloy, Europe had been, since the end of the
fifteenth century, a "kind of large republic, divided into many
states," each of them "corresponding to the others." By that last
phrase, Laloy explains, Voltaire meant to say that, because they
made up a family, those maturing nation-states invariably
agreed to maintain "constant relations, in war as in peace."

Needless to say, in Voltaire's time, the European family of
middle-sized powers did not yet include politically organized
Italian or German nation-states, and his own France was very
pleased that it did not. United Germans always made the
French fearful. That was because German kings usually thought
of themselves as emperors first, which meant, according to a
tradition as old as Charlemagne, that they had to be kings of
Italians as well as Germans, since Italy's Rome was originally the
only place in the world where German kings could be transformed as if by magic into Roman emperors, while at the same
time being anointed to make them holy as well.

Mere national kings, like those of France, England, Portugal, and Spain, were supposed to obey anointed emperors for
Christ's sake. And so, from the point of view of national kings,
especially French kings whose kingdom lay so close to the
German and Italian imperial territories, it seemed that for the
good of the entire family of middle-sized powers the Germans
and Italians remain divided forever. That attitude changed,
finally, only after Napoleon very graciously buried the mori-
bund Holy Roman Empire in 1806. Thereafter, as a result of
Napoleon's conquests, Italians, Germans, and other fragmented
or conquered peoples, especially in Eastern and southeastern
Europe, were powerfully inspired to assume separate and
juridically equal stations as sovereign nation-states.

No one can deny that, since Columbus' time, "international
democracy" (critics call it anarchy) has reigned among the
states of Europe that have qualified as middle-sized powers.
Every effort to pull the family together by force, for the sake of
peace or for any other reason, has invariably failed. That was so
in the case of Charles V and his son Philip, who were sent

packing by the National Confederacy of the Dutch. England's Henry VIII dreamed of giving it a try, hoping to turn his Reginald Pole into a pope for that purpose; but all he could manage was to break off a piece of the universal church in order to make himself a pope-king on his little but mighty island. A couple of ambitious Scandinavian kings tried it, as did Louis XIV of France, then Napoleon, and finally Adolph Hitler, with his Third Reich, named not only after Bismarck's Second Reich but also after the First Reich of the Hohenstauffen Holy Roman emperors of the twelfth and thirteenth centuries. Those emperors had imperial capitals in Sicily as well as in the Germanies and have been immortalized in Dante's *Divine Comedy*.

All that came of Hitler's effort to bind the family of sovereign nations under the discipline of his "New Order" has been German people again divided — a Germany with little hope that the new Titans of East and West will ever let them be united again, except as part of some secular equivalent of the repeatedly revived empire that Charlemagne and Pope Leo III invented, in A.D. 800, as a means of educating the still-barbarous Germano-Europeans of that "dark age."

Alluding to such details in his discussion of Europe as a "fatherland of middle-sized powers," Laloy presumed to ask in effect: Why would anyone want to put an end to a democratic, family-like approach to international relations like the one we have just described? It is, after all, an approach that has already stopped a long line of would-be European "federators with a sword," who have always preferred peace on their terms to peace subordinated to the demands of freedom. That question lay at the heart of an article that Laloy contributed to the October 1972 issue of *Foreign Affairs* under the provocative title "Does Europe Have a Future?" By "Europe," Laloy meant, of course, his continent made up of middle-sized powers or nation-states. And he was asking whether it had a future in the face of expectations, widely shared at the time among European intellectuals, that the European Community might succeed in putting an end to such powers through its "peace-by-pieces"[2] approach to economic integration and eventual political integration.

II. The European Community That England Did Not Join

Laloy's article was written in anticipation of England's entry into the Community, which was, in October 1972, just a few months off. The Conservative government of Britain's Prime Minister Edward Heath had just gained the approval of the House of Commons to join the market, and England's official "swearing in," together with Ireland and Denmark, had already been scheduled for January 1, 1973. Laloy observed that with the "entrance of the United Kingdom into the European Community" the new "European idea," which had animated that Community from its beginnings in the 1950s, would "soon take a new form."[3] The Heath government's white paper making the case for England's entry carefully assured the lower house of Parliament that the Community would hereafter have a form differing radically from what it had previously been, back in the days when England had first been invited to join its six-member market as a seventh founder but had flatly declined.

Why had England refused to join the Community in the 1950s, and why did she apparently change her mind in the 1970s? The answer is very complex, for reasons we must take up in a moment, but the Heath government's white paper is clear enough in its reply to the second half of the question, even as it diplomatically makes no reference to the first half. The main argument of that paper appeared under a section headed "Maintenance of sovereignty." There it explained that "the practical working of the Community," at present, "reflects the reality that sovereign governments are represented around the table"; and, more particularly, that "on a question where a government considers that vital national interests are involved, it is established that the decision should be unanimous."[4]

As those words imply, things were different back in the 1950s when England had refused to join. Then, according to the terms of the Treaty of Paris signed in 1951 to launch the first of Western Europe's famous "three communities" — the European Coal and Steel Community (ECSC) — decisions made by the vote of a qualified majority of members were to be binding on all members. That meant that a country could not "veto" such decisions and remain in the Community. The rule had been introduced by the founders of the Community, Jean Monnet and Robert Schuman, the former a famous French political economist specializing in international organizations, the latter France's foreign minister at the time. They had spelled it out in their Declaration of May 9, 1950, which proposed that West Germany and France, on France's initiative, would begin the process on their own as a two-power agreement. The ex-foes of World War II would agree specifically to put their "entire coal and steel production under a common High Authority whose decisions will bind." Other Western countries would be invited to join the resulting Community, after which other communities would have started in other sectors such as atomic energy, agriculture, and defense. And all of that would then constitute, in the words of the Declaration, the "first stage toward European federation."[5]

That was how today's European Community began. There can be no doubt about its ultimate purpose in those days. It was designed to put an end to Europe as the fatherland of middle-sized powers, not by the sword, however, but by a slow process of economic integration that could eventually become political integration. Before negotiations of an authorizing treaty were completed in 1951, Schuman, as minister in charge of implementation for the Declaration, was asked: "How many countries are needed to make the plan work?" He replied without hesitation: "If necessary, we shall go ahead with only two."[6] That proved unnecessary. Italy, Belgium, Luxembourg, and the Netherlands, for reasons having to do with the injustices inflicted on them during the war, quickly volunteered to join France and West Germany in the Community enterprise. The result was the "Original Six," as they soon came to be called. But, as already indicated, England was invited in 1950 to become a seventh founder. Monnet and Schuman went to London to extend the invitation, although they did not expect proud England to join. They journeyed there to make a point.

The British expressed concern about the nature of the proposed "common High Authority whose decisions will bind." They were informed that the Authority's members, appointed by their national governments, would take an oath of "higher loyalty" to the Community, pledging to "exercise their functions in complete independence" and agreeing "neither to solicit nor accept instructions from any government" in reaching their binding decisions.[7] Declining to join, the British observed simply that the proposed decision-making procedure would constitute an unacceptable infringement on England's traditional prerogatives of sovereign nationhood. That British "no" was handed to the French on May 27, 1950. A week later, on June 3, the Six announced their full acceptance of the decision-making procedure rejected by the British. As Richard Vaughan puts it in his *Twentieth Century Europe: Paths to Unity*, it was "the omission of Britain which was the truly decisive event in the formation of the Six"; and then for the record, he adds: "Henceforth, the Europe of the Six was in existence; the history of the European Community began on 3 June 1950."[8]

III. The Challenge: National or Supranational

Our purpose in this article is not to examine the history of the European Community in any detail. It is, rather, to focus on the challenge that a supra-nationally conceived Community presents to our modern Western ideal of "governments by discussion" that secure their freedoms by means of delicately calibrated internal checks and external balances of power. Internal checks on separated governing powers are necessary to secure individual or personal freedom. External balances of power are necessary to prevent totalitarian states from gaining hegemonic power over other freer peoples.

That delicately calibrated system requires enlightened loyalty on the part of citizens who enjoy the freedom it helps secure. When political integration of free nations for the sake of "peace in our time," or to "prevent a nuclear holocaust," is advanced as something worthy of a "higher loyalty," the result is inevitably an undermining of national loyalties. Yet those loyalties, as expressed by Charles de Gaulle throughout his career, and by Britain's Iron Lady, Margaret Thatcher, today, must inevitably reassert their necessity, when the full consequences of acting on a presumably higher loyalty are widely experienced. At that time, government by violence, as Edmund Burke predicted in the days of the French Revolution, necessarily replaces government by discussion until the internal checks and external balances of power needed for ordered freedom are fully restored.

Yet before we turn to the fuller implications of our subject, it will be useful, here, to provide a brief account of the European Community's development before and after England's entry in 1973. Later we will focus on major turning points in that development that will help clarify our central argument.

We begin with England's entry in 1973, under the conditions defined in the Heath government's white paper, because that is the central turning point of the entire development. But here we are obviously *in medias res*, as befits an epic tale. The terms defined in that white paper are now technically the norms of membership in the Community. That was not so in the beginning. And now, since the post-1985 ascendancy of Jacques Delors as president of the European Commission (the Community's top executive organ), an all-out propaganda campaign is going on, with "Europe 1992" as its revolutionary cry, to turn the Community back to what it was when England refused to join it. Today that propaganda campaign is being most conspicuously resisted by Margaret Thatcher. That is all part of this epic tale, for which we must now provide an introductory framework or catalog of basic facts.

IV. The Three Communities and the Luxembourg Compromise

There is much good to be said about the European Community as a traditional international organization of the kind described in the Heath government's white paper. The Community had indeed been an international, not a supranational, organization since 1957, and, on a practical level, perhaps since 1954. But, before 1954, it had plainly had a supranational character. The supranational element was very deliberately stripped away when the Six created two new communities, each with a separate authorizing Treaty of Rome, in 1957. The two were the European Atomic Energy Community (EAEC or

Euratom) and the European Economic Community (EEC), now known as the Common Market. The terms of those 1957 treaties transformed the Community into a traditional international organization, at least according to the letter. Yet, because of the continued existence of the ECSC's High Authority (replaced in 1957 by a commission), practical transformation of the whole enterprise required a little time. And it became the task of de Gaulle's twelve-year tenure as the president of France's new Fifth Republic (1958-1969) to make the transformation a reality.

Between 1958 and 1966, strong efforts were made by top Community officials, and particularly by Walter Hallstein,[9] as president of the European Commission, to undo in practice the effects of the 1957 EEC treaty. During those years, the EEC was absorbing, as planned, the governing institutions of the other two communities into its own so that if changes could be introduced altering decision-making procedures in the EEC they would eventually become applicable in the Community as a whole. Glancing ahead, it may be noted that the process of absorption would be completed and made official in 1967 by the terms of a so-called Merger Treaty. Thereafter, the three communities could justifiably be viewed, administratively, as constituting a single European Community (EC) without further qualification. (The three communities did retain their separate legal identities – a fact destined to acquire great importance after 1985, when efforts began to revive past procedural practices.)

While the merger was in process, however, Hallstein sought to transform the top governing organ of the Community – its Council of Ministers representing the sovereign member governments – into an independent supranational entity. He hoped to accomplish that by changing its rule of decision-making from a requirement of unanimity to one of a qualified majority-vote. Hallstein pointed to an apparent loophole in the 1957 treaty that allegedly permitted such a transformation. A change of that order would have made the Council of Ministers what the old High Authority of the ECSC had been, before its absorption into the EEC's Commission. Had the scheme succeeded, it would have been a tremendous victory for Monnet's most ardent supranationalist partisans.

De Gaulle insisted all the while that there was no such loophole in the 1957 treaty. And when Hallstein persuaded the other five members to side with him against de Gaulle, France's president countered by boycotting all Community proceedings, demanding nullification of the majority's contrary stand. The boycott lasted for six months during 1965, ending finally when de Gaulle threatened to pass from nullification to secession. Everyone recognized that, without France, the EC could not last. England's refusal to join in the early 1950s over the same decision-making procedure had reduced to zero the prospects of recruiting new members. Had France been forced out in 1965, the result for the five remaining members aligned with Hallstein would have been but a Pyrrhic victory at best. The five persisted in claiming that Hallstein was right and de Gaulle wrong about what the 1957 treaty allowed on decision-making procedures. They nevertheless agreed that France could, if she insisted, exercise a veto on all majority decisions and still remain in the Community.

That agreement has since been called the Luxembourg Compromise.[10] Its meaning was precisely expressed in the passages previously cited from the Heath government's white paper of the early 1970s. Yet there is a well-known irony to be noted here. During the 1960s, while de Gaulle was exacting his Luxembourg Compromise out of the Community's majority, he was also exercising the prerogatives of sovereign nationhood, guaranteed by that compromise, to prevent England from entering the market. England applied twice in the 1960s: first in 1961 and then again in 1967. On both occasions de Gaulle vetoed the applications. He did so, he said, in France's national interest, because, in his view, England was still too world-minded in her interests and not yet reconciled to becoming a middle-sized, responsible member of the European family. The other five market members eagerly sought to override the French veto: They wanted England to be admitted, assuming that when and if she entered, she might then admit the virtue of a procedure that could overcome the stubbornness of de Gaulle. But they were mistaken. Even if it had been possible for the five to override France's veto, England would not have joined at all — for the same reasons given in 1950.

V. Enlargements: From Six to Nine, to Ten, and Then Twelve

Thus, England entered a market in 1973 that had been fashioned to her liking by de Gaulle. She entered on January 1 of that year, together with Ireland and Denmark, both of which had earlier indicated that they would enter when England did or not at all. For all three, as for all subsequent new members, the Luxembourg Compromise ranked as an essential part of the Community's fundamental law. That completed the first phase of the Community's enlargement.[11] After twenty-two years of having been a Community of six, it had at last become a Community of nine. And furthermore, since the new members were all northern European countries, the market now possessed a decidedly northern "tilt." Efforts were quickly made to recruit three counterbalancing southern European countries. Greece entered on January 1, 1981, increasing the number to ten. And finally, after a painfully long delay, Portugal and Spain, the poorest of poor relations in the market, entered in December 1985, although their formal swearing in did not occur until January 1, 1986.

It was, incidentally, by way of welcoming those two poor Iberian relations into the market as its eleventh and twelfth (which is to say, its last) members that the target date for eliminating all remaining technical, physical, and fiscal barriers was set. That date is the last day of the Columbus quincentenary: December 31, 1992. The mysterious-sounding Single European Act was proposed at that time to accomplish full economic integration over a seven-year period. Its chief sponsor was, of course, Jacques Delors. It was to be a prolonged but nevertheless single act designed to turn each and every citizen of twelve independent and very unequal states into a true European one at last, with all Europeans equal, as citizens in a "people's Europe," soon to replace the old "Europe of states."

Before long — it was said in December 1985 — there would be "European" passports for all, a European flag, and a national anthem (Beethoven's "Ode to Joy," from the Ninth Symphony, of course). And there would soon cease to be any "ranking by nationalities," as there still was in the Community, for instance, where the Original Six ranked first and Portugal and Spain last, according to their dates of entry. After "Europe 1992" all the different nation-states would begin to lose their hold on their citizens as "nationals." Those citizens, upon recognizing themselves as "Europeans," would retain only their treasured national cultures and languages. Nine cultures now rank as official in the Community: Danish, Dutch, English, French, German, Greek, Italian, Portuguese, and Spanish (with a tenth, Irish, added for especially solemn occasions or to record for posterity the most sacred Community texts, like the Single European Act).[12]

The Columbus quincentenary was targeted in December 1985, and the cry of "Europe 1992" then raised, undoubtedly in order to inspire the last two members admitted to the market, Portugal and Spain, to approach the difficult challenge of complete economic integration with a Columbus-like spirit of leadership. If they for now ranked eleventh and twelfth in the market, "Europe 1992" would remind them of a time when they ranked first and second among the chief maritime powers of Western Europe. They had been the second and third homelands of Columbus,[13] after Genoa, and had done much more than Genoa, Italy, or any other cities or countries, to prepare the great navigator for his daring attempt to reach the fabulous riches of the East quickly and cheaply by sailing West. And after Columbus's return to Spain in 1492 to tell his royal patrons about all that he had seen and done, with "six Indians in native dress" at his side ready to be baptized, all of Europe soon turned to the Iberian countries for leadership in that bright dawn so full of promise of things to come.

Their coasts jutting out geographically into the Atlantic, and already skilled in ocean sailing, the Portuguese and Spaniards led the way. But the English were soon at their heels, with the French and the Dutch moving up quickly. Soon they were all "making history" together by literally bursting out of the old continent's bounds. Each, in turn, sent its boldest seamen, merchant adventurers, and soldiers out onto the seas. They crossed the Atlantic, of course, but they also circled the southern tips of Africa and the new South American continent; and finally they circumnavigated the entire globe. Before long, the great fleets of those seafaring middle-sized powers had for the first time made the whole world an open, if not yet a common, market.

That had been the spirit of "Europe 1492." Marvelous things had been done abroad. The world in those days was divided into great spheres, and even hemispheres, of influence, with demarcation lines drawn from pole to pole. And yet — leaders of the European Community were thinking and saying in December 1985 — what a terrible legacy those adventures overseas had bequeathed to Europe in later years! Ever since, Europe has suffered national rivalries, contests, and disputes; and, of course, wars, wars without end. But now, in the age of the great bombs, the wars must end. And why shouldn't the Portuguese and Spanish citizens of today, if not their states, feel moved by memories of past greatness and take the lead again, if they can, in the proud new mission of "Europe 1992," which is to "sail toward peace for all mankind," in tomorrow's stateless world?

Behind the spirited cry of "Europe 1992," first raised in December 1985, was a renewal of the efforts of Monnet and Schuman to use the Community idea as a means of getting rid of Europe's divided sovereign nation-states, incessantly engaged in wars. And behind the high-sounding rhetoric the particular means proposed were again those of Hallstein in his struggle against de Gaulle. Delors, in December 1985, was insisting that to integrate the market completely it would be absolutely necessary to radically amend the authorizing Treaty of Rome with respect to decision-making procedures. But England's Thatcher was there, and with the ghost of Charles de Gaulle beside her, she objected. She fully approved of economic integration. But she insisted that all of the more than three hundred proposed reforms could and should be "achieved without revisions to the Treaty."[14] Delors would not hear of it. He went about at that time fervently pleading for amendments on decision-making procedures. "Let us hope," he had typically said, that the member states will find the wisdom to turn their backs on their present "fatal ways of behaving," and finally give-up "their obsession of unanimity."[15]

Thatcher plainly understood the purpose behind that plea. Delors was not interested in economic integration any more than Monnet. Economic integration was to be just a means. The goal was to strip national states of their sovereign prerogatives. And she viewed Delors's attempt at pursuing such a means so late in the game as blackmail. He assumed that England and other like-minded states in the Community had invested too much effort already to follow de Gaulle's example of threatening secession as an alternative to accepting what England had refused to accept in the beginning: supranational control of vital national resources.

VI. On the Motives of the "Original Six"

Turning to particulars, we must now ask exactly why the Original Six, and particularly the French, should have been willing to accept the kind of supranational control over their coal and steel production that England, and then de Gaulle, rejected. One can readily understand why Italy and West Germany — the ex-Nazi/Fascist Axis powers — should have been eager to participate in such an enterprise. They had been reduced to unconditional surrender, out of which, as Vaughan puts it, they had "become sovereign in name only." By joining France as equal partners in such a Community they could only improve their international status, gaining rather than losing recognition as sovereign in that respect. As for the three Benelux countries, which were stripped of their sovereignty by Hitler's *Blitzkrieg* in matter of hours, they possessed centuries of experience at turning international economic cooperation to the advantage of the only narrowly-defined measure of independence (with administrative capitals of their own) that they presumed to claim.[16]

But what about France? De Gaulle had forced the "Big Three" victors — England, the United States, and the Soviet Union — to accept France as a fourth victor, entitled to a fourth share of the territorial spoils in the occupation. It is true that, at a certain moment, it was made clear to him that "France after 1945 was in the victors' camp only by courtesy of the United States and Britain."[17] Yet, for whatever reason, France had in the end qualified as a victor. What could she have had in common in the early 1950s, therefore, with the ex-Axis powers and the Benelux countries? Under de Gaulle, immediately after the war, and then again in the 1960s, France proved herself to be exactly what Laloy means by a responsible middle-sized state, as distinct from excessively large states that are "irresponsibly" strong superpowers and small ones that are "irresponsibly" weak, because they are either physically or morally impotent.

Yet, as Laloy reminds us in "Does Europe Have a Future?" when Monnet and Schuman started their ECSC in the early 1950s de Gaulle had been out of French politics, in so-called retirement, from 1947 to 1958. De Gaulle, it should be understood, had from the beginning strongly opposed Monnet's idea of a "Europe of communities." He saw it as a "Europe of losers" that no self-respecting nation could honorably join, structured as it had been in the beginning with its plainly supranational High Authority. He never wavered in expressing contempt for Monnet's having pressured France to agree to decision-making by majority vote. He made radio broadcasts against it while he was out of power, and expressed himself with a vehemence that has been matched only very recently by Thatcher. She now defends de Gaulle's position in an ongoing quarrel with Monnet's avowed disciple, Delors, now in his second four-year term as president of the European Commission.

But, during de Gaulle's retirement, the government of France's Fourth Republic had been in the hands of the faithful partisans of Monnet and Schuman. And they were immensely proud of the Community they had built. In fact, the French leaders actually welcomed de Gaulle's opposition, as they welcomed England's. To countries like England, and to leaders like de Gaulle, who treated their cause and achievement with disdain, these leaders said — good riddance! For, in their hearts, they believed that, win or lose, their cause was right, while the opposition was wrong to the core, and most wrong when they had the power to make things go their "sovereign" way.

Monnet was especially proud, as he repeatedly stated, that there were only six in his original Community, for that made them an elite, morally superior six, who had proved their superiority by acknowledging that loyalty to a European Community was a higher loyalty than any mere national loyalty. And he often explained why he was proud. After the Original Six had negotiated and signed the 1951 authorizing Treaty of Paris, for instance, Monnet and Schuman were widely congratulated for having brought off such an apparently complex piece of traditional diplomacy so smoothly. Monnet impatiently replied that he and Schuman used diplomacy and statecraft only as an unfortunately necessary national means for accomplishing their supranational ends — means that he fervently hoped might soon cease to be necessary.

"Nous ne coalisons pas d'états," Monnet liked to say, *"nous unissons des hommes"*: We don't combine states, we unite human beings![18] As for the collaboration of the great industrial corporations involved in the first community, he once exclaimed: "I don't give a damn about coal and steel, what I am after is European union." States would be used, and great corporations would be used, he explained, but only to facilitate the essential work of unifying human beings. Before long, the "supranational institutions" — like the High Authority of the ECSC — would, as he put it, inevitably "erode the existing nation-state systems, gradually replacing them with a federal regime."[19] We have already noticed how such terms and ideas recur today in the arguments of Delors. They illustrate what Paolo Taviani has aptly called the "revolutionary attempt to pass from the international to the supranational."[20]

Praise for the successful launching of the ECSC poured in from committed federalists everywhere. Hans Morgenthau in the United States, for instance, hailed the ECSC as the greatest supranational breakthrough in the history of modern international organizations, surpassing in that respect both the UN and NATO. He predicted that if Monnet and Schuman could manage to carry out the rest of their plan with as much success, it would mark the dawn of a new era in international cooperation. Monnet and Schuman, Morgenthau noted, had structured the ECSC as the model for a series of similar communities in "other operational fields, such as agriculture, transport, electricity, military forces," for example; he then concluded, approvingly, that, with many such communities finally "established as going concerns, sovereignty will have been transferred to a common European government by gradual steps, without the individual nations really being aware of it."[21]

In Monnet's and Morganthau's words we have, plainly, an answer to the question raised in our opening paragraphs. There are indeed many persons and groups in our midst determined to put an end to what Europe has been for the past five hundred years. But we need to glance again at motives. Obviously neither Monnet nor Morgenthau are contemplating forceful destruction of Europe's family of middle-sized powers. They speak of erosion, of gradual steps, and even of nations failing to notice what is happening, until it is, perhaps, too late. Those who know what the wartime European Resistance was all about will understand what kinds of dangers are at issue here. Monnet and Schuman very early on associated themselves with resistance leaders who came out of the war with no other purpose in their hearts than to destroy the nation-state system of international relations. And as the war drew to a close, this purpose appeared to have widespread support.

VII. Atomic Bombs and the Price of Sovereignty

The timing had been ripe: The United States dropped its first atomic bombs not on Germany but in distant Asia — indeed on that legendary Cipango, where Columbus had hoped to make a first landing. In the American academy, popular historian Thomas A. Bailey summed up the situation in his book, *Diplomatic History of the American People*:

> A thousand years were telescoped into that fraction of a second when the first atomic bomb exploded at Hiroshima. Many old concepts of diplomacy . . . were blown up in a billowing cloud . . . . It is no longer One World but One Room. We must dispose of the maniacs and learn to live with the rest of our fellow men . . . . The statesmen in charge of American foreign policy, as well as the better-informed citizens, know . . . that we must meet the other fellow half way, sometimes more than half way; and that we must invest some of our precious sovereignty in

effective world organization — perhaps some kind of world government.[22]

That view, as we all know, soon became official American policy, at least in theory. And it has continued to be given lip service, as proof of good intentions, by many presidential candidates and their chief advisers for national security affairs. Typical of the shared views of such civilian strategists are two books by Walt Rostow, published in 1960, just before he went to Washington to become, in time, the chief national security adviser for President Lyndon Johnson. In his *Stages of Economic Growth*, for instance, Rostow argued that "war, ultimately, arises from the existence and acceptance of the concept of national sovereignty." On the strength of that argument he then declared his conviction (elaborated in *The United States in the World Arena*) that it is, in the nuclear age, a "legitimate American national objective to see removed from all nations — including the United States — the right to use substantial military force to pursue their own interests." And then, in words echoed in the subtitle of this article, Rostow concluded that, "since this residual right" to use substantial military force in the common defense "is the root of national sovereignty and the basis for the existence of an international arena of power, it is, therefore, an American interest to see an end to nationhood as it has been historically defined."[23]

All of that is consistent with Monnet's views on sovereign nationhood — views that he had drawn largely from his long acquaintance with distinguished leaders of the wartime European Resistance. By the time of Hitler's defeat, the major resistance groups had long since revealed their plans for postwar Europe. Armed only with pens and words, they had never hoped to contribute much to Hitler's physical defeat. Where they expected to be of service, however, was in defeating that "other foe" — the European system of sovereign nations — which, they claimed, caused Hitler to pursue, and eventually rise to, power. As they put it in their famous Geneva Declaration of July 7, 1944, at no time during their long underground propaganda war against the Nazi tyranny had their purpose been to vindicate the sovereign independence of the national states of which they had been citizens. On the contrary, their purpose had always been to condemn those states for having "triggered two world wars" in a single generation, while permitting the rise of Mussolini and Hitler in between. "We must attack this anarchy," their Declaration had said, "by creating a federal order for the peoples of Europe."[24]

Why hadn't that been done right after the war? At first the victorious superpowers seemed to back the idea. Each had suitably supranational rather than a national name, as if they intended to keep making additions to their united states and union of republics. Yet each obviously had a rival plan for world order. So, instead of helping the resistance leaders build a new "people's Europe," the United States and the Soviet Union put their rival ideological commitments to global peace aside to deal with the world in accordance with traditional practices of power politics. In "liberated" Eastern European countries, the Soviets established regimes led by dedicated Marxists committed to revolution; and similarly in the West, the liberating armies of England and the United States brought with them almost all of the national governments in exile to which they had given asylum during the war. They did not seek out inexperienced partisan leaders, full of words and plans and hatreds. They turned instead to proud émigrés, like de Gaulle and many others, who had been planning for years their triumphant returns to their battered homelands, bringing fully staffed governments with them, and clinging more fervently than ever to the traditional prerogatives of sovereign nationhood.

From the standpoint of the resistance leaders this proved to be a terrible blow. Hitler was gone, but the other foe, the system of sovereign nation-states, was back in business. Their resistance, those leaders gloomily concluded, would have to be extended into the postwar era of so-called peace. The phenomenon has been much studied. In his classic essay, "European Federation in the Political thought of Resistance Movements During World War II," Walter Lipgens, for instance, identifies the basic obstacles to the development of a federated "people's Europe" as a replacement for the old "Europe of states." First and foremost, he insists, was England's refusal to participate in any supranationalist undertaking, although English leaders often made speeches encouraging the European states to do so. Of less importance but still a factor was the refusal of the four so-called neutral states spared by Hitler during the war — Spain, Portugal, Switzerland, and Sweden — to participate in federalist or supranationalist movements. And last but hardly least were the émigré national leaders, like de Gaulle, whose return to power had the most direct repressive impact.

As Lipgens explains, neither England nor Spain nor Portugal had a "direct share in the catastrophic experiences under totalitarian rule"; for this reason they were "unable to understand the conclusions which the Resistance on the continent had drawn from those experiences." Thus, while the Resistance had earlier persuaded many governments to insert clauses in their constitutions "accepting limitations on national sovereignty" and obliging them to join international movements dedicated to maintaining peace, little was ever done to actually implement any of that — except in the case of the six countries who responded to the Monnet-Schuman Declaration of 1950.

VIII. Targeting De Gaulle as Hitler's Heir

The brightest time for the war-time resistance federalists, Lipgens continues, was undoubtedly the period from 1947 to 1958, when de Gaulle was out of power in France and Monnet and Schuman were free to build their communities as "stages toward European federation." But even then, he acknowledges, the "example of Britain," in refusing to join the Community; the "economic recovery made possible by the Marshall Plan"; the "beginning of a relaxation of East-West tensions," which seemed to minimize the need of Western states to act together; the "increasing strength of national governments on the continent"; and finally, de Gaulle's "coming to power" again in 1958 all worked, as he puts it, to "prevent these governments from taking the decisive step to federation." Since then, he concludes, "the European federalists have had no choice but to embrace once again a situation with which they are quite familiar; namely, that of resistance."[25] That is a startlingly frank confirmation of de Gaulle's view that the Original Six of Monnet and Schuman really made up a "community of losers."

Just how formidable a foe de Gaulle eventually became during his years as president of France from 1958 to 1969, from the standpoint of Monnet and the European federalists generally, is most pointedly suggested in the title of a well-documented book published in 1969, when the great French war hero finally resigned his office to await death, which would come the following year. The book, Hans A. Schmitt's *European Union: From Hitler to de Gaulle*, ends with a brief summary of what de Gaulle appeared to have accomplished between 1958 and 1969 as a "destroyer" not only of European but also of Western unity in general, meaning the unity fostered by the United States and England apart from the European Community. De Gaulle surely did all he possibly could, Schmitt argues, to prevent the governments of Europe in his day from "taking the decisive step to federation," as Lipgens had expressed it. But even worse, de Gaulle seized control of the very institutions the federalists had created — namely the three European Communities — for use as policy instruments to pursue the sovereign concerns of French nationhood as an end in itself.

During de Gaulle's years as president, Schmitt stresses, "the European Economic Community and its common market continued to develop on schedule" as if "political unification" had never been its goal, while prospects of "a European government" and of "military integration had stood still." In other words, according to Schmitt, de Gaulle managed to block all advances toward European unity "without losing the benefits accrued from the actions of his weaker and more cooperative predecessors." In fact de Gaulle, after thoroughly scandalizing those predecessors with his deeds, forced those seeking unification to finally pursue their supranationalist and federalist goals by means that amounted to subterfuge, as many had done during the days of their resistance against Hitler. Once again, with frontal attacks against de Gaulle rendered futile, they were forced to resort to cunning and underground propaganda techniques to work their way around his obstructiveness. Schmitt's final assessment of the 1958-1969 period reads: "Immobility became a most prominent terrain feature on the western European and Atlantic stage. De Gaulle's policies were the actions of a declining power that was not yet resigned to decadence."[26]

Once again, we have the image of European unity being something for losers, for nations "resigned to decadence" and not resisting it, as France certainly did while de Gaulle was its leader. Monnet, who survived de Gaulle by many years, later took note of the difference in commenting on a passage in his adversary's memoirs recording his first impressions of the Monnet-Schuman call for France and Germany to pool such precious national resources as coal and steel. Had it been done, de Gaulle observed, for the aggrandizement of Germany and France, what a splendid idea it might have been. But as a means of permitting five weak states to control a strong Germany through the procedural rules of a supranational High Authority, that, said de Gaulle, is a piece of treachery unworthy of a victorious France that still treasures the spirit of the ancient Strasbourg Oaths of A.D. 842, oaths that were sworn and exchanged by the grandsons of Charlemagne in French and German — in which French and German nationhood spoke quite literally for the first time.

Still, despite his contempt for Monnet's goal — to end sovereign nationhood — de Gaulle admitted that the means proposed were daring. From a patriotic French perspective, de Gaulle wrote in his memoirs, such Franco-German collaboration might have been a good idea. "If one were not constrained to look at matters coolly," we read, "one would be dazzled by the prospect of what could be achieved by a combination of German and French strength, the latter embracing also Africa." If the thing proposed were really done right, de Gaulle concluded, it would "mean giving modern economic, social, strategic and cultural shape to the work of the Emperor Charlemagne."[27]

After 1958, when he returned to power, de Gaulle appeared to have more than half a mind to give it a try, together with his old friend, West Germany's Chancellor Konrad Adenauer. The proposed Franco-German Community, in other words, might have been something very different from the "Europe of Six Losers," that it became in the hands of Monnet and Schuman. One must recall de Gaulle's notes on his conversations with Adenauer in 1963. "We discussed Europe at length," he wrote. "Adenauer agreed with me that there could be no question of submerging the identity of our two nations in a stateless institution."[28]

Monnet, as we mentioned before, believed to the end, as Delors evidently believes today, that his side in the contest against England and de Gaulle was right, whether it prevailed or not. All the other side could ever claim for itself, in Monnet's view, was not right but might. Monnet and his disciples therefore concluded that, in the long run, what they sought would prevail. They only had to be patient. The future was theirs. De Gaulle on the contrary, while he was transforming the Community into a traditional international organization in which members maintain and exercise their sovereign prerogatives, remained persuaded that Monnet's vision belonged to the past not the future; that it represented a latter-day return to the premodern, medieval effort to suppress the sovereign independence of the nations under the universal order of the so-called Holy Roman Empire.

IX. A Community Haunted by Ghosts of Roman Emperors

Charlemagne, it has been said, and the Holy Roman Empire that grew out of his legacy passed on to his grandsons have haunted the European Community from the very beginning. And we turn to that subject now, for the European Community, as conceived by Monnet and Schuman, and as defended today by Delors with his "Europe 1992" crusade, is not so much forward-looking as backward-dreaming; dreaming of a unity utterly alien to all that is genuinely European, taking Europe to be, indeed, the "fatherland of middle-sized powers," the "place where such powers were born."

Today, in the spirit of "Europe 1992," we are witnessing a final desperate attempt to do the same old thing — force the sovereign nations to give up their sovereignty — only this time by novel means that Monnet and Delors and their partisans like to call "European to the core." Every serious scholar who has studied the beginning of the European Community acknowledges its "debt" to the Holy Roman imperial tradition. But let us take a moment here to cite a few sources. And we may suitably start with Dick Leonard's widely used *Pocket Guide to the European Community*. Aiming to shock his readers in its opening sentences, Leonard begins by acknowledging that "Adolph Hitler was the main catalyst of the European Community," even though, today, "none of its leaders would readily admit him as a founding father." But then he explains: "Like Charlemagne and Napoleon before him," Hitler undeniably "brought together, by the sword, virtually the entire land area of the original EEC, destroying in the process the self-confidence of the nation-states from which it sprang."[29]

Leonard's geopolitical observations are consistent with the conclusions drawn by Geoffrey Parker in his *Political Geography of Community Europe*, which is by far the most thorough account of the Community's Carolingian background. Late in his book, Parker predicts that a European Community truly "engaged in the process of unification . . . would not be a reactivation of the empire of Charlemagne, still less that of Napoleon, but a kind of secular Holy Roman Empire possessing firmer institutions and without its expansionist Prussias or Austrias."[30]

On another level, stressing the essentially non-European nature of the Carolingian legacy, is the European Community parallel that Vaughan draws on the first page of his previously-cited *Twentieth-Century Europe: Paths to Unity*. Vaughan warns his readers that "European unity should not be read into situations which had little or nothing to do with it." For instance, while Europe undoubtedly owes ancient Rome a unifying cultural debt, that cannot in the least alter the fact that "there was little European" about Rome's empire, "which was mainly Mediterranean." And something of the same sort, he adds, may be said about "Charlemagne's empire, which has been compared, territorially, to the Six of the original EEC, because its boundaries did more or less embrace the area now occupied by France, Germany, Italy, Belgium, the Netherlands and Luxembourg." But Vaughan is then careful to note that there was really nothing "European" about Charlemagne's empire, as Charlemagne himself well knew. Charlemagne considered himself to be a second Julius Caesar, completing the Roman conquests of northern Europe. And so the empire he shaped was, in Vaughan's words, "by no means European in spite of the Carolingian court poet Angilbert's application to its ruler of the epithet 'father of Europe'; whatever unity it may have had was Christian or Western, not truly European."

Vaughan's insights can help us unravel the ambiguities inherent in the "Europe 1992" rallying-cry. A yearning for peace as an end in itself has long been recognized as a pre-European Roman legacy transmitted to Europe by the medieval church. Of the "recurring idea" of European unity, Vaughan reminds us that the chief interest of its advocates has been "not in Europe, but in peace." And then, pointing directly to the founders of the European Community, and their most loyal supporters, like Delors, he notes that "their federal schemes, their dreams of European union, were not dictated in the first place by a vision of unity, but by a desire to avoid war."[31]

X. Europe's First Community: An Alien Roman Legacy

We noted that, in speaking of Europe as the fatherland of middle-sized powers, Laloy was acknowledging that the old continent had to have been something else, feminine as well as masculine, before any *birth* of nation-states could have occurred. To this day, our best guide to what Europe had earlier been remains James Bryce's remarkable book, *The Holy Roman Empire*. It is perhaps the only book that has ever focused directly on what we may call the internal "labors" of a pregnant Roman Christendom that finally gave birth, against her will, to Europe's large family of nation-states.

Bryce reminds us that the Church of Rome, whose bishops survived the empire's fall, did not like to deal with Germano-European ethnic tribes. Even after such tribes had settled as conquerors in the West, those bishops held fast to the ghost of Rome's universal order and kept up an unbroken relationship with the emperors in the East right down to A.D. 781, when those emperors themselves finally gave up trying to keep an "Italian office" open in the West. Between A.D. 781 and 800 the papacy for the first time since the days of Constantine was without its "rulers of all the world," whose universal sway is called in Holy Writ the "fullness of time," providentially ordered to prepare the entire world for conversion to the preaching of Christ.

Those nineteen years without an emperor proved to be too much for the Roman Church to bear. The many different Teutonic ethnic tribes that were competing to establish rival national kingdoms — such as the fierce Longobards who wanted to unite all of Italy and call it "Lombardy" — really frightened the Successors of Peter. And so one of them, Pope Leo III, at last "commissioned" a king of the Franks, mightiest of the German nations, to come down from his embattlements in Aachen and be made over into a Roman emperor (holy, of course) in A.D. 800, by being crowned and anointed in Christian-imperial Rome.

The papal commission given to Charlemagne was to start immediately to train all the rest of "his kind" for a new way of life. They were to cease at once being what they natively were — fearless Teutons — and start behaving like good little Romans, eager to "bend their knees to peace," as Rome's imperial poet Virgil put it, and do whatever the new universal emperor (with his Pope ever at his ear) asked them to do. Christian chivalric oaths were sworn up and down across the continent to that effect, and the first "European Community" — a Christianized Roman imperial revival dedicated to peace on earth as an absolute value — came into being.

Summing up the achievement of Charlemagne, Bryce says that, in "one sense," it has "scarcely a parallel" in the history of the world. Many great events, like the assassination of Julius Caesar, or the conversion of Constantine, or Columbus' voyage of 1492, or Emperor Charles V's efforts to silence Martin Luther, come to be seen in retrospect as belonging to a chain of circumstances that would have run their course toward the same end even if the particular event identified had not occurred. That cannot be said, in Bryce's view, of Charlemagne's achievement. On the contrary, he insists, "if the Roman Empire had not been restored in the West in the person of Charles, it would never have been restored at all, and the endless chain of consequences for good and for evil that followed could not have been."[32] And Bryce then notes that, in the teaching plan of the papacy, as universal pastor of the faithful, all the institutions of imperial governance (none native to the Germano-European peoples) were to serve as instruments of education that were designed primarily to tame the native violence of the Germanic converts.

XI. A Greco-Roman Legacy of Sub-National City-States

Yet the non-European supranational imperial legacy of the Church of Rome is really only half of what that benign alma mater bequeathed to her Germano-European adopted children. The other half, as Bryce carefully stresses, was another non-European inheritance, only in this case with an ultimate origin that was undoubtedly pre-Roman. Anyone at all familiar with the history of those "geographical expressions" known as Italy and Germany before their national unification in the 1860s is aware that, during the middle ages, when those territories were not actually united by the Holy Roman emperor's strong hand, they consisted of sovereign cities and ports, like Genoa and Venice in Italy and the Hanseatic cities of Lubeck, Hamburg, and Bremen (now in West Germany), and Danzig (now Gdansk, in Poland). The models for such ports, as also for their inland industrial and commercial companions, were undoubtedly the city-states of ancient Greece.

The ancient Greeks were great colonizers. Wherever their ships could take them, they would set up colonial cities, which invariably became independent political units. Cicero, writing just before the collapse of the Roman Republic — a collapse into the arms of Julius Caesar — used a splendid image to describe the string of colonial cities built by the Greeks all across the Roman Mediterranean world. He said that when you pictured them linked together, those cities formed a "Greek fringe woven round the coast of the barbarian," upon which each was decoratively placed, "like the golden tassels on a Roman senatorial toga."[33]

In most of those Greek cities, and in the many new cities built on the same pattern by the Romans, the church set up its overseers or bishops. And when Charlemagne organized his new empire in the Germanic world, the bishop of Rome, through his administrators, helped him and his *missi* to set up comparable cities in the new territories. Those cities were sub-national centers of local administration without which the supranational empire couldn't function effectively. They were "imperial cities," serving the empire, to be sure; but, like their Greek ancestors, they were also able to maintain themselves on their own when the imperial administration failed, which was often. Today, one can think of Brussels, Luxembourg, and Strasbourg — the European Community's "Eurocities" — in such terms.

There were cities outside the territories of the Germans and Italians, of course; and many of them were bishops' sees. But their situation was very different. For when the imperial administration failed, those cities found that their local na-tional kings would simply take up the imperial slack and tighten their hold on those sub-national administrative centers. That could not happen among the Italians and Germans because their king was invariably also their emperor; and his failure as emperor meant, even more, his failure as king. One has only to read Dante on the subject to appreciate the difference. Dante was the poet of one of the great inland cities of the empire, mighty Florence, destined to remain Europe's cultural and financial center for centuries. Yet Dante despised his beloved Florence for her vaunted independence, just as he despised all the other proudly independent Italian cities from Genoa and Venice in the north, to Naples and Palermo in the south.

Dante never dreamed that the answer to medieval Italian disunity could be an Italy united nationally on its own. Italy's cities should obey a universal emperor, and he curses them for not doing so. In one of the most moving pages of his *Divine Comedy*, Dante exclaims: "*Ahi, serva Italia!*" — "Oh, servile Italy You used to be a proud Mistress of Provinces." He then says: "But now, you've become the brazen Madam of an Italian whore-house." Italy has become an anti-imperial brothel, he says, whose "emancipated" cities prostitute themselves left and right, in order to keep up their *dolce vita* at all costs, while the Holy Roman imperial order crumbles.[34]

Moreover, Dante blamed the papacy for the arrogance of the imperial cities. The popes encourage them, even as they encourage the national kingdoms, Dante says, to defy the imperial authority. And they do it because they want to have the last word as the highest authority in all of Christendom, as if the empire were not just as holy, just as faithful as they, and although it was often more faithful. Dante foresaw — and it is the theme of his epic poem — that, if the papacy, the cities, and the national kingdoms kept up what they were doing, the empire would indeed fall, Europe would be divided into nation-states and warring cities, and then the universal church — alma mater herself — would be broken up, its pieces again becoming captives, harlots, of national kings.

All of that happened quite as Dante had predicted. And Bryce, in the most famous passage of his book, sums up the lesson of the entire failed attempt of "Mother Church," through Charlemagne, to make herself the supreme educator of the war-like tribal Germano-Europeans, in order to train them in the habits of peace. Bryce starts his account with the breakup of Charlemagne's empire after its division among his three grandsons. "In that day, as through all the Dark and Middle Ages," he writes, "two forces were striving for the mastery." On the one hand was a Germanic "instinct of separation, disorder, anarchy"; and on the other, a "passionate longing of the better minds for a formal unity of government, which had its historical basis in the memories of the old Roman Empire, and its most constant expression in the devotion to a visible and catholic Church."[35]

In the end, the native Germanic element, the European element, prevailed; but not before the medieval memory of imperial Rome and the pastoral care of its medieval church had, in Bryce's words, "tamed the barbarous races of the north, and forced them within the pale of civilization." In other words, supranational imperial unity, says Bryce, was a civilizing ideal, although foreign to the essential European spirit. It was pre-European, a legacy of the ancient world through the church. Late in his history, Bryce speaks of the empire's having "kept alive, in the face of national prejudices, the notion of a great European Commonwealth," but also of its having "fostered, while it seemed to oppose, the nationalities that were destined to replace it," each established, in Bryce's words, "as a free self-governing community." The empire fostered those national, self-governing communities, he explains, by preparing them to use "national independence aright" — in doing so, however, it was also "abolishing the need for itself."[36]

The "notion of a great European commonwealth" is thus the medieval empire's chief legacy to the nationalities organized as "free self-governing communities" in the modern world. Medieval political universality values peace above freedom; modern nationhood values freedom above peace. Each offers a distinct way of creating orderly relations among diverse peoples. In the case of Europe, the notion of a great European commonwealth (or European community) suggests that it be organized, as Charles Burton Marshall has ably put it, "through subordination of its parts to one center of authority." The notion of self-governing nationalities requires, instead, organizing the continent "through free association among juridically equal components."[37] There is no escaping those alternatives. A single center of authority is incompatible with a "free association among juridically equal components." One center of authority means that the component states must be, at best, reduced to the condition of Kansas, Pennsylvania, and Ohio in the American federal union. Is that the sort of status a politically integrated European Community means to confer on Denmark, Italy, or Greece, for example, after "Europe 1992"? Could England be content to play the part of a European Hawaii or Puerto Rico for the sake of perpetual peace? Not if Thatcher has her way.[38]

In her quarrel with Delors, England's prime minister dismissed as "fairy-fairy" and "absurd" his view that the European Community "needed to move toward a unified Western European government" as soon as possible. It really "angered" her, she said, to hear heads of state in Europe talking like Delors and saying: "Let's have a European union." That, too, she dismisses as "fairy-fairy" talk, yet it bothers her. "I can't see any of you dissolving your own countries into a United States of Europe," she snapped. "When I go to Europe, I am answerable to my own parliament and therefore to my own people. They're proud being British, and so am I."

Perhaps more to the point of this article, Prime Minister Thatcher has repeatedly reminded critics in the Community of her government's long-standing position on supranational control of shared economic resources. When the 72-year-old tory Lord Cockfield, a British appointee to the European Commission, started criticizing the British government publicly for opposing the creation of a "European Central Bank" — feeling justified by virtue of his commissioner's oath of "higher loyalty" to the Community — the Iron Lady promptly fired him. Accepting such a bank, she said, would mean surrendering "fundamental economic decisions to another country." And that, she concluded flatly, "I will not do."[39] Delors deplores such an attitude, of course, as the unhappy effect of that "fatal obsession of unanimity" that still permits a de Gaulle or a Thatcher to frustrate a Community majority at will. He, like Monnet and Schuman, clearly prefers a Europe organized "through subordination of its parts to one center of authority." Thatcher, like de Gaulle, on the other hand, prefers a Europe organized "through free association among juridically equal components."

XII. The Checks and Balances of Peace with Freedom

But here we must allow the last word to Walter Bagehot, who has taught so much on the ultimate responsibilities of genuinely free "government by discussion." Writing about President Lincoln's war to save the American Union, and about the Italian and German wars of national unification that occurred at the same time, Bagehot generalized on the experience of all three by noting that "half the wars in history have been caused by the desire of strong states to annex weak ones," and that most of the remaining wars have been caused by what Bagehot calls the movement of "nationalities," pulling weak states together to prevent foreign annexation or to overthrow a weakened foreign master.

The alternative to such a condition is a system of middle-sized states, most of whose members are relatively equal in power, so that no one of them can hope to dominate the others on its own. That, Bagehot says, is a truism. Yet the advocates of peaceful international arbitration, of leagues of united nations, of world federalism and world government (of the European

Community today) have all along stubbornly resisted its truth. They try to conceal from themselves the fact that powers capable of resisting any effort made by others "to force them to keep the peace will inevitably meet force with force; and that is war, not peace." Accordingly Bagehot concludes: "The condition of Europe most unfavorable to war is one in which the great majority of states are preserved from annihilation by their intrinsic vigor, and the few remaining destructible ones are preserved by the common interest, the common respect, and the common guarantee of all the stronger powers."[40]

Bagehot's point is that the spirit of diverse "nationalities" that leads them to form self-governing nation-states — occupying separate and juridically equal stations in relation to one another — is indomitable. One hears of a moral imperative to sacrifice all of that for the sake of peace in the nuclear age. It is very ancient talk — and medieval, too — having little to do with the reality of nuclear weapons. At issue, rather, is the civilized business of securing peace with freedom through internal checks and external balances of power. It is a civilized business because it presupposes, as we indicated earlier, two highly civilized truths. The first is that international order enforced through subordination to one center of authority is incompatible with freedom in any meaningful sense of the term. And the second civilized truth is that a balance of power can be maintained (when free and equal human beings organized as sovereign nation-states are disposed to keep it), whether the weapons are sticks and stones or hydrogen bombs.[41]

NOTES

1. Jean Laloy, "Does Europe Have a Future?" *Foreign Affairs* 51, N. 1 (Oct. 1972): 161.

2. Geoffrey Parker, *A Political Geography of Community Europe* (London: Butterworth, 1983),1-17,131,134.

3. Laloy, "Future?" 154.

4. Frances Nicholson & Roger Frost, *From the Six to the Twelve: The Enlargement of the European Community* (Chicago: St. James Press, 1987), 69.

5. Hans A. Schmitt, *European Union: From Hitler to de Gaulle* (New

York: Van Nostrand, 1969), 114.

6. Christopher Tugendhat, *Making Sense of Europe* (New York: Viking, 1986), 31.

7. Schmitt, *European Union*, 119.

8. Richard Vaughan, *Twentieth-Century Europe: Paths to Unity* (London: Croom Helm, 1979), 108.

9. Dick Leonard, *Pocket Guide to the European Community* (London: Blackwell, 1988), 11.

10. Leonard, *Pocket Guide*, 35-36.

11. Nicholson & Frost, *From the Six*.

12. Panayiotis Ifestos, *European Political Cooperation: Towards a Framework of Supranational Diplomacy?* (Brookfield, Vt.: Avebury, 1987), 608.

13. For versions of the Columbus/Age of Discovery saga that stress the nation-state aspect, see *Columbus: Selected Papers on Columbus and his Time* A. & H. Paolucci, eds. (New York: Griflon House, 1989).

14. Nicholson & Frost, *From the Six*, 262.

15. Ifestos, *European Political*, 349.

16. Vaughan, *Paths*, 80.

17. Tugendhat, *Sense of Europe*, 31.

18. Ifestos, *European Political*, 57.

19. Schmitt, *European Political*, 62.

20. Vaughan, *Paths*, 116.

21. Hans Morgenthau, *Politics Among Nations* (New York: Knopf, 1954), 498.

22. Thomas A. Bailey, *A Diplomatic History of the American People* (New York: Appleton-Century-Crofts, 1950), 906-907.

23. Walt W. Rostow, *Stages of Economic Growth* (Cambridge: Cambridge University Press, 1960), 105-108; *The United States in the World Arena* (New York: Harper & Row, 1960), 549.

24. Schmitt, *European Union*, 102.

25. Walter Lipgens, "European Federation in the Political Thought of Resistance Movements During World War II," ed. F. Roy Willis, *European Integration* (New York: New Viewpoint, 1975), 15-16.

26. Schmitt, *European Union*, 82.

27. Parker, *Political Geography*, 17.

28. Tugendhat, *Sense of Europe*, 76.

29. Leonard, *Pocket Guide*, 31.

30. Parker, *Political Geography*, 118.

31. Vaughan, *Paths*, 13.

32. James Bryce, *The Holy Roman Empire* (New York: Shocken Books, 1961; orig. 1904), 51.

33. A.H.J. Greenidge, *Greek Constitutional History* (London: Macmillan, 1911), 38.

34. Dante, *Divina Commedia, Purgatorio*, VI, 11. 76-78.

35. Bryce, *Roman Empire*, 50-51.

36. Bryce, *Roman Empire*, 443.

37. Charles Burton Marshall, *The Exercise of Sovereignty* (Baltimore: Johns Hopkins Press, 1963), 100.

38. Leonard, *Pocket Guide*, 180.

39. *New York Times*, 31 July 1988, IV. 1-2.

40. Walter Bagehot, *Complete Works*, VII, ed. N. St John-Stevas (London: *The Economist*, 1974), 155.

41. Henry Paolucci, *War, Peace, and the Presidency* (New York: McGraw-Hill, 1968), 200.

ABOUT HENRY PAOLUCCI

At the time of his death, on January 1, 1999, HENRY PAOLUCCI had been retired for eight years from St. John's University and held the title of Professor Emeritus of Government and Politics. He had also continued to serve, until his death, as Vice-Chairman of the Conservative Party of New York State.

He graduated from The City College of New York in 1942 with a BS degree and promptly joined the United States Air Force as a navigator. He flew many missions over Africa and Italy and, toward the end of the war in Europe, was placed in charge of 10,000 German prisoners of war. In that capacity, he remained in Italy for over a year. Immediately after his discharge, he resumed his education and received a Master's Degree and a Ph.D. from Columbia University. In 1948 he was chosen Eleanora Duse Traveling Fellow in Columbia University and spent a year studying in Florence, Italy. In 1951, he returned to Italy as a Fulbright Scholar at the University of Rome.

His wide range of intellectual interests was reflected in the variety of subjects he taught, including Greek and Roman history at Iona College, Brooklyn College, and The City College; a graduate course in Dante and Medieval Culture at Columbia; and, from 1968 until his retirement, graduate and undergraduate courses in U.S. foreign policy, political theory, St. Augustine, Aristotle, Machiavelli, Hegel, astronomy and modern science at St. John's University.

A frequent contributor to the *Op Ed* pages of the *New York Times* and magazines like *National Review* and *Il Borghese* (Rome), Professor Paolucci wrote numerous articles for the Columbus quincentenary and helped prepare three volumes of *Review of National Literatures* from materials drawn from the massive eight-volume work of Justin Winsor, the great historian of early America. He translated Cesare Beccaria's *On Crime and Punishments*, Machiavelli's *Mandragola* (in 34th printing), portions of Hegel's massive work on the Philosophy of Fine Arts, in a volume titled *Hegel and the Arts*, and edited Maitland's *Justice and Police*, as well as a notable collection of *The Political Writings of St. Augustine* and, first of its kind, selections drawn from Hegel's entire opus into a single volume, *Hegel on Tragedy*. His books on political affairs and foreign policy analysis include the classic *War, Peace and the Presidency* (1968), *A Brief History of Political Thought and Statecraft* (1979), *Kissinger's War* (1980), *Zionism, the Superpowers, and the P.L.O.* (1964) and *Iran, Israel, and the United States* (1991).

In 1964, he was urged by William F. Buckley to accept the New York State Conservative Party nomination for the U.S. Senate, running against Kenneth Keating and Robert F. Kennedy. His stimulating campaign drew considerable interest, and he was written up in the *New York Times* as the "Scholarly Candidate." In 1995, the Party honored him with its prestigious Kieran O'Doherty Award.

Founder and President of The Walter Bagehot Research Council on National Sovereignty (a non-profit educational foundation), Professor Paolucci was for many years the chief editor of its newsletter, *State of the Nation*, and organizer of the Council's annual meeting at the American Political Science Association. He contributed also to the international series *Review of National Literatures* and its companion series, *CNL/World Report*.